CONTENTS

INTRODUCTION 13

Part One — Our First Steps   15
Making the decision to go   15
Who's going (15), How to go (16), When to visit and how long
to stay (21), How much does it cost ?(23), First Steps (24),
How to get there (33)

Part Two — Easing the Shock: Where Have We Landed?   36
Accommodation (36), Food and drink (37), Domestic
transportation (38), Personal security (40), Local currencies
(41), Altitude — how to cope with thin air (43), Discounts for
students and young travelers (44), Behaviour and manners
(44), Keeping in touch (45), Shopping and souvenirs (46),
Overland border crossings (47), Taxes and custom duties
(48), Working hours (48), Holidays and festivals (48)

BOLIVIA 49

History (49), Geography and climate (54), Population (55),
Economy (56), General information (59)

P *ERU*

P *ERU* 121

History (121), Geography and climate (124), Population,
education and culture (125), Economy (127), General
information (129), Personal security (134)

I *NDEX*

BOLIVIA
PERU

MICHAEL'S GUIDE

BOLIVIA PERU

Series editor
Michael Shichor

I NBAL
Travel Information Ltd.

Inbal Travel Information Ltd.
P O Box 39090 Tel Aviv Israel 61390

Intl. ISBN 965-288-085-X

Text: Michael Shichor
Cover photo: Moshe Frankfurter
Photos: Moshe and Joana Frankfurter,
        Amos Kreiner, Miki Kreiner
        Avi Maromi

Distributed in the United Kingdom by:
Kuperard (London) Ltd.
9, Hampstead West
224 Iverson Road
West Hampstead
London NW6 2HL

U.K. ISBN 1-85733-031-5

*T*ABLE OF MAPS

Preface

Writing this guide, we have aimed at coming out with a comprehensive, in-depth companion for the tourist who wants to get to know the South American continent in a direct and personal way.

The modern traveler is interested in a significant, relevant, first-hand experience when touring foreign lands. He wants to get to know new and different worlds and is well aware of the effort involved. This book is written for this traveler — curious, intense, experienced and open-minded — the tourist who really and truly wishes to meet South America, face-to-face.

While writing this guide with special emphasis on enlarging upon and clarifying general areas, it was not done so at the expense of the plethora of practical details which are of vital import, if you are to fully succeed in your venture and truly enjoy the experiences awaiting you. An attempt has been made to create an information pool, which would combine material relevant to understanding the **what**, while contributing to the practicalities of the **how**.

Aware of the responsibility involved in being guide and companion to all who choose to see South America "through our looking glass," we have tried to compile as many facts and details as possible. From this pool of information, let each person take what fits best, what is most appropriate.

In the course of this work, we have labored to separate the wheat from the chaff and have tried to be as precise as possible. Naturally, many of the impressions and recommendations included in the guide are subjective. However, the guide do contain those elements which will fulfill the expectations of the kind of tourist mentioned, and will guide and assist you in making the most of your trip, in as enjoyable, comprehensive and pleasant a way as possible.

Michael Shichor

Using this guide

In order to reap maximum benefit from the information concentrated in this guide, it is advisable to read the following material carefully and act upon it.

Before setting out, it is important to read the Introduction in its entirety. The information contained there will supply you with details which will help you in making early decisions about your trip. Once you arrive at your destination you will already feel familiar and comfortable there, more so than would otherwise be the case.

In the chapters dealing with the individual countries you will find a broadly-based Introduction, whose first section deals with general topics, while the second part includes practical information about the country, its customs and ways.

The country's capital is the next section in the chapters. The information here — suggestions, recommendations and advice about the city — will guide and assist you from the time you arrive and until you leave.

From here on, the chapters are organized geographically: the different regions are presented in logical sequence, with each region surveyed along major touring routes. Following main sites noted, you will find suggestions for touring the areas around them — using the site as both your point of departure and return. In each of these touring sub-sections too, the sites are noted according to their geographical order rather than their importance, so as to make it easier to follow along the way.

As you read through, you will notice that similar information is mentioned in more than one place. This is meant to assist tourists who decide to start their tour from a particular place along the way, but have not arrived at this point via the route described or suggested in the guide, and with no prior knowledge. This allows for greater flexibility in planning your tour, without being tied to the geographical divisions or considerations of this guide.

For travelers crossing borders by land, you will find in each border town discussed a section on the procedures required for continuing into the neighboring country. Treat this as you would treat a plan to go from one site to another: read the material dealing with both places — the place from which you are coming and the one to which you are heading.

At the end of this guide we included a short vocabulary, and an alphabethic index of sites and places.

When mentioning information about transportation, accommodation, food, etc., we have tended to simplify and have preferred to give general guidelines, placing more emphasis on existing possibilities than on variable specifics. It is always disappointing to find that what you have counted on seeing or doing is not available once you finally get to the location. We have therefore tried to avoid giving specific details about subjects given to frequent change, preferring rather to advise you of those places where relevant, here-and-now information can be obtained once you are actually on the spot.

Therefore, an important rule of thumb should be to consult the local Tourist Office in each place you visit. Their addresses are mentioned in the text. They can advise you of the latest updated information for the specific time of your visit.

As for updating — this kind of guide to this part of the world cannot afford to march in place. A technical update from year to year is not enough, either. A finger on the continent's pulse is ever necessary. Up to the day this guide went to press, we attempted to confirm its relevance and up-to-dateness. However, it is only natural that due to frequent changes which occur, travelers will find certain time-related facts somewhat less than precise when they arrive at their destinations, and for this we apologize in advance.

To this end, cooperation and assistance from you who have enjoyed the information contained in this guide, is necessary and vital. It ensures, first and foremost, that those who travel in your wake will also enjoy and succeed in their ventures, as much as you have. For this purpose, we have included a short questionnaire at the end of the guide and we will be most grateful and appreciative to those of you who will take the time to complete it and send it to us.

Have a pleasant and exciting trip!

*I*NTRODUCTION

A Special Place for Tourists

South America's exciting, exotic charm combines forces with the veteran tourist's natural curiosity. When these are reinforced by a significant drop in the costs of touring and by a constantly developing tourist infrastructure, it's no wonder that South America has become a new and captivating destination for travelers. Here is a continent that offers innumerable experiences, sights and impressions. On the one hand, it has incredible untamed scenery — canyons, deserts, mountains, jungles, rivers, and glaciers; on the other hand there's an astonishing and varied "human landscape" — a blend of cultures and races woven into a fragile and enchanting social fabric. Anyone seeking an encounter with rare worlds — a fascinating harmony of nature and scenery, man and animal, progress and antiquity — will find it here.

A trip to South America, whether for business or for pleasure, is wholly different from a trip anywhere else. Before we set out we must prepare, investigate, interpret, comprehend. As we travel, too, we engage in a process of learning, becoming acquainted and adjusting. Our ordinary ways of life and thought, attitudes to time, people, and things are simply not the same as those found in South America. Its languages, foods, clothing and customs are all quite remote from those we know. As we head for South America, we must disabuse ourselves of many biases; we must open ourselves up, both emotionally and intellectually, to wholly different messages and impressions. Though it's certainly true that the transitions are not so sharp between New York and Caracas or between Paris and Buenos Aires, the contradictions remain in full force. They accompany the tourist every step of the way, and place him in daily confrontation with his own values, opinions, and habits. The greatest return one can expect from a trip through South America is the knowledge of the existence of another world, one which lives, thinks and behaves differently, a world no better and no worse — merely different.

South America invites the tourist to share numerous experiences and ordeals — cosmopolitan cities, ancient villages that have not changed in centuries, untamed scenery of mighty grandeur, massive power projects, and all the rest. Here you'll find a fantastically wealthy elite beside shameful poverty, incomparably primitive scenes alongside technological wonders. Wonderful outings on foreseaken trails will take you to Indian tribes who still go about naked, fish with harpoons, and hunt with bows and arrows. Other journeys will lead you to some of the world's best-known and most important archaeological sites.

South America has it all — for the family on their annual vacation, for the youth out to wander with a backpack, or for the retired couple on their second honeymoon. Each will find what he is seeking here. There's enough here for everyone, on every topic and in every field. On every itinerary, every form of travel, visitors are sure to find what they want — and more.

It is important to mention again that the substantial difference between "North" and "South", which accounts for Latin America's exotic splendor, requires fundamental and thorough preparation. The sharp transition obliges you to be open and tolerant, and to reinforce those qualities with advance study and suitable intellectual and emotional preparation. These guarantee a successful tour, out of which you'll get the most enjoyment; in their absence you're liable to encounter many difficulties which may well spoil your pleasure. Under all conditons and in any event it's worthwhile to behave with great patience and to accept South America for what it is — beautiful, wild, fascinating. This, after all, is the purpose of our visit, one unequalled anywhere on Earth.

*I*NTRODUCTION

Part One — Our First Steps

Before we set out we must consider a number of important points: deciding upon our route, destinations, and the like. The paragraphs that follow will guide you in these matters.

Making the decision to go

Who's going

Anyone can visit South America. Due to the great variety of sites, plentitude of things to see, and abundance of areas of interest on the way, there's almost no one who won't find what he's seeking. A great many **young tourists** spend several months exploring South America from one end to the other, wandering along the roads with backpacks and a few coins in their pockets. It's a nice "timeout" from the rat race, in addition to being an enjoyable and fascinating experience. These backpackers, known in local parlance as *mochileros*, come to know the continent perhaps better than most natives, and enjoy unrestricted mobility on all of South America's highways and byways.

More and more **middle aged** tourists have been frequenting South America in recent years, generally after having come to know both the United States and Europe. Now, in search of new and interesting places to visit, they've packed their bags and wandered to the faraway southern continent. Faraway? Not really. For the tourist, South America is closer today than it's ever been. It's no longer a backward continent, but rather a bustling and popular place, connected to the rest of the world by excellent air service.

There is no longer anything to fear about going to South America, as far as you arrange your immunizations before arrival and avoid focuses of disease. Sanitary conditions and the public services offered tourists are constantly improving, and today are not significantly inferior, in the large cities, to those we're used to in the West. Transportation services, hotels and restaurants have also conformed to a great degree to the new tourist's demands and, though difficulties still occur, the experienced tourist has no reason to refrain from visiting. Vacation and resort sites, too, are flourishing, and many people combine rest and recreation with their visit.

*I**NTRODUCTION***

As trade between Latin America and the rest of the world expands, a great many **business people** have been combining business and pleasure, enjoying the experience of getting to know different economic systems. The Latin American business world is lively and effervescent, and has adopted Western work patterns and behavior in the large cosmopolitan cities. Grand hotels, superb restaurants, and office, guide and rent-a-car services are available for the businessman and tourist of means. The South American ambience, the "flexibility" of the clock, and tendency to do things lightheartedly and at leisure leave their impact here, too, though when you get down to it, business is conducted strictly and thoroughly.

Bringing the children along requires special preparation. In many places — mainly in Andean countries such as Bolivia, Peru, Ecuador, and Colombia — it is difficult, for example, to obtain milk products. Sanitary conditions are not the best, and are liable to cause problems for adults as well. At the same time, do not hesitate to take children from the age of 7-8 years old to the large cities or the famous tourist sites. These are served by convenient access roads beside which you'll find visitors' facilities. There is no problem in touring with children in Argentina and Chile — quite the contrary.

How to go
The most comfortable way to go is, of course, with **organized group tours**. Many companies specialize in providing this kind of service — generally rather expensive — in a number of Latin American countries. Here you'll be assured that your trip will involve a minimum of difficulties and breakdowns, though you'll be deprived of personal contact with the natives, the ability to set your own timetable and itinerary, and more. It's nevertheless important to remember that there are few English speakers in South America, and visitors who don't speak Spanish or Portuguese are liable to find themselves in tight spots, especially when meandering in remote locations outside the cities.

South American group tours are varied and diverse, so that it is hard to relate to them as a single unit. Every visitor should draw up a list with a number of destinations and objectives, carefully examining the means by which he'll reach them with the greatest success and least expense.

Another way of going, of course, is the private, individual trip, where you're free to choose your own dates, destination, pace, budget, etc. Indeed, there's no greater freedom than that of a long, extended tour, where one has no obligation to preset an itinerary and timetable, but can suit these to the needs and desires of the moment.

*I*NTRODUCTION

Backpack tourism is especially popular among the young, and the young in spirit. Many spend several months in South America, making their way through the continent from country to country and site to site. It's a fascinating and pleasant way to travel. Most such visitors pick up some Spanish or Portuguese en route, get to know the natives, and get to interesting places that few visitors reach.

Backpack tourism is cheap, pleasant, and easy. The visitor should not expect many difficulties, and excluding a few countries where the police pick on tourists — such as Peru, Colombia and, to a certain extent, Argentina — it's highly improbable that you'll encounter any problems that will mar the pleasure of your trip.

Mochileros, with their packs on their backs, are usually received cordially. Tourists of all nationalities tend to meet anywhere on the continent and continue together.

Women, too, have nothing to fear in South America. Apart from several places which I wouldn't advise young women to enter alone, and apart from the fact that they shouldn't go about in dangerous urban areas late at night, I find no reason to be deterred. Traveling in pairs or small groups helps a great deal to solve these problems.

By traveling in this manner, you won't have to carry a lot of money; a few ten dollar bills per week will enable you to get along fine and in relative comfort. At the same time, bear in mind that such a journey does involve difficulties: the means of transportation you'll use aren't very good, the hotels will offer no more than the bare essentials, and so on. Hence, you'll need extra time, more strength, and lots of patience, openness, and good humor.

Well-off tourists, and those whose time is limited and who want to get in a lot of sites comfortably without wasting precious time on the road, can get the most out of their visit by careful advance planning and by making reservations. One should carefully select the sites you consider most important to visit, and draw up a timetable for your trip.

Reservations are not always essential, a fact which allows for greater flexibility en route. In this guide we've noted the places, routes, and dates that attract crowds. If you've placed these on your itinerary, be sure that you have a reliable travel agent make reservations before you set out. Make sure he obtains written confirmation since overbooking is a common phenomenon in South America and is liable to cause you great unpleasantness.

Business people would do well to arrange all matters

*I*NTRODUCTION

beforehand. The big cities frequently experience unexpected pressure on hotels, flights, and car-rental firms; though ordinary vacationers would hardly notice these problems, they are apt to cause delays and annoyance to a businessman on a tight schedule.

Where to go

In our opening paragraphs we noted that South America is rich in all kinds of places to visit. Therefore it is important to determine and locate the types of places that attract you in particular.

Mochileros setting out on an extended visit can expect to discover many of the beautiful continent's hidden secrets on the way, and will meet and enjoy its abundant treasures. Others, especially those whose time is limited, will prefer to designate one or several countries, and do them throughly. Both sorts of tourists might give preference to subjects in which they are particularly interested, and plan their trips so as to achieve the maximum in these spheres. We will survey below a number of categories in which we'll try to sketch out various directions of interest. Individual tourists will choose the categories that attract them, and draw up a plan that includes one or several.

The first possibility involves those **natural and scenic attractions** which are found throughout South America. They are divided into several types:

Glaciers and lakes are located chiefly in the continent's southern section, in southern Argentina and Chile. Here you'll find some of the world's most beautiful tour routes, enchanting scenery, friendly people. Many Andean peaks in the region feature well-developed ski areas, in top condition, because here the seasons are reversed. In Europe, holiday-makers are tanning themeselves on the beaches. North of Lima, Peru, in the vicinity of Huaraz, you'll find lovely hiking trails that demand good physical condition, the ability to adapt to unusual climatic conditions and a willingness to live primitively. All these routes require first-class camping gear.

For a pleasant stay on the **seashore** there's nothing like Brazil. Resort towns with pristine beaches abound along the Atlantic coast, especially between Vitoria and Puerto Alegre and in the Nordeste (North East). These are especially popular among Brazil's wealthy, and tourists frequent them primarily at Carnival time in February and March. Their great advantage — like that of the ski areas — is in the reversed season. Here you can swim and sunbathe from January to March, while most of Europe is buried in snow. The few coastal sites in Argentina and Chile serve mainly the local population. Peru and Ecuador have lovely beaches, though these lack a developed service infrastructure. There are developed beaches in Colombia and Venezuela, with the popular ones located along the Caribbean. Hotel occupancy and prices are high during the summer months (June-August), and it's important to make advance reservations.

A long strip of exclusive resort clubs has sprouted along the Caribbean coast, where you can spend a seaside vacation under ideal conditions, renting gear for fishing, sailing, diving, and more. Some of the beaches, especially those in the Caracas area, are rather neglected; their level of upkeep has deteriorated perceptibly.

About one-third of South America is covered with thick **jungle**. On the exceedingly popular jungle excursions tourists can encounter out-of-the-way cultures and get a first-hand impression of ancient ways of life that are rapidly disappearing. It's important to remember that jungle trips require special effort, organization, and experience. You can take such trips in Brazil, Bolivia, Peru, Ecuador, Colombia and Venezuela. Each of these countries has extensive jungle regions.

The jungle's harsh and unpleasant climate — an oppressive combination of high temperatures, high humidity, and frequent rainfall — explains to a large extent why the area has not been settled, though it also deserves credit for the lush wild vegetation. This flora, watered by giant rivers such as the Amazon, the Orinoco, and their tributaries, is of decisive importance in reducing air pollution and maintaining the natural environmental equilibrium in all of South America. An outing to the jungles must be planned carefully and with great caution. Though most of the jungle is free of malaria, it is recommended taking medication against that disease, along with water purification tablets and mosquito repellent.

Travelers visit the jungle cities of Peru and Brazil in great numbers, either on organized tours or on their own. Though the former are very expensive, it's worth remembering that the "unattached" visitor, too, will find a visit to these areas far from cheap. Prices in and around the jungle towns are far higher than elsewhere as goods must be imported from far away. Be prepared for this, and bring along a sufficient amount of the local currency.

The jungles in Ecuador's eastern region are home to a number of Indian tribes, and are accessible as a relatively "short hop" from the capital. The jungles in Ecuador offer a maximum return of enjoyment and interesting experiences while demanding minimum investment of time, effort, and expense.

INTRODUCTION

Wildlife: Though the jungle might appear to be **the** place for observing wildlife in its natural habitat, this is in fact not the case. It is true that jungle tours can give you a glimpse of thousands of strange and varied species of birds, insects, butterflies, and even reptiles, monkeys, and wild boars, but you can't assume so. You must penetrate deep into the jungle, and there's no guarantee that you'll find what you've come for there, either.

By contrast, the Galapagos Islands off Ecuador are famous for their abundant wildlife, most of it unique. It is rather expensive to visit, and it's best to make reservations for a flight to the islands, and on the ships and boats that sail among them. The lovely nature reserve on the Paracas Islands off central Peru has thousands of birds and sea lions, and is far less expensive and more convenient to visit. Bolivia and Chile, too, have nature reserves with a multitude of wild animals, primarily of the llama family.

In Brazil, in the area of the Bolivian border, there are vast stretches of marshes known as the Pantanal, inhabited by an abundance of birds, alligators and other animals. The best time to visit here is during the dry season, between May and September, when one can really appreciate the variety and profusion of wildlife.

The Valdéz Peninsula in southern Argentina is another fascinating reserve, with penguins, whales, sea lions, and more. The best time for visiting it is October or November, when the animal population reaches its annual peak.

Another planning strategy places the emphasis on South America's **complex social structure**, concentrating on sites from **the continent's past**, as well as those which accent its special present.

Archaeology: The glory of pre-Columbian settlement in the southern half of the Americas is, of course, the Inca Empire and its center, the city of Cuzco, Peru. From these, the Inca (emperor) and his men dominated the tribes from Ecuador in the north as far as central Chile in the south. Few pre-Incan remains have survived in South America. Remains of what is thought to be the oldest settlement in all the Americas have been discovered at Puerto Varas (Southern Chile), and are being studied thoroughly. Pre-Incan civilizations existed primarily in Tihuanacu, Bolivia, around the village of San Agustin in southern Colombia, and in various locations in Peru. While the tourist will certainly want to visit San Agustin and Tihuanacu, the pinnacle of his archaeological experience will undoubtedly be a visit to the Inca sites, with the lost Inca city of Machu Picchu as the highpoint.

*I*NTRODUCTION

Folklore and folk culture: Age-old Indian traditions have blended with the Spanish influence to produce a unique and extraordinary compendium of folklore and culture. All of South America, and the Andean countries in particular, excel in uncommonly beautiful handicrafts of unique character and style. Visiting these countries is like an extended shopping trip. This activity centers on the marketplaces — in large cities, country towns, and remote villages. In some, the barter system is still practiced. The markets of South America are colorful, effervescent, lively, and enchantingly beautiful. Most commerce is carried on by women, and they are most skillful at it. As you meander through the markets choose carefully, check quality, compare prices, and bargain, **always** bargain.

Most South American countries have a rich and varied folklore. Folk music varies from country to country: while quiet cowboy songs typify Argentina and Venezuela, Brazillian music is usually stormy and rhythmic. Music and dance in the Andean countries draw on Indian sources; typical musical instruments are the *charango*, the drum, and the reed flute. Music and dance dominate Latin American life. Numerous holidays and festivals are celebrated on the continent every year, and there's hardly a month when some part of the continent isn't gearing up for a festival. National festivities reach their peak with folk festivals, most in February or March. The largest and most famous is the Brazillian Carnival, unequalled anywhere in the world for beauty and joy. The most important festivals in Peru and Bolivia are held in February-March and June-July.

When to visit and how long to stay

Getting to know South America inside and out is a matter of month after month of intensive touring. The first condition for success is command — albeit of the most rudimentary nature — of Spanish (or, for Brazil, Portuguese). *Mochilero* touring of this sort usually lasts from three months up to more than a year, and allows you to visit most countries on the continent, exploring them exhaustively and comprehensively. Eight to ten months seems the optimal length for such a trip, broken down more or less as follows: two to three months in Argentina and Chile, three to five months in the Andean countries (Bolivia, Peru, Ecuador, and Colombia); two to four months in Brazil; and one more month for the remaining countries.

The tourist with this much time available can fix his original port of entry at whatever point is cheapest to reach, and move around in accordance with weather conditions and the various special events that take place throughout the year.

Argentina and Chile

The period from September to March is best; plan to visit the southernmost regions close to the middle of that period, when the weather there is best. Before September and after March the continent's southern reaches suffer harsh and unpleasant wintery weather, when touring is almost impossible. These countries' central and northern areas can be visited the year around.

Brazil and Venezuela

The period from October to June, the hot season, is recommended. Then you can go most places with ease, tan on the beach, roam the jungles, visit the cities, and so on. The desire to participate in the Carnival, celebrated annually in February or March determines for most tourists when they go to Brazil, and this is how it should be. Participating in the Carnival is undoubtedly an experience not to be missed; what's more, it's held at the best time of the year for a visit. Yet, this is the peak of the tourist season, and you better make reservations well in advance for hotel and other tourist services.

The Andean countries

These may be visited the year round, though the summer months (November-February) are the wettest, with showers liable to mar your enjoyment. During those months excursions to the mountains and jungle are difficult, so it's a good idea to make the effort to come during the winter (May-September), when although it's a bit cooler, the skies are clear and the weather excellent.

On the Galapagos Islands (Ecuador), as in the countries along the equator (Ecuador, Venezuela, and parts of Brazil, Colombia, and Peru), the weather is stable the year round, with no extreme differences among the seasons.

These climatic details describe somewhat generally the course of the season according to a rough division of the continent, and are meant for those traveling for extended periods. Those making shorter visits will find a more precise description of the climate in the chapters on each country; furthermore, a section dealing with local weather is included for each of the large cities.

Tourists who want to know as much as possible of South America within a limited time period, may opt for a number of different possibilities, according to their special interests. In all events, it seems that any visit to South America, even if you wish to focus on a certain region and a simple field, requires at least three to four weeks. It's most desirable that it be planned with enough flexibility to allow for possible changes in your intinerary.

None of this applies, for example, to those coming for a week-long organized tour of Brazil to attend the Carnival, or for ten days of sailing among the Galapagos Islands. But apart from such limited frameworks you should allow a longer period. The great distances, extreme variation from place to place, range of sites, and tour and holiday possibilities make this much time necessary. One must always bear in mind the chance of delays on the way, so that a packed and precise timetable — reminiscent of one's last visit to Switzerland — would be wholly inappropriate here.

How much does it cost?

Since the mid eighties, fierce competition among the various airlines has led to tremendous cuts in airfares to destinations in South America. Today they are not much higher than for flights of similar length to other destinations and we are the fortunate beneficiaries.

Another factor which played a role was the depreciation of the local currencies. The difficult economic situation of the Latin American countries finds expression in inflation and frequent devaluations of their currency against the dollar, which has gained greatly in strength in recent years even in comparison to stable European currencies — and all the more so in comparison to the South American currencies, which generally serve as legal tender in rickety economic systems that have been in a distressed state for some time.

From the tourist's point of view, of course, there's a distinct plus to this situation. Domestic price rises do not always keep up with the rate of devaluation, and sometimes people with dollars or a stable European currency to spend will find prices for meals, lodging and shopping which may appear ridiculous when judged by Western standards. However, local people, earning local incomes, can not always afford even minimal needs.

South America is, therefore, a better tourist bargain then ever before. On the one hand, airfare is cheaper than in the past; on the other, expenditures for transportation, accommodation, food, shopping and so forth are far lower than they used to be. The cost of living is not uniform everywhere, and prices, of course, vary from country to country. The cheapest countries to visit are the Andean ones, while the most expensive are Venezuela, Uruguay, and Paraguay. Even the last three, however, which in the not-too-distant past were expensive even by European and American standards, have become significantly cheaper, and a visit there today is no more expensive than an intermediate-priced tour in Europe or North America. Countries once considered prohibitive, such as Argentina, Chile, and Brazil, have become much less expensive, and the devalutation of their currencies gives you the chance to enjoy a tour of reasonable standards.

When dealing with luxury tourism, there's almost no gap with the West. The best hotels in Bogotá, Caracas, Lima, Rio, São Paulo, Buenos Aires and the like are rather expensive, especially at peak tourist season or at holiday or Carnival time. Car rental rates resemble those the world over, but first-class restaurants tend to be less expensive than their counterparts in the Western world.

In conclusion, it can be said that the range is broad; each of us must choose a path in accordance with our means. On every budget, though, tourists will find South America open, ready to meet them, and easy on the wallet.

First Steps

Once you've decided how, when and where to go, all that's left is to make practical preparations for the journey. The next section deals with these matters, spelling out everything that must be done before leaving home, in order to make the trip as successful, easy, comfortable and inexpensive as possible.

Documents and papers

Anyone going to South America requires a valid passport, except for citizens of certain South American countries who may cross into neighboring states with nothing more than an identity card. Some of the Latin American states require that your passport be valid for at least six months beyond your date of entry. It's best to get your passport some time prior to your trip, for some of these countries require you to obtain an entry visa in advance, and issuing this visa generally takes several days.

In our chapters on each country, we've spelled out the relevant regulations and documents you'll need; study them before you go. We should again mention that immigration regulations in the South American countries are in a constant state of flux; you **must** consult the embassy, consulate or tourist bureau of the country you intend to visit, shortly before your trip, in order to obtain up-to-date and reliable information.

Countries that require an entry visa have fixed procedures for issuing them. You'll need to present a passport, an entry and departure ticket, a photograph, and relevant travel documents (reservations, a letter from your place of work, etc.) The visa takes from one to three days to be issued, and usually involves no difficulties. All visa matters should be seen to in your own country, but if necessary, they can be obtained en route, in each of the countries you visit on the way.

A tourist card issued by airlines or distributed at frontier posts to those arriving by land has replaced visas in many cases. This card, which is free, must be filled out before you land or at the border station, and handed to the immigration officials along with your passport. A stamped copy will be attached to your passport, and returned when leaving the country.

We must stress that, as a rule, government clerks, police and military personnel check documents punctiliously, so keep them on you at all times, properly stamped and arranged. Many tourists have found that letters of reference (for example, a letter confirming that you were sent on business by your employer), various certificates (preferably with your photograph), and documents that have an official look to them are frequently of help in getting pesky clerks or policemen to leave you alone.

Due to frequent changes, find out before arrival which immunizations are required at your destination country, and how long before departing you need the vaccinations. This is specially true for cholera.

A tourist's national driver's license is accepted in most South American countries, on condition that a Spanish translation has been attached. Even so, we recommend that you obtain an International Driver's License and make sure that one of its languages is Spanish.

A Student Card is good for certain discounts and benefits. In Argentina and Chile students are granted discounts on public transportation, though foreign students may have to engage in lengthy bargaining to receive them. In Peru, significant discounts are given to students on tickets for museums, archaeological sites, and more. Venezuela discounts certain domestic flights. The essential condition for using your Student Card is that it be valid and bear your photograph.

One should not go to South America without an **insurance policy** covering health and baggage. Theft is a common occurrence throughout the continent, and the uninsured tourist is liable to suffer great financial damage. The matter of health insurance, however, is even more serious. Because disease is rife, and medical care and drugs are expensive, under no circumstances should one leave a matter as important as health insurance to chance or luck; no knowledgeable tourist would ever set out without being properly insured.

Though it can hardly be described as a document, you'll find in your travels that an MCO card is as important as if it were one. An MCO is a flight voucher issued by airlines that are members of IATA, and is honored by all other IATA members. At many border points where you'll be asked to show a departure card, and when you apply for a visa, an MCO will satisfy the requirement in most cases. It's important to check that its value is specified in dollars and in no other currency, for the voucher is calculated according to the value in the currency in which it was paid. At the end of your trip you can apply your MCO to pay for the flight ticket you want, or you can redeem it where it was issued or at the airline office.

Health

Most serious diseases have been totally eradicated in South America, and linger on only in the most remote jungles. Malaria no longer strikes in the cities and towns, though those wishing to penetrate deep into the jungles should bring malaria pills as a preventive measure.

Intestinal diseases are very widespread in South America, due to the poor sanitary conditions and inappropriate food storage methods. Be prepared for the near certainty that at some stage you'll come down with intestinal trouble. It's worth your while to bring along any medication you're used to taking. Don't hesitate to consult a doctor in serious cases, for common diseases such as hepatitis are liable to cause you great distress if not discovered in time. Bear in mind that in 1991 the colera attacked many countries in South America, especially in the Andean countries, where the epidemic killed thousands of people.

Avoid fresh vegetables (eat only boiled ones) and fruits. Drink bottled water only, and make sure that it wasn't opened before. Despite the fact that in most large cities the water undergoes filtration and purification, it's still contains pollutants and bacteria, which not infrequently cause stomach aches and more serious ailments. Carbonated drinks and bottled water will help you overcome the problem (we're not referring to mineral water but to ordinary water that has been boiled and purified). When you're in the country or in places where bottled drinks are unavailable, boil your drinking water and purify it with chlorine tablets.

Mosquitoes and other flying pests are especially common in tropical areas, and are a real menace. **Don't go there** without large quantities of mosquito repellent and — no less important

— ointment to spread on the bite when the repellent fails to work. A visit to Asuncion, Paraguay, or the jungles of eastern Ecuador cannot but end with dozens or hundreds of painful bites.

Every tourist must bring along a small kit with first-aid supplies and medicines. Many kinds of medication are hard to find in South America, and those which are available are expensive and not always usable due to their age or storage conditions. Before you set out, see your doctor in order to obtain an adequate stock of essential medications. A short list of essential drugs and medical items follows:

Medication for intestinal diseases.
Painkillers.
Fever pills.
Anti-malaria pills.
Chlorine tablets for water purification.
Antibiotic ointment.
Antiseptics.
Gauze pads, bandages and adhesive tape.
Medication for chronic illnesses.

The chronically ill, and heart and asthma patients, should consult their doctors concerning the treatment they may require in the climatic conditions and altitude of the lands they're going to visit. Asthmatics should be doubly cautious when going to high elevations, where even healthy people find it hard to adjust to the thin atmosphere.

Women should bring tampons and birth-control pills in sufficient quantity since these items are difficult to obtain in Latin America, except in some of the large cities.

Before setting out, it's best to have a thorough checkup to ascertain that your health permits you to take the trip. Medical care in South America is generally not of the highest quality, and it's best to try not to need it. See your dentist for preventive treatment to forestall problems that might arise during your tour. South American dental care is definitely not recommended, except in truly urgent cases.

For the trip itself, I'd recommend bringing an extra pair of eye glasses and the lense prescription. Contact lenses, though generally convenient to use, are liable to cause problems and discomfort in dry areas and at high elevation.

Thus far we've been speaking of the continent in general. It's obvious that in certain places — mainly cosmopolitan capital cities — the sanitary conditions are good and medical services advanced. Nevertheless, do yourself a favor and set out well-equipped and prepared for most eventualities.

*I*NTRODUCTION

Finances

The most popular and convenient currency to use and exchange in South America is the U.S. dollar, recognized and sought after everywhere; converting it presents no problem in the large cities. The Pound Sterling, Deutsch Mark, and Swiss Franc are also recognized, but exchanging them can involve problems, especially on the black market.

Currency laws vary from country to country. How much money to take and in what form depends to a great extent on the regulations in effect in the countries you decide to visit.

In most South American countries a black market in foreign currency is active. For cash dollars, moneychangers will give you local currency at higher rates than the banks offer. When visiting these countries, it's worthwhile to carry more cash and fewer travelers' checks. Credit card transactions and bank transfers involve the official exchange rate, since charge slips are calculated according to that rate and the transfers are paid in it — in local currency. Given that the difference between the official and "black" rates may reach 50% and more, it's only wise to avoid using these financial means.

The theft epidemic that has spread through some of the South American countries — especially Colombia, Peru, Brazil, and Venezuela — has led many banks to refuse to cash travelers' checks out of fear that they may be stolen, and, at times, tourists are put through an exhausting bureaucratic procedure. A letter of credit is not efficient either; getting it honored is a slow and complicated affair and here, too, and payment is made at the official rate.

Those traveling for short periods can make it easier on themselves by carrying cash, whereas long-term travelers would do well to divide their resources into a number of baskets, to minimize risk.

In certain countries — Uruguay, Venezuela, and at times Bolivia and Ecuador — travelers' checks can sometimes be converted into cash dollars for a fee, but the regulations in these matters are always changing and cannot be relied upon. This point is particularly important for tourists who want to stock up on cash en route to countries with black markets.

It's worth your while to bring a credit card. Their use is widespread throughout South America, and can be used to purchase goods, services, and for cash withdrawals. It's important to note that cash withdrawals involve a 4%-5% commission; you should consider whether this service is worth the price. In any case, using your credit card is worthwhile only in countries where there is no black market, so that your account will be debited at the same rate as that at which you would change money on the spot.

The alternative to carrying cash or using a credit card is travelers' checks. We recommend using small denominations — nothing over $50; hundred-dollar travelers' checks are harder to cash. In small towns, it is difficult to exchange travelers' checks in any case; not only is the exchange rate low, but there is a high commission as well. It's best to stick to travlers' checks issued by *Bank of America*, *Thomas Cook*, and *American Express*.

Always keep your money, credit cards, and documents **well-hidden** in your clothing. Guarding against theft here requires precautionary measures that we're not accustomed to in Europe and North America; nevertheless they are essential, and mustn't be scorned.

What to take

As a general rule, the less you take the better. The advantages of traveling light far outweigh the satisfaction of a few extra clothes — after all, you're going on a trip, not a fashion show. When all is said and done, a large portion of what you take never gets used in any case, and you quickly learn that most of what you took along was quite unnecessary.

Remember, whatever you need — you'll manage to find during the trip — perhaps not of the same type, model, or quality you are used to, but I have yet to meet a traveler wandering around the world. During the trip you'll be picking up many souvenirs and presents, so you should really take along the bare necessities — but plenty of resourcefulness.

Clothing depends on your destination and the season. Businessmen must be smartly dressed, although a jacket and tie are not usually necessary. In the large cities, appropriate evening dress is customary for both men and women, and sportswear for young people and children. *Mochileros* will feel most comfortable in jeans and casual wear, although they should also take along more festive wear for events that require this.

Lightweight and simple clothes are always appreciated, and are easy to wash and carry. Avoid taking elegant evening attire that requires careful transport and special care. It just isn't worth the effort.

I wouldn't suggest taking along more than one backpack or suitcase. These too should be at the most average in size. Baggage weighing more than 15 kg can be a real burden, and more than 20 kg can be even expensive. Many airlines are strict about the baggage limit, and travelers with overweight have to pay for it.

Comfortable walking shoes are perhaps the most important item. These are appropriate for any type of trip or travel. It is not an exaggeration to say that a bad pair of shoes can utterly ruin a trip. So make a point of getting good walking shoes and don't skimp.

Camping Gear

Those embarking on an extended tour and intending to explore the entire continent should put everything in a backpack, including camping gear. When buying camping gear, be sure that its quality is appropriate for your needs. Remember that it must serve you for long months, and that cheap equipment, saving you money at the time of purchase, is liable to prove a painful impediment when you're on the road.

A list of essential items follows:

A lightweight **backpack** with **internal** metal frame, lots of pockets, and laces to which a sleeping bag, mattress, and other gear can be tied.

A **sleeping bag:** Chose one appropriate for the season and the area to which you are headed. For a lengthy trip through a number of climatic zones you should get a warm sleeping bag (-5 or -20 degrees Centigrade) made of down. It must be of excellent quality, well sewn, and with a reliable zipper. Sleeping bags come in various sizes and shapes; be sure that yours matches your dimensions. The "mummy" style, wide at the shoulders and narrow around the legs, is the best of all. It holds body heat well and is easy to carry. Synthetic-filled sleeping bags are much cheaper, but are much larger, bulkier, and heavier. Remember that you'll have to carry it on your back — week after week and month after month — and the inconvenience will outweigh your savings. On the other hand, bear in mind that the down bag has one great disadvantage: when it gets wet, it loses its efficiency and special qualities; sleeping in it then is downright unpleasant.

A **mattress:** To soften the bed of rocks on which you'll spend many a night, we recommend — highly, if you've got a down sleeping bag — an easy-to-carry mattress. There are two common types: foam-rubber and inflatable (especially made for capming). The latter costs more, but provides comfort and ensures a good night's sleep, essential after a full day of walking.

A **tent:** We recommend a two-man, two-layer model with a floor. A one-man tent isn't enough, for you're unlikely to find yourself alone on outings into the country. A two-layer tent provides better protection against rain, retains heat, and repels moisture.

INTRODUCTION

A **cooking stove:** This is essential on hikes through the countryside, and economical in town. Since gas for camping stoves is almost unavailable in South America and comes at great cost when it is at hand, we think it best to use a kerosene stove. The most popular models are made by Colman and the Optimus company of Sweden. They are reliable, safe, and easy to carry. Remember to exercise great caution when using them. Flammable materials may cause disaster if you don't treat them with the caution they deserve.

Utensils: Bring the minimum, but choose good ones. Metal or aluminium is best. Food should be kept in plastic or cloth bags, since cans take up more space in your pack.

Miscellaneous: Pocketknife, flashlight, rope, etc.

Buying equipment represents one of the largest expenditures of your trip. It's therefore worthwhile to do some comparison shopping and not buy hastily. At the same time, I must again stress that economy must not be at the expense of quality, for the "saving" is liable to cost you dearly on the road. It's also worth noting that camping equipment is in great demand in South America, so that at the end of your trip your gear can be sold for a reasonable price; not much lower than what you paid for it.

The traditional centers for buying camping gear are London and New York, where you'll find the widest selection and the most attractive prices. Though London has many stores that handle camping gear, the best, in my view, is the Youth Hostel Association store at 14 Southampton Street (Tel. 836-8541). This is a gigantic store where you'll find it all — from shoelaces to emergency dehydrated rations. A tourist could enter this store stark naked and come out a few hours later with everything needed for a trip around the world. YHA members receive a 10% discount on all purchases.

In New York you can pick up your gear at any of hundreds of camping and sporting goods stores. The largest, Paragon, offers a seemingly inexhaustible selection of merchandise, at prices suitable for all budgets.

Photography
One of the most enjoyable aspects of a trip is taking photographs. It is worth making your photographic preparations in advance, acquiring appropriate equipment, and learning at least the basics of how to use your camera.

Many tourists wander through South America with sophisticated and complicated photographic equipment. South America is a photographer's paradise, fertile ground for expression and creativity. Those who are familiar with the secrets of the art will come equipped with several cameras, lenses, and a range of film.

If, however, you wish to commemorate your trip without lugging a mobile studio around with you, it is recommended to take one camera with three lenses: a standard lens (50mm), a wide-angle lens, and a telephoto lens. A good lens that combines all three functions is the 35-210 zoom. Buy good and reliable equipment, and remember to wrap it well and to insure it. Avoid taking fancy and expensive equipment, since it is likely to get knocked about on the way. Such equipment can also attract thieves. Film is expensive in most South American countries, so take along plenty of film, since you can always sell what you don't use. As a general rule, use ASA 64 film, which is suitable for almost every type of light and weather conditions you'll encounter in South America. ASA 400 film is also worth taking, since it is hard to find, and particularly expensive when available. If you have to buy photographic supplies in South America itself, do so only in the large cities, since elsewhere, not only is film hard to come by and exorbitantly priced, most of it is also likely to have long since past its expiration date.

In South America film is developed in various sorts of laboratories, and it's not always worth taking the risk. As a rule, it's better to develop films in the United States or Europe. In some locations, such as Buenos Aires, São Paulo or La Paz, you can have your film developed with relative safety in Kodak laboratories. Slide film whose purchase price includes developing should be sent directly to the company laboratory, which will return it directly to your home address.

For those carrying video cameras, keep in mind that in some countries Betamax is more popular than VHS, and Video 8 is not always available, nor are the accessories (filters, batteries, etc.). Bring with you all the necessary equipment. When using rechargeable batteries, remember that some countries use 220V and others 110V. Bring along an adaptor with the proper amperage. Those who buy pre-recorded video-cassettes, pay attention to the fact that some countries use the NTSC (American) standard, while others use the more widespread PAL (German). Check the labels before you pay!

Language
You won't have any language problems in South America's large cities. Most people dealing principally with tourists have sufficient command of English to help you get what you want, and it can be assumed that shortly after your arrival you'll

pick up enough of the local conversational "code" to express basic needs. The problems begin when you venture outside the professional tourism framework, and even on its fringes — taxis and restaurants. Few taxi drivers or waiters speak English. Communication is in Spanish only, as are most restaurant menus.

It's even worse in outlying areas. English-speakers are few and far between in the towns, and in villages — nonexistent. On the roads, too, and even in tourist bureaus, airline offices, and banks, it's hard to find someone fluent in the language of Shakespeare, Keats and Milton, or even with enough English to understand a request for a glass of water.

Nor will a command of Spanish or Portuguese solve the problem altogether. In many places — Paraguay, northern Bolivia and the mountain towns of Peru, for example — ancient Indian languages are used. Although most locals speak Spanish at one level or another, it's hard to maintain verbal communication with them in the accepted sense of the term.

Those who've set their hearts on a long, thorough exploration of the secrets of the South American continent absolutely must acquire the basic linguistic skills before setting out. It's true that one picks up a language during a trip, and that within a month or two one is able to carry on a basic conversation with the locals, but advance preparation will make things much easier and increase your enjoyment. No less important is the fact that advance study will establish a correct grammatical foundation, to which a large vocabulary will be added as you go. On-the-road study, though easier, is built atop a shaky foundation, which will demand great efforts to repair afterwards.

How to get there

By air: Most European airlines maintain service between their respective capitals and various destinations in South America, as do the national airlines of the South American countries. The latter also fly to various destinations in the United States, as does *Eastern*.

A number of ticket options are available to and from South America; their terms and fares vary from airline to airline and from country to country. Excursion tickets, limited in time, are generally the cheapest, followed by youth and student tickets. The most expensive are ordinary tickets sold at IATA prices. A combined ticket, by which different sections of the route are flown on different airlines, is usually more expensive than flying all sections with the same airline.

*I*NTRODUCTION

Planning your flights requires thorough preparation and comprehensive market research. Careful investigation and resourcefulness can save lots of money and cut the price of your trip. The open market and fierce competition have led to a situation in which passengers aboard the same plane on the very same flight may well have paid completely different fares.

As a rule a round-trip ticket is worthwhile, unless you're making an extended trip and don't want to commit yourself about where and when it's going to end. Airline tickets bought in South America are subject to excise taxes at rates that vary from country to country; this makes them significantly more expensive. A round-trip ticket purchased outside the country from which you're returning is exempt from tax.

Those who want a one-way ticket should check which routes and combinations may make the trip cheaper. Such routes, for example, go via the Carribbean islands, Central America, and so on. Certain destinations are traditionally more expensive than others. Flights to São Paulo, Buenos Aires, Santiago, La Paz, and elsewhere are far more expensive than those to Lima, Rio de Janeiro, and Bogotá. Relatively low-cost flights reach the latter group of cities from London, Paris, and Miami. It's a good idea to inquire at travel agencies which specialize in these destinations about the cheapest and best way to get there.

Ordinary tickets are more expensive one-way than round-trip. Their great advantage lies in the fact that they are calculated on a mileage basis. Holders can change dates and arrange for stopovers on the way, so long as these remain within the permitted mileage. Thus, for example, a New York-Buenos Aires ticket gives one the right to stop over in Miami, Caracas, Belem, Rio, and São Paulo at no extra cost.

London and Miami are known as preferred ports of departure for Latin America; here you can usually find the cheapest tickets. A significant portion of these tickets are sold over-the-counter only, and travel agents in other countries are not permitted to sell them. A stopover in one of those cities and a visit to some of these agencies may be worth your while, even though you must remember that two days in London cost money too, as does a separate ticket to London. At times it may be cheaper to buy a slightly higher-priced ticket where you live, with the margin offset by the savings in time, stopover expense, and the effort involved in getting around a foreign city.

The national airlines of Venezuela (*Viasa*), Colombia (*Avianca*) and Peru (*Aero Peru*) are known for being less expensive than the other South American flag carriers. They fly to numerous destinations, but you must change planes in their respective capitals. European airlines such as *Air France, Iberia,* and the Portuguese *TAP* also offer seasonal packages worth taking advantage of. Never buy until you've checked and compared prices!

When buying discounted tickets, be very careful about their validity and reliability. Remember that any change involves additional payment, and it's best to know how much is in question in advance. Avail yourself of the services of reliable travel agents — there are charlatans in this field too. Best of all are travel agencies that specialize in tourism to South America, and have package deals with various airlines.

By land: An overland trip from North America via Central America is a unique experience. It can be done by car, bus, or train, and you'll need to do the Panama-Colombia stretch by sea or air. The highway there still isn't suitable for traffic, and is impassible several months out of the year. Due to political tensions in Central America, you should check exactly when and how to cross various countries, and, even more so, when and how not to. If you're driving, bring along plenty of spare parts, and have somcone along with mechanical knowledge. Your car papers must be in good order, since they'll be inspected every time you turn a corner.

INTRODUCTION

Part Two — Easing the Shock: Where Have We Landed?

Previous sections of this introduction have dealt with the preparations and arrangements necessary before the trip begins. Now we shall survey some relevant details concerning the trip itself, to make the experience of landing in this alien world a bit easier. The material we're about to present is meant first of all to facilitate your adjustment to South America, but reading it before you go may be of great importance in determining the form and nature of your tour. Here you'll find much **useful information** about all spheres of your trip which will help you overcome quickly, comfortably, and efficiently the range of problems liable to arise at the very beginning of your trip.

The paragraphs that follow offer some general advice, and in the chapters on each respective country, you'll find more specific information on those countries and their sites.

Accommodation

South America offers a wide variety of accommodation possibilities. All the large cities have luxury hotels, some of which belong to the world's great hotel chains; standards here equal those in the Western countries, with prices set accordingly. In the large cities you'll also find locally owned luxury hotels, whose prices are lower although the level of service is in no way inferior.

Intermediate-class and inexpensive hotels abound. Almost all hotels outside the cities charge intermediate or low rates, and many are very inexpensive. Lodging is significantly cheaper in the Andean countries than in the lowland countries (Brazil and Venezuela), but conditions there, too, are far worse.

Be careful when choosing a hotel that is not first-class. In many places these are not regulated in any way. At the same time we must note that the Ministries of Tourism in most South American countries are making an effort to enforce hotel regulations. In the large cities and major tourist centers you'll find that most hotels are clean, reliable, and altogether satisfactory.

Away from the big tourist centers and along the roads, there are always places to stay. Almost every village has a house that serves as a hotel, but don't expect much here — at best a creaky bed and rickety chair. Sanitation and cleanliness, too, are not the best.

Youth hostels aren't popular in South America, though you will find them in some places. On the other hand, it's customary to put up young travelers in churches, schools, youth clubs, and even fire stations — for no charge.

Camping grounds are rather rare. In some countries — mainly Argentina, Chile, and Brazil — they do exist and can serve the tourist public. They aren't organized along North American lines, and the tourist must provide his own tent and sleeping equipment. On many routes tourists spend their nights under the stars in improvised campgrounds and an informal atmosphere.

Food and drink

In the culinary field, too, we've landed in a very strange place. We've all heard the legends about Argentinian steaks and Brazilian coconuts, but we should also be ready for what comes along with them — guinea-pig (*cuy*) in Peru, eel in Chile, and similar terrors elsewhere.

The South American cuisine, like everything else on the continent, combines Indian tradition with Spanish influence, and its national character is determined by what's grown where. A lot of meat is eaten in Argentina, Uruguay, Paraguay and Venezuela; lots of fish and seafood in Chile and Peru; and tropical fruit in Brazil. Potatoes and rice are standard side-dishes in every restaurant; so is soup, a very popular item throughout the continent and many varieties are served.

Milk products are hard to get in the Andean countries, in contrast to Argentina, Chile, and Brazil where they are plentiful — and excellent. *Empanadas* (stuffed pastry), *mate* (South American tea), and many other delicacies are only some of the contents in the bursting menu of excellent food and drink enjoyed by the local populace. We'll cover them in detail and at length in our Introduction to each country.

South American restaurants are innumerable. Every second house serves as one, and every streetcorner has two more. In the cities, a variety of food is served at all levels of quality, while in towns and villages native and peasant cooking is the most common fare. Hygienic conditions aren't the best, but that's something you get used to as time and upset stomachs pass... Western manners and dress are customary in the better restaurants, while the more popular ones favor a free and

*I*NTRODUCTION

informal atmosphere. Eating at streetside stands, kiosks, and market stalls is a common practice. It's a quick and cheap way to get a meal, and how most of the locals get their nourishment. Try it, but remember to check how clean, or perhaps how "undirty" the place is. Mealtimes vary from country to country, according to the climate.

Fruit and vegetable lovers will have problems in the Andean countries, where most produce may be tainted with various diseases. Even if they appear healthy to the eye, their insides are liable to be infested. You must therefore adopt an ironclad rule about fruit and vegetables: peel them, cook them, or throw them out. If you can't peel or cook it, **don't try it!**

Vegetarians will manage quite well. Although vegetarian restaurnts aren't very common, the major foods on which a vegetarian diet is based are available in abundance, and can be prepared yourself.

Domestic transportation
Airlines link the South American countries with one another. International flights are frequent and convenient, and prices resemble those of short international flights in the West. Domestic flights are another story. Here the range is broad, complications are rife, and confusion reigns.

In Brazil, Argentina, Peru, and Colombia the airlines offer an open ticket for unlimited flights during a predetermined time period. In these countries, where covering distances overland requires many days, this is an offer certainly worthy of consideration. To go from Rio de Janeiro to Manaus or from Buenos Aires to Bariloche takes days or weeks by land, and the cost of an individual flight is high. In addition, *Aerolineas Argentinas* has reduced-price night flights, which cost about the equivalent trips by bus. You must therefore weigh the alternatives well and decide accordingly. An unlimited-flight ticket may be bought only **outside** the country in which you intend to fly.

The armed forces of the South American countries also operate flights that carry civilian passengers. These are cheaper than their civilian counterparts, but take off at irregular intervals and generally involve antiquated aircraft.

Another typical problem of domestic flights is overbooking. Airlines are not reliable when issuing tickets, and frequently sell more tickets than the number of seats at their disposal. You must therefore get to the airport early; otherwise the flight is liable to fill up and leave you waiting for another. Cancellations,

*I*NTRODUCTION

delays, and changes of routes are also common occurrences, for which the tourist must be prepared.

Be very sure to mark your gear, although even this doesn't guarantee that it will reach its destination. The care of passengers' luggage, especially in Peru, is negligent and contemptuous. Try to carry as much as possible, and relegate to the baggage compartment only the necessary minimum, **after** you've packed and marked it properly.

Driving a private or rented car is widespread in all South American countries. More and more tourists choose this way to get around, and avail themselves of the large international car-rental companies or local firms.

If you want to bring your own car, you should stock up on spare parts and make sure your documents are in order. Bureaucratic difficulties are especially frequent at border crossings, and garage services are rare in the hinterlands. Consult Auto Club experts in the United States or Europe before you set out for up-to-date material, including maps and the addresses of local Auto Clubs (which we've provided in the chapters pertaining to each country). Auto Clubs in South America are very active, and their personnel provide assistance and guidance to members of similar clubs abroad.

Your car must be in top mechanical condition before you set out. In the Andean countries many roads reach thousands of meters above sea level, where engines must be specially tuned. Note that the road networks of Colombia, Venezuela, Brazil, and Bolivia are undeveloped (apart from main highways) and difficult to drive on. It's better to avoid driving there, and find another way of getting around. When traveling off the main roads, be sure to have enough fuel for the return trip, plus spare parts — service stations are almost nowhere to be found. A breakdown here is both unpleasant and expensive.

Car-rental rates vary from country to country, but usually they are around an international average for mid-sized cars in the large agencies. Local agencies can sometimes be cheaper, but do not offer the same level of service. The minimum age for renting a car is 22 (25 in some countries), and the customer must leave a sizeable deposit or a credit card. It's important to insure the car when you rent it.

River boats are a common means of transportation in a number of areas, especially the eastern portions of the Andean countries and northwest Brazil (the jungles). Here you'll find that the only way to get from one settlement to another is by boat or ship along the river, and not infrequently you'll have to rent your own to reach your destination. Rental fees are high, but energetic bargaining will drive them down to something almost reasonable.

The major means of **public transportation** include trains, buses, trucks, and taxis. **Trains** operate only in some of the countries, and most are old, slow, and uncomfortable. They are not as common a way of getting around as they are in Europe, so don't plan a tour based on the railways. **Buses**, by contrast, are the most popular form of transportation, and connect all places of settlement. In several countries — Brazil, Chile, Colombia and Argentina, for example — the buses are modern and comfortable; in others they're motorized crates. Differences in quality and service are extreme, precluding a uniform and precise description. On some routes, you'll find smiling stewardesses; elsewhere you'll find terrible overcrowding and rampant theft. In any case, the bus remains the cheapest and most efficient way of getting around on land. **Shared taxis and minibuses** run on many intercity routes. Their fares are higher than the buses, but their advantage lies in far greater speed, comfort and safety. **Trucks** (*camiones*) carry passengers mainly in the poorer countries, where they ply remote dirt roads with their loads of shoulder-to-shoulder animals and people, the latter seated on piles of freight and clinging to their baggage lest it tumble off. It's a unique experience by all accounts — a cheap way (sometimes the only way) of reaching many remote places.

Hitchhiking is common in Chile and Argentina, chiefly in their southern regions. Hitchhikers there — especially women — get lifts easily, and vast distances can be covered quickly and cheaply. In the Andean countries, an accepted practice is to demand payment from a passenger, even if he thought he was getting a free ride. In Brazil and Colombia tourists have been attacked and their gear stolen: avoid hitchhiking in these countries by no means!

Urban transportation is efficient in most large cities. Bus lines, subways, taxis, and *colectivos* (shared taxi service) contribute to mobility in densely-populated urban areas and are usually rapid and reliable. In many countries, particularly the Andean ones, taxis have no meters and the fare must be agreed upon with the driver — **before starting out.**

Personal security

One of the most severe problems that visitors to South America are liable to encounter is protecting themselves and their

*I*NTRODUCTION

belongings. A combination of social and political ferment, plus the desperate poverty, makes violent outbursts all too common. Sometimes these are directed at the authorities, in the form of hostile underground activity, and sometimes aimed at the tourist, whose valuable baggage attracts thieves. The problems are especially serious in Colombia, Peru, Brazil, and Venezuela — in that order. In the Introduction to each of those countries, we have included guidelines on appropriate behavior and preventive measures. Argentina, Uruguay, Paraguay, Chile, Bolivia, and Ecuador are considered to be tranquil and relaxed; have no fears about touring there.

Local currencies

The various South American currencies are noted for their worrisome instability. In recent years they've been considerably devalued against the dollar; for the tourists, this has lowered the cost of a stay there significantly. If on an extended visit, you'll find that for every dollar you change on your last day you'll receive more local currency than you got when you arrived. Accordingly, it's worthwhile to change money only to cover your immediate needs since within a few days you are likely to get more for your dollars.

Banks and moneychangers (*Casa de Cambio*) change currency; the latter usually offer a slightly higher rate and far less bureaucratic red-tape than the former. Though several countries do not allow private dealing in foreign currency, and restrict activity to the major banks, black-market moneychangers will always find a way to offer you a more attractive rate. Be extremely careful about dealing with them — verify their reliability and be sure to count what they give you.

Most airports also have some arrangements for converting foreign currency. If you've arrived on a weekend or holiday, change enough to cover your needs until the next business day. In the city itself you probably won't find a bank open, and may be forced to change money at a poor rate. Cash dollars are always preferred, but it's best to hold onto these for countries where a black market operates, and use travelers' checks elsewhere.

When entering a new country by land, don't change more money at the border checkpost than you'll need to reach the nearest large city, where you can expect to get a better rate. In any event, check and compare rates carefully with a number of moneychangers before you decide; differences among them are by no means small. Count the money you're given very carefully, making sure you get what you paid for.

Many moneychangers will try to exploit your innocence by holding back a few bills from the stack they hand you.

When leaving a country, get rid of any remaining local currency; it's worth considerably less in other countries, even those right across the border, and sometimes in the country itself, if you are back the next day.

Tourist services

A well-arranged and efficient system of services awaits the tourist in most South American countries. As tourism increases, governments become more aware of its tremendous economic impact. They have begun investing in expanding and improving the infrastructure and services which will help tourists get oriented and acclimated. This infrastructure includes not only hotels and restaurants, but also information centers, transportation services, guides, various publications, and more. Major airports will greet you the moment you touch down with counters to provide information, hotel reservations, car rental, and baggage checking. The bus and taxi fares from the airport into town are usually fixed by the government.

Almost every city has a tourist information bureau which offers guidance, maps, and other material. One of the noticeable drawbacks of these bureaus is the lamentable fact that their personnel often speak only Spanish, so that a tourist who cannot get along in that language will find it hard to avail himself of their services.

In addition to the tourist bureaus, several other organizations offer tourists information and assistance. The most important are the various Auto Clubs (*Automóvil Club*), which will keep you updated in matters of transportation and tour routes. There are also the military geographical institutes (*Instituto Geográfico Militar*), where you can obtain maps for hiking tours, the nature reserve authorities, etc.

Medical and health services

The most common health problems that a tourist to South America is liable to suffer are intestinal problems and difficulties in adjusting to the thin air at high altitudes. In both cases you'll probably need nothing more than short and routine treatment, which can be obtained at any regional clinic.

For more serious problems you'll have to go to a hospital. In national capitals and other large cities there are British or American hospitals, to which tourists should turn in case of need. In other cases, it's best to turn to English-speaking private physicians to whom you can describe your ailments, though you must be cautious about accepting treatment which seems inappropriate to you.

First-aid services in South America aren't the best, and still can't treat many health problems. You must therefore be doubly careful, and seek out qualified medical help in any case of suspected illness.

Dental treatment that can be put off should be put off. When that is impossible, visit a qualified dentist who has modern equipment.

Altitude — how to cope with thin air

The high elevation of South America's mountains requires one to take appropriate measures. Remember that the atmosphere is thin at these altitudes. The amount of oxygen is less than at sea level, upsetting the body's equilibrium. If you breathe at your normal rate you'll simply take in less oxygen, and consequently suffer from asthma-like sensations of choking and weakness. A certain amount of attention or caution may alleviate the problem and lessen its impact. Common side-effects are dizziness, nausea, headaches, and at times fainting. To avoid these reactions — which involve a certain discomfort even if they are not dangerous — you must take a number of precautionary measures.

First, it's best to reach the mountains by an overland route, in order to moderate the rate of ascent and give your body a longer period of time to acclimatize. If you arrive by air, there will be a sharp transition which results in a quicker and stronger impact. In any event, be sure to set aside the first twenty-four hours for rest, relaxation, and reduced food intake. This will grant your body a suitable interval to adapt to the lower percentage of oxygen in the atmosphere.

At high elevations you should refrain from physical effort, including that considered insignificant under normal conditions. Walk slowly, do not run or carry heavy loads, slow down even more when walking uphill or climbing stairs, and take frequent rest stops. Keep physical activity to a minimum: don't smoke, and avoid large, heavy meals. If necessary, you can buy special medication in drugstores which expand the blood vessels, thus increasing the amount of oxygen supplied to the body. Asthmatics, heart patients, and pregnant women tend to suffer more at high altitudes and it's recommended that they stay away from these areas as much as possible.

In most cases, as we have said, rest will help but sometimes this may have to be augmented by medical care and short periods of oxygen treatment. Hospitals, clinics, and even ordinary institutions recognize the problem, are experienced at treating it, and will be glad to help. As time passes, the body grows accustomed to the new situation and can resume normal activity — if more slowly and cautiously, and less strenuously.

Discounts for students and young travelers

In South America students are eligible for discounts on public transportation and admission to various sites. The discounts are not offered on all occasions, and certainly not automatically. For details, consult the section on documents, and the text, where you will find these discounts mentioned wherever they are offered.

In regard to accommodation, few places offer reduced youth rates and those which do, are mentioned in the relevant chapters.

Behavior and manners

The rules of manners accepted in the West apply here as well. The "dress code" is similar, though less formal. Both men and women wear sporty evening wear for official events, concerts or dinner in an elegant restaurant. In the daytime, light and airy clothing is wholly acceptable. For men, shorts are out of place except on the beach. In certain places, such as Caracas, the police can fine anyone who's improperly dressed in public. In Brazil, seashore dress is acceptable, but only in town and not on an intercity bus, for example. Women should dress modestly and avoid revealing garments. At holy places, those improperly attired are not allowed to enter.

Behavior toward women is somewhat archaic here, a matter which carries with it a certain grace and charm. Among descendants of the Indians as well, whose women bear the brunt of the physical burden, women are accorded respect and are treated with great consideration.

Latin Americans are friendly and hospitable. Many tourists are warmly welcomed into local homes, where they are made to feel at ease.

Among the European communities in Argentina and other countries it is customary to greet guests with a friendly kiss on the cheek. It's a gesture of friendship, and expresses no intimacy of any kind. The South American way of life is conservative and restrained; conspicuous permissiveness is nonexistent here.

In Spanish it is accepted practice to address people with the formal *usted* rather than the familiar *tu*. This serves to express respect and esteem rather than distance and estrangement.

It's customary to tip restaurant waiters (10%-15% of the bill) and service personnel (a small amount). Taxi drivers with whom you've negotiated a fare at the beginning of your trip do not expect a tip.

Keeping in touch

Postal and telephone services in Latin America are far from efficient. They are slow and clumsy, unreliable, and some are even expensive. An airmail letter sent to South America is liable to spend an extended period (up to several weeks) en route, perhaps not arriving at all.

Poste Restante (General Delivery) service is available in national capitals, but one shouldn't rely on it too much. Mail which arrives for you at the post office will only be kept for one month. *American Express* offices accept mail for their customers, and we recommend this method: have your correspondents send letters to an *American Express* office, where they will be kept for you until you get there.

Sending postal items from South America also requires attention. Mail letters only at post offices; use airmail, preferably registered. Film and important items should be sent registered, and only from main post offices. Avoid stamps in favor of a post-office cachet, since stamps not infrequently catch the eye of the sorter, who appropriates them for himself; more seriously, he destroys the contents. Letters encounter prolonged delays on the way, and if your tour lasts for two or three weeks your letters are likely to reach friends and family when you're already back at home, planning your next vacation.

Sending parcels involves much effort, time, and trouble. Parcels must be of fixed weight, and need to be boxed and wrapped. Those weighing more than one kilogram require inspection by a customs clerk, who sits — of course — somewhere other than the post office. The parcel has to be left open for inspection; only then can you seal it. Parcels may be sent by air or surface mail. The former is fast and sure, but is immeasurably more expensive than surface mail. Though surface is cheaper, it is far slower, and your parcel may spend many months in transit. It also happens that surface-mail parcels "get lost" and do not arrive at all. Surface mail is considered reliable from Argentina,

*I*NTRODUCTION

Chile, Ecuador, and the Brazilian coastal cities, but not from Peru, Colombia, or Bolivia.

South America has telephone links to the rest of the world. International phone service is slow and expensive, but the connections are usually of satisfactory quality. Placing an international call from your hotel is liable to involve a wait of several hours. It's therefore wise to make most such calls from the telephone exchange found downtown in the large cities. These have several booths to which callers are summoned, each in his turn. The minimum length for such a call is three minutes. Collect calls are not always possible; it depends on where you are and to where you're calling. (This is not the case in Brazil, where the International phone service is quick and efficient, and one can make collect calls from any public phone.)

Shopping and souvenirs

Any tour of South America will add many kilograms of souvenirs and purchases to your luggage. Whether it's a Dior suit from Buenos Aires, a poncho from La Paz or jewelry from Brazil. Every traveler, even the most frugal, will end up buying at least a few of the innumerable souvenirs encountered on the way. And this acquisitiveness is perfectly justified.

In South America you'll find an amazing concentration of crafts and other artifacts, called *artesanía*, most hand-made — the glory of local craftsmen and artists. Their beauty and the special character of these items will have you digging into your wallets time and again.

Those touring only one or two countries will find information on the characteristic wares of each country in the relevant chapters, and will soon discover the wealth of possibilities. Keep in mind a number of important rules so as to avoid later problems with budget and weight (or rather excess weight).

Firstly, remember that all of South America resembles one gigantic market. It's hard to find a product exclusive to a single place, though there are, of course, differences in quality, types, and the like. Accordingly you'll be able to compare styles, prices, and quality, to ponder the various options... and to bargain! Bargaining is essential here; if you accept the stated price, not only will you pay more than you should but you'll also hurt the vendors' feelings, for they look forward to this give-and-take with their customers.

Each of the South American countries has its own characteristic forms of *artesanía*. These give artistic expression to the economic condition of the country in question and the sources of its treasures. Thus Chile abounds in metalcrafts, Argentina in clothing, Brazil in precious stones, and the Andean countries in woollen fabrics and woodcrafts.

Andean *artesanía* is noted for its strong Indian influence. In this region you'll find lovely woollen products, musical instruments, pottery, and astonishingly beautiful woodcarvings. Wall hangings, various garments, and antique fabrics are only some of the local treasures, and it's only natural that we'll cram them into our suitcases in considerable quantities. If you are travelling many months, it's best to send these home by mail (see above), for otherwise they're liable to interfere with the rest of your trip, getting in your way and causing problems.

In the cities you'll find tourist shops that offer top-quality merchandise at prices to match. As you travel you're bound to find these where they're made, closer to their natural environment and at their natural prices.

Overland border crossings

To explore South America properly, we must cross borders rather frequently. Whether during a combined tour of Argentina and Chile, a journey from Colombia to Ecuador, or on any other route, we'll encounter a number of traits common to all these inspection points.

All frontier stations are staffed by immigration officers in charge of the gates to their respective countries. They allow traffic to pass only during certain hours, which vary from station to station. In most cases border crossings are open from morning to nightfall, sometimes closing for an afternoon *siesta*. Some stations are open for only half a day on weekends. Check out the situation thoroughly before you reach the border, so as not to lose a full day's touring.

The main crossing points have separate lines for tourists and local citizens; crossing procedures here are simpler and quicker. In most countries you'll have to fill out a tourist card, stamped by the immigration clerk, which indicates how long you are permitted to stay. Always be sure to request the maximum time allowed — generally 90 days. Though getting an extension once you're in the country is possible, it can be very time-consuming.

Moneychangers congregate near crossing points. When changing money with them beware of being misled as to the exchange rates or in counting the bills.

Border posts can be reached by taxi or local bus. Direct bus routes from one border town to its counterpart on the other side are more expensive. It's therefore best to get to the border, cross on foot, and continue by vehicle on the other side after having taken care of the formalities.

Taxes and custom duties

Tourists must pay duty only on valuable items brought in as gifts, cigarettes and alcohol in excessive quantities, or commercial samples. These excluded, tourists can bring in personal belongings, including all required gear.

Among the many taxes imposed in South America, tourists are obliged to pay two: a port tax when leaving the country, and in some countries an excise tax on air tickets purchased there. Port taxes vary from country to country, as do the rates of the air ticket tax. When planning your return trip, it's therefore convenient to find out where to end it according to the tax you will have to pay. Sometimes these taxes can add more than 10% to the price of the ticket.

Working hours

The afternoon *siesta* is almost the Latin American trademark. In every country, businesses, shops, and offices close for two or three hours in the afternoon; during that time it's hard to find a seat in a restaurant, and even the streets seem more crowded.

Most businesses open early in the morning and stay open until evening. Office reception hours are usually only before noon. On weekends most businesses and offices are closed. Shops are open half-day on Saturdays, and are closed Sundays. Many museums are closed on Mondays.

Holidays and festivals

South America's holiday season, on a continent-wide basis, lasts the entire year, though most special occasions tend to be concentrated in February-March, June-July, and December, when you can celebrate the carnivals in Rio and elsewhere, *Inti Raimi* (the Sun Festival) in Cuzeo, Peru, and Christmas everywhere. During those seasons, much of the local population are themselves on vacation, and the general ambience isn't conducive to business. On national holidays, most services and many institutions are closed. When planning your tour, be sure to keep the dates of holidays in mind, and arrange matters so that your visit won't suffer on their account.

B OLIVIA

Bolivia is certainly one of the most interesting countries in South America. Its geography, from the dense jungles in the east to the arid Andean plains in the west, and its Indian population, make it a fascinating country to visit.

Bolivia offers the rare opportunity of entering a strange, wonderful world, whose value system, customs, and outward appearance are unlike anything we are used to. Here primitivism, simplicity, a slow pace of life and an almost stoical apathy still reign. It is difficult to believe that Bolivia has experienced more political instability and unrest than any other country in the world.

Everything seems to be a century behind. If we were to take away the cars and electricity, we would be thrown back five hundred years in time. Even in the suburbs of the large cities, single-story adobe houses, unpaved roads, wells, earthenware vessels, wood-burning stoves and other such relics from the past, are still very much in existence and will probably be present in the future too.

History

Existing settlement atop the mountains, in the region currently known as the Altiplano, apparently dates back to the seventh century. Before then, the Tiwanaku culture flourished in the area, with a high level of social and material development.

Controversy surrounds the origins of this culture, and researchers have come up with dates hundreds of years apart. However, it is clear that the Tiwanaku civilization disappeared several centuries before the arrival of the Spanish conquerors. (See "Short trips around La Paz — *Tiwanaku*").

When the Spaniards arrived in the 16th century, they found a large agricultural population in this region, who spoke mainly Aymara and Quechua. The Indian tribes warred among themselves, especially the Aymara against the Quechua. The Incas, upon conquering the area, settled in large numbers, intermarrying with the local Aymara people and thus laying the foundations of the Bolivian nation as it exists today.

BOLIVIA

When silver and rich deposits were discovered near the towns of Potosí and Oruro in the Altiplano (or Upper Peru as it was known then), the importance of the area soared. The Spanish, rejoicing in these promising discoveries, set thousands of workers to mine the metals and ores for export to Europe. Prosperity reached its peak in the mid-17th century, at which time Potosí, then the largest city on the American continents, had some 150,000 inhabitants, living mainly off the mines.

B OLIVIA

The Spaniards founded other cities, including La Paz and Chuquisaca, later renamed Sucre. These towns were intended to strengthen Spanish unity, while at the same time supplying the needs of the mining towns. In 1776, when Upper Peru was transferred from the jurisdiction of the Spanish Viceroy in Peru to the Spanish Viceroy in Argentina, the precious metals were exported through Buenos Aires. At the same time, the University of Chuquisaca developed into an important intellectual center, promoting ideas that had considerable influence in the more distant South American countries. In 1809, the call for independence rang out from Chuquisaca, calling for revolt against Spain, which was under the heel of Napoleon's conquering army at the time. Even though the revolt was suppressed by the legions of the Viceroy in Peru, the call was sufficient to kindle the spark of rebellion in neighboring countries, with the result that Argentina, Paraguay, Chile and Uruguay all declared their independence within a few years. Bolivia continued to bear the yoke of the Spanish, who refused to give up the rich mines. Only in 1825, one year after the young General Antonio de Sucre routed the Spanish in battle in Peru, did Simon Bolívar, one of the continent's foremost leaders and thinkers, declare the independence of the country that today bears his name. General Antonio de Sucre was elected as the country's first president.

Upon achieving independence, the newly-founded country was immediately confronted with serious economic problems, which, apart from short periods of prosperity, have dogged Bolivia to this day. These problems are largely responsible for her continuing reputation as a poor and backward country. The root of the problem lies in the fact that the national economy was almost exclusively based on mining, so that the country is at the mercy of the international market, with its sharp fluctuations and instability. As if to prove the point, at the end of the war of independence which had drained the national coffers, there was a significant decline in the world demand for silver, and Bolivia, as a result, entered a troubled economic and political era. In an attempt to solve these difficulties, President Andres de Santa Cruz sought union with Peru, but the protests of his Chilean neighbors thwarted his efforts. Chile continued "showing an interest" in its undeveloped neighbor, and when rich deposits of sodium nitrate were discovered in the Atacama desert — then Bolivian territory — Chile began exerting considerable pressure in order to gain a share in the profits. When these pressures proved ineffective, the five-year War of the Pacific broke out (1879-84). The Chilean army defeated Bolivia and Peru, captured the Atacama Desert with its mines, and reached the outskirts of Lima.

B OLIVIA

As a result of the war, Bolivia lost her outlet to the sea, and was henceforth dependent on her neighbors for exporting her goods. Consequently, more attention was given to internal affairs, and this internal political consolidation gave rise to social stability and tranquility, which in turn encouraged foreign investment and the development of the mines. New mining techniques were introduced and a railroad was laid. Towards the end of the 19th century, when there were signs of another decline in the world silver market, the demand for tin increased significantly among industrialized nations. Bolivia, which till then had neglected this metal, began investing considerable efforts in the development of her tin mines. To this day, tin constitutes an important export.

The change of emphasis from silver to tin mining had social as well as economic repercussions, since it lowered the status of the silver-mine owners. Development continued into the present century, and Bolivia began to deal with her social problems. However, this respite did not last long. Bolivia's neighbors continued exerting pressure in the border areas, coveting districts that seemed economically promising: Argentina annexed part of the Chaco, Brazil appropriated a large, rich stretch of land in the east, later forcing Bolivia to "sell" it to her, and Paraguay claimed a foothold in what was left of the desolate Chaco. The Bolivian government adopted a tolerant stance and conceded these territories. As compensation for damages incurred, Bolivia signed dependency and compensation agreements with her neighbors, which included the laying of railway lines from Bolivia to ports on the Pacific Ocean, to Argentina, and to Brazil.

During the First World War the mining industry reached its apex, but the ensuing prosperity brought with it political power struggles. In the early 1930's, when the economic situation deteriorated due to the 1929 Wall Street crash, fresh border skirmishes broke out with Paraguay. The Bolivian government, seeing war as a way of diverting public attention from economic problems, provoked a war that lasted for three years (1932-35). The war, having claimed thousands of lives, ended with the total defeat of the Bolivian army, and led to the loss of most of the Chaco. The ensuing domestic turmoil, brought about by this traumatic defeat, encouraged extreme political trends. The army seized power and subjected Bolivia to ten years of chaos and bloodshed (1936-46). The fascistic National Revolutionary Movement, which was the main political force of the times, led to the appointment of Colonel Villaroel as president in 1943. He remained chief-of-state till 1946, when another violent revolt broke out, in the course of which Villaroel was hanged in the square facing the presidential palace.

Since 1946, Bolivia has suffered from continuing social and political strife, and except for short periods of peace, the country has been subjected to violent changes. Bolivia has had more than 180 (!) governments in less than two centuries of its independent existance, with military men and civilians alternating as presidents. The most significant of these vicissitudes took place in the early fifties, when the National Revolutionary Movement again seized power in a bloody revolt. They nationalized the mines, instituted comprehensive reforms which altered the balance of power and the distribution of land, and established universal suffrage. However, their inability to stabilize the economy, together with rampant inflation and the ferment caused by groups who had suffered from these reforms, once again brought about a state of anarchy.

In the 1960's Bolivia was the place chosen by Che Guevara to create a focus of guerilla and establish a new revolution in Latin America. He was killed during confrontation in October 1967, and the repression was cruel. During the 1970's the power of the army as a moderating and stabilizing influence grew. In the early 1980's the country was again in a state of agitation, and in 1982, after protracted student riots, the army transferred the reins of power to an elected civilian president.

During 1983-1984 the government attempted to deal with the critical economic situation, but it was not backed. Finally, in August 1985, the newly elected administration succeded with an economic plan which reduced inflation from 25,000% to less than 20% a year(!), one of the lowest rates in South America. Thanks to this success, the democratic institutions advanced steadily, and transitions were quite smooth ever since.

Geography and climate

Bolivia extends over an area of 1.1 million km in a distinctly tropical region. Since the loss of the Atacama desert in the war with Chile in 1884, Bolivia has been landlocked between Peru and Chile to the east, Brazil to the north and east, and Paraguay and Argentina to the south. Even though 70% of its territory lies to the east of the Andes, most of the population is concentrated in the *Altiplano* (high plain), which is wedged between two parallel mountain ranges: the Eastern Range (*Cordillera Oriental*) and the Western Range (*Cordillera Occidental*). The Altiplano is a deep and narrow valley, 3500-4000 m above sea level, bordered on east and west by high mountains. Some 65% of the population live in this area, which is 800 km long, 130 km wide, and constitutes only 10% of Bolivia's total area. The weather is always chilly, both in winter and in summer, with an average temperature of 10°C (50°F). The annual rainfall of 600 mm is concentrated in the summer months; the rains drain into Lake Titicaca in northwest Bolivia. The Altiplano is arid, and the shrubs and groundcover which grow here are seasonal. Agricultural yields are sparse, and such crops as do grow require irrigation from the rivers flowing into Titicaca, or from the lake itself.

The towns of Oruro and Potosí are the center of the mining industry. These cities, like the rest of the Altiplano, are dependent on other parts of the country, in particular El Oriente (east) for food. El Oriente extends east of the Cordillera Oriental over 60% of the country, yet only 15% of the population live here. Although fertile, its geographical isolation makes it difficult to transport its agricultural produce to the markets of the large cities. A large part of El Oriente is covered in thick tropical jungle and mosquito-infested marshes. El Oriente is divided by a network of streams and rivers which together form part of the southern watershed of the Amazon.

The northern part of El Oriente, the Beni region, is one of the remotest parts of the country. This is an untamed jungle region with many wild animals. Farms were set up in its endless expanses, but it was only in the late 1970's, when the Trinidad-La Paz road was opened, that significant development occurred, as it then became possible for local produce to be marketed in the large cities.

To the south of El Beni, in the area north and east of the city of Cochabamba, is the rich and fertile Yungas region. The climate here is hot and humid, with an average temperature of 25°C (80°F). Heavy rain falls throughout the year (1300 mm annual average). The natural vegetation of the Yungas is luxuriant, and its forests are inhabited by a large variety of animals. The Cochabamba region is known for its fertility and its agricultural produce feeds the entire country.

The Chaco region — or that part of it which Bolivia managed to hold on to after her defeat by Paraguay in the 1930's — lies in the southeastern part of the country near the borders of Paraguay and Argentina. The climate here is hot and heavy and the land is arid. During the summer, when the rain falls, the Chaco turns into one huge, green marshland, but reverts to its former savanna appearance as soon as the rains cease.

Bolivia is divided into 9 administrative districts, each with its own capital.

Population
Some 75% of Bolivia's total population of approximately 7 million

are Indians, and only 5-10% are of European extraction. Perhaps this disparity, which is the largest in South America, explains the unique character of the land. Although Spanish is the official language, it constitutes the mother tongue of only half the population. The other half still speak the languages of the pre-Columbian period — Aymara and Quechua.

Although more than 90% of Bolivians identify themselves as Catholics, Indian traditions from pre-Spanish times are still observed alongside Christianity. The ancient rituals are commonly practiced throughout the country, especially in rural areas. The Indian population, which is concentrated in the Altiplano, lives mainly off agriculture and mining. Most of them have distinctive facial features, and their clothes, houses, language and customs all reflect their strict adherence to ancestral traditions. The native costumes of the Indians, especially the women, are exceptionally colorful and unusual.

Only one third of the population are town dwellers. The rest are scattered among thousands of small, extremely undeveloped villages, most of which have no electricity or plumbing. The educational and medical infrastructures are slowly but surely making headway, and cholera and malaria have been almost totally eradicated. In spite of this, the infant mortality is still very high, average life expectancy is less than 60 years, and about a third of the population are illiterate.

Since the agrarian reform that accompanied the 1952 revolution, settlement patterns have altered somewhat, and many former tenant-farmers are now landowners. Technological advances have led to a significant increase in output, but their distribution is restricted to the vicinity of the cities and to settlements that can be reached by road or rail. In many villages, especially the more remote ones, you will still find the barter system being used.

Economic pressures and low income have led to massive emigration: it is estimated that hundreds of thousands of Bolivians are now living in neighboring countries.

Economy

National economic development along Western lines began in Bolivia only several decades ago. Previously, most of the population followed a regime of self-sufficiency. More than three-quarters of the population lived on subsistence agriculture, without participating in the national market, providing for their own needs through a system of barter. Only in the wake of the reforms of the early 1950's did an economic awakening make itself felt among this sector of the population, so that they too, like the urban sector, began consuming imported goods. The growing interest in industrial products among the exclusively Indian village population has led to the establishment of small factories, mostly textile plants, which supply cheap alternatives to imported clothes. However, in spite of the demand, industrial development has more or less remained static, and is unable to satisfy local consumption. The power plants that were erected have also failed to give industry the needed impetus. Although Bolivia has the potential to enlarge its power supply, there have been no significant developments in this sector.

On the national level, the Bolivian exports are based on the traditional natural resources, metals in particular. Bolivia is currently the Americas' most important ore producer and this alone explains the continued assistance of the United States. The country is the world's second largest producer of tin-ore and a significant supplier of other minerals. Ores constitute a significant part of the total exports, but since the world market is subject to severe fluctuations, the government encourages the development of other products and branches of the economy, in order to overcome the chronic instability. Oil and natural gases have been extracted in the area around Santa Cruz for several decades, but production has declined in recent years. In the agricultural sectors, development is fast; domestic productions satisfy local consumption and exports are constantly increasing.

The settlements in the Yungas and El Beni supply the Altiplano with most of its agricultural needs, but transport problems and the isolation of these areas make it difficult to transport food, so that food prices are high. In view of this situation, the government is attempting to expand the road network in order to reach places that are inaccesible by rail.

During the 1970's, Bolivia enjoyed a short-lived economic respite. Later, the political unrest discouraged foreign investors, and only the generous assistance of the International Monetary Fund and the United States prevented a total monetary collapse.

The frequent changes at the top of the political pyramid during the late seventies and early eighties caused a rapid devaluation in the national currency, and the dollar exchange rate rose thousnads of times in the space of a few years, leading to social unrest, strikes and riots, which caused to the premature fall of the first-elected government in 1985. That year's inflation was estimated at 25,000%(!). Since then, a new liberal plan helped to reduce inflation to less than 20% a year in 1991. The currency was stabilized, thus bringing new investments and creating a new economic climate. For many experts, Bolivia is the real success story of the South American economy of the early nineties.

Bolivian trade — Barter system

B OLIVIA

General information

How to get there

By air: The national airline *LAB* (*Lloyd Aéreo Boliviano*) flies to most Latin American countries and to the United States; all South American companies have at least one flight a week to La Paz. There are daily flights from Brazil, Argentina, Chile and Peru. From Europe, *Varig* flies via São Paulo or Rio, and *Aerolíneas Argentinas* flies via Buenos Aires. *Lufthansa* has flights from Europe to La Paz with at least one intermediate stop. Most flights to La Paz also stop at Santa Cruz. When leaving Bolivia, you will have to pay an airport tax. Air tickets purchased in Bolivia carry a tax.

By land: There are five rail routes between Bolivia and the shores of the Pacific and Atlantic Oceans and all are used by passenger trains. Buses travel along parallel routes, but given the bad condition of Bolivia's roads you should, if possible, avoid traveling by bus.

From **Chile** you can take a train from Antofagasta or Arica to La Paz — a long but fascinating journey. The first part of the journey is through dusty desert, but as the train climbs upwards to over 4000 m in its ascent through the Andes, the weather becomes extremely cold. Frequent buses also cover the same route.

From **Peru** most traffic goes via Lake Titicaca or the road that runs along its perimeter. There are daily buses between La Paz and Puno in Peru, which continue on to Arequipa, Cuzco and Lima. From Puno you can cross Lake Titicaca by boat to Copacabana on the Bolivian side, and then continue by bus to La Paz.

The train between Santa Cruz and São Paulo in **Brazil**, passes through the Brazilian border town of Corumba. The stretch of track between Corumba and Santa Cruz is extremely old, and problems with the rails — especially in the marshy areas where derailing is not an uncommon occurrence — have earned it the nickname of "death train", though this is rather an exaggeration. Buses link the large towns of both countries, but from the point of view of technology and comfort they leave much to be desired.

The way to **Paraguay** passes through northern Argentina, since there is no public transport over the Chaco road. Thus, to travel directly to Asunción you must drive or hitchhike, but in any case **not** during the rainy summer season. If you are hitchhiking, lifts are scarce and you will need plenty of food and patience. Take more than enough food with you, since once in the Chaco you will be unable to buy any, and you may have to wait several days by the roadside.

The train from Buenos Aires to La Paz takes three days. Buses also cover the same route. From Villazón on the **Argentinian** border there is convenient transportation to most Bolivian towns. We suggest that you take the train from Villazón to La Paz. There is a train every day, and the journey lasts 24 hours.

Documents

Although regulations change periodically, holders of European and U.S. passports do not usually require a visa, and may stay in Bolivia for 90 days without a special permit. The immigration officials at the border will give you a visa valid for 30 days, which can be renewed at the Immigration Office (on González Street near Avenida Acre in La Paz), for a further 60 days.

At the border check point you will be required to fill out a tourist card, which you should always carry with your passport, and which you will be asked to hand back when you leave the country.

No immunization certificates are required to enter Bolivia.

When to come; national holidays

The tourist season is generally the winter, when the skies are clear and temperatures low. The summer months, especially December and January, are quite rainy. During these months you will be more or less city-bound, since the mainly unpaved roads turn to mud with the first rains, making travel difficult if not impossible.

The most important national holiday, Independence Day, is the 6th of August. Folk festivals are celebrated in the various towns and villages, especially in the Altiplano. The **Fiesta del Gran Poder** (Festival of the Great Power) is celebrated in La Paz in early June. This is one of the most beautiful folk festivals of South America. Many people dress up in costumes and the day is spent in dancing and relaxation. Thousands of stands selling food and sweets spring up around the city and people stroll about in obvious enjoyment. The fiesta reaches its climax in a gigantic dance parade along the main streets which are lined with thousands of spectators.

Other colorful celebrations are the *Fiesta de Santa Ana* in El Beni, end of July; the festival of the *Virgen de Urkupiña* in

Quillacollo in mid August; the *Phujllay de Tarabuco* in Sucre in March and of course the *Carnaval* in Oruro.

Where to stay

Accommodation is easy to find, but really good places to stay are far more difficult to come by. Hotels worthy of the name are found only in the four large towns, and even there not without difficulty. In all other small towns and villages the most you can expect to find is a modest — and with any luck, clean — hotel, hardly ever with a private bath.

The larger hotels in La Paz are of a reasonable standard. The smaller ones, used mainly by backpackers (the *mochileros*), will provide you with a small, dilapidated room, a bed, a closet and occasionally — a sink. During the big inflation days they were extremely cheap for Western visitors, but the more stable the currency, the narrower is the gap of prices.

Some hotels can be found which are ridiculously cheap, but the bedding and mattress are liable to be bug-infested. Extra caution should also be exercised in public showers and conveniences, which are far from clean. In most of the small hotels, shower water is heated via an electric element attached to the water pipe, which you must turn on yourself. Beware! The appliance is dangerous and caution should be exercised to avoid electrocution. In most of these places, the level of maintenance leaves much to be desired and the appliances are neglected, so that even a small amount of water can cause a short-circuit and disaster.

Camping is not common except when hiking in the countryside. If you do camp out, be sure to take a good tent and a warm sleeping bag! Spending a night in the Altiplano without suitable equipment will remain etched in your memory as a veritable torture.

Wining and dining

In this sphere Bolivia is well provided for; indeed, sometimes every second building seems to house a small restaurant. The large cities have many quality restaurants that serve a wide variety of continental and popular food. In the small towns and villages, and by the roadside, you will come across numerous eating places, whose culinary arts are mainly restricted to soup, rice and beef, and the level of hygiene is deplorable. Soup is usually the most tasty and safest dish to eat here.

Due to the low sanitation standards in Bolivia, you should avoid tapwater as much as possible, and stick to mineral water (or fresh stream water when hiking through the countryside). In

Fiesta in Tarabuco

Fiesta in the Altiplano

particular avoid eating fresh fruit and vegetables without first peeling them. Worms and other pests are a common occurrence, and even vegetables that seem to be clean are likely to be infested with germs. Stomach-aches and intestinal upsets are practically unavoidable in Bolivia; remember this and be suitably prepared. It is recommended to take basic medicines to Bolivia, since some are hard to obtain outside the large towns. The same rule is valid for some trivial things such as solutions for contact lenses or contraceptive pills. When leaving towns, you should stock up on canned goods, beans and durable foods, and do your own cooking.

Most restaurants throughout the country serve two meals — lunch and supper. Usually there is a fixed-price menu for each meal. If you order a la carte, you will pay more. Lunch (*almuerzo*) is served from 11:30am-2pm, and supper (*cena*) between 6-9pm.

In the Altiplano, and especially around Lake Titicaca, trout fried in oil is a popular dish. This is a local delicacy and is highly recommended. Bolivian food, especially in the Altiplano, is spicy and hot. Most dishes are seasoned with *ají* (red pepper), which is the most popular spice and served along with each meal.

Once you get used to its sharpness, you will become addicted to it.

Meat is served in much smaller portions than in Argentina or the other lowland countries, and is of much lower quality. Steaks are usually thin, dry and tough. On the other hand, the soups are extremely rich, well-cooked and both filling and nutritious. Typical South American foods and beverages such as *empanadas* (pastry filled with meat or cheese) and *mate* (South American tea — pronounced ma-teh) are standard here too, and usually accompany local dishes. A uniquely Bolivian beverage is *api*, fermented from corn, which is commonly sold on city streets and markets.

Hygiene and health
Malaria has been almost completely eradicated. Nevertheless, we would advise you to take prescription anti-malaria pills if you are planning to visit areas like El Beni region or the Yungas. Usually these pills should be taken for a week before you enter a malaria zone, and continued for six weeks after you leave the area. When staying in these places, be very careful regarding what you eat and drink. Water must be sterilized by both boiling and chemical means (chlorine tablets). Make sure that the water source is not contaminated.

El Oriente is infested with mosquitos and bugs, so take along mosquito-repellents and soothing ointments. Even if you apply these liberally, you will no doubt be bitten as never before in your life. But if you do not use them and do not wear protective clothing (long sleeves, socks, scarf, etc.) you will be exposed to bites that will cause prolonged suffering and illness. At night, you should sleep under a mosquito net.

From a hygienic point of view, Bolivia is certainly far from satisfactory. Sewage networks exist only in large towns and villages; all other places, including city suburbs still use open sewer pipes and water is brought to the houses from central wells. You should be extremely cautious with food and drink since the cholera hit badly the Andean countries in 1991.

Living on high
Given the elevation of the Bolivian Altiplano, suitable precautionary and preventive measures must be taken. (see "Introduction — Altitude — how to cope with thin air".)

Currency
During the 1970's and the first half of the 1980's, the national currency was subject to constant devaluation and the economic

instability was proverbial. In December 1986 six zeroes were taken off the *peso*, and the new currency became the *Boliviano*. The old policies kept restrictions on the purchase of foreign currency, causing the black market to flourish the differences of rates were very high. The new ultra-liberal policy on the subject nullified the differences, and the open offer for change decreased a great deal. Moneychangers (*casas de cambio*) can sometimes be prevailed upon to cash travelers' checks into cash for a commission.

The use of credit cards is not very widespread, and you should not rely exclusively on them when planning your traveling budget. Check well the commissions to be paid before you order a bank transfer, since they can be very high, unproportionally to small amounts.

Business hours
Banks and commercial offices are open to the public both morning and afternoon. Nearly all places are shut between noon and 2pm. Shops reopen then until 7pm. Outside the large towns, the *siesta* can be a little longer.

Most places are open half-day on Saturdays. On Sundays the entire city is at a standstill and even traffic almost ceases.

Domestic transportation
Buses and Trucks: Buses run between all the large towns and to most villages that are accessible by road. The roads are of poor quality, narrow, uncomfortable and incredibly crowded. Generally speaking, you should be at the bus station an hour before the bus leaves, since, although the driver will in all likelihood set out much later than scheduled, all the seats will be taken long before the official departure time. On interurban routes, tickets are sold a day or two in advance, so make sure to buy one in time. Bolivia's cheapest and most popular form of transport is the truck, into which dozens of passengers are squeezed, not to mention freight and animals. Although this is an interesting way to travel, it is by no means uncomfortable.

Travel by bus or truck is extremely cheap, but drawn-out, uncomfortable, and unreliable. Nevertheless, it is also the most authentic way of traveling, and if you don't mind "roughing it" you should certainly give it a try.

Train: Bolivia's rail system has improved considerably over the past few years and modern carriages now run on the antiquated tracks. Trains run only between the large cities, and are cheap, fast and comfortable. Night journeys on the Altiplano are very cold and you should be suitably prepared. There is

Bolivian transport

also *ferrobus* service. This consists of two first-class carriages only, and is fast and comfortable. It is available only on inter-city lines.

Private and rented car: Bolivia is not the kind of country in which if you rent a car upon arrival, this solves all transport questions. Most of Bolivia's roads are unpaved and in bad condition. Service stations and garages are scarce and one must stock up with fuel cans before leaving the large cities. For certain trips, a rented four-wheel drive car is recommended, but remember to take large quantities of fuel, at least two spare tires and repair tools! The rental companies usually require your passport as a deposit, or $500 in cash, for which you will get a receipt.

There are many road-blocks along the way, but most are not interested in tourists. Travel permits can be obtained without difficulty at any police station.

Plane: *LAB* has daily flights throughout Bolivia. Price is relatively low for some routes, but they are heavily booked. You should reserve a place as early as possible, but bear in mind there may be delays, or even cancellations, due to weather problems, floods, etc. — especially in El Oriente, El Beni and the Yungas. Flying is the quickest and most comfortable method of interurban travel.

Shopping
Bolivian products most in demand are local handicrafts and artifacts. These include attractive sweaters made of llama wool (coarser and cheaper) or of alpaca wool (finer and softer but more expensive), wall hangings, small sculptures and *mantas* (a special kind of intricately woven fabric). The Bolivian *mantas* are the most beautiful in South America, and the older they are, the more expensive they are too. The "antique" *mantas* are particularly beautiful, and if they are also in good condition and the embroidered patterns complete, they will in all likelihood be extremely expensive.

Although the sweaters and woolen goods are beautiful, they are of medium quality. They must be washed in cold water and hung out to dry, without wringing, in a shady place.

Bolivia has many unusual markets. The giant market of La Paz is the largest, containing everything you could possibly wish for. Woven goods are cheaper elsewhere, such as the villages where they are made or in the market held on Wednesdays and Saturdays in Cochabamba. A market is also held on Sundays in Tarabuco, near Sucre, which is one of the most beautiful in South America. Prices are high, but can be bargained down to 20% of the initial quote. As a general rule **bargaining** is essential in the markets, and you should make a point of doing so everywhere.

Measurements; electricity and time
The metric system is used. The standard voltage throughout Bolivia is 220V, except for La Paz, where the power grid supplies also 110V. Bolivian time is GMT-4.

A suggested itinerary for touring Bolivia
La Paz is the starting point for most tourists. There are many places you can visit from La Paz, whether in the immediate surroundings, in El Oriente (jungle tracks and mountain villages), or in other towns. You can make the rounds of the cities and their surroundings beginning and ending in La Paz, or on your way to or from neighboring countries. Suggested excursions accompany the section on each city.

La Paz

Although La Paz is not the official capital of Bolivia, it is the de facto one. The presidential palace, government offices and other national institutions are located here. Bolivia's largest city (nearly one million inhabitants) is the political, economic and commercial center of the country, and is the main tourist attraction.

This enchanting city nestles in a valley carved out of the mountain by a gigantic prehistoric glacier. The city center lies at the bottom of the valley, about 400 m below the Altiplano, and on either side clusters of small adobe houses ascend the steep slopes. The downtown area is modern: its main road, the Prado, has multi-story buildings and traffic is heavy. The first thing you notice is the walking pace of its inhabitants — a pace which is slower and more relaxed than in any other city. This phenomenon has its roots in the city's altitude. The thin atmosphere rules out strenuous exertion and a slower pace has become second nature. More than half of the city's population are Indians who have come from the surrounding villages, and they still wear their traditional garb and black hats (including the women). Many women carry their children in an embroidered cloth sack which they wear on their backs, and breastfeed their infants in public thoroughfares. Others sit on the sidewalks of the main streets selling sweets and cigarettes displayed on *mantas*.

Seen from above, as you look out of the train on its approach to the city or from the taxi bringing you from El Alto airport (the highest civilian airport in the world, over 4000 m), your first impression of La Paz will be of a walled city. Although from afar the red-brown of adobe appears to be the dominant color, when you reach the city you will marvel at the wonderful variety of colors, the like of which few cities can boast. The small streets, even those near the main avenues of the city, are exceedingly beautiful and picturesque, radiating simplicity and uniqueness. The inhabitants are friendly, and you can stroll safely through the streets at all hours of the day and night. Behind the city, which was founded on October 20, 1548, looms Mt. Illimani. Its snow covered peaks rise proudly to a height of 6700 m.

How to get there
El Alto, La Paz's somewhat old-fashioned airport, serves all

La Paz

domestic and international flights. Although it has no banks, you will immediately be approached by moneychangers who will be happy to change your dollars. The 20-minute taxi trip to town, traveling on a wide freeway, will afford you an enchanting view of the town below.

Trains, buses, and trucks travel right down to the city center. The central train and bus stations are within walking distance of the main street, but because of the altitude it would be wiser to take a cab and avoid carrying your luggage. Trucks and buses usually go as far as the central Plaza San Francisco, or to the area near the cemetery.

Where to stay
There are many hotels and pensions scattered throughout the city, covering all the range of prices and services. In cheaper hotels, ask to see the room before you accept to take it.

Expensive
Plaza: Av. 16 de Julio 1789; Tel. 37-8311; fax 34-3391. Five-star hotel, excellent restaurants, a health club with sauna, good location. Recommended.
La Paz Hotel: Av. Arce; Tel. 35-6950; fax 39-1593. Once the local branch of the Sheraton chain; its location is not as good as the Plaza's.

Hotel Presidente: Potosí 920; Tel. 36-7193; fax 35-4013. On a high spot, the view is breathtaking. Very good restaurants.
Los Tajibos: Edificio Hermann, reception at the 4th floor; Tel. 32-1455.
Gran Hostal del Rey: Av. 20 de Octubre 1947; Tel. 36-7759.

Moderate
All the hotels in this category have private baths, telephones, room service and restaurants.

Sucre Palace: Av. 16 de Julio 1636; Tel. 36-3453; fax 39-2052. Close to the Plaza in Paseo El Prado. More expensive than the others in this category.
El Dorado: Av. Villazón s/n; Tel. 36-3355; fax 39-1438. Close to the University, recommended.
Copacabana: Av. 16 de Julio 1802; Tel. 35-1240. Opposite the Plaza (Paseo El Prado).
Gloria: Potosí 909; Tel. 37-0010/8; fax 39-1489. Opposite the Hotel Presidente, on the corner of Sanjines.

Inexpensive
Neuman: Loayza 442 (between Potosí and Comercio); Tel. 32-5445. Very well situated, quite new with pleasant rooms and friendly. Recommended.
Hotel Panamericano: Av. Manco Capac 454; Tel. 34-0810.
Torino: Socabaya 457; Tel. 34-1487. Large, simple and cheap, very popular among backpackers, but one of its drawbacks is that it locks up at midnight and latecomers are not allowed in.
Residencial Independencia: Comercio on the corner with Bueno. Clean, neat and quiet, with helpful crew. Recommended.

What to eat, where and when
There are several superb restaurants in the city, where you can get a meal at lower prices than a similar will cost you in the Western world. Therefore a wise tourist — and even thrifty one — would do well to indulge. It should be stressed that in spite of the low prices, dress and etiquette requirements are the same as in New York, Paris, or Rome.

The *Plaza's* roof restaurant serves a limited selection of main courses, mainly beef, chicken and fish, all of superb quality. The restaurant also has an open salad bar. Prices are moderate and the service excellent. The fantastic panorama from the windows is enough to justify a meal here, and when you add the excellent food and attractive prices, it is a special experience.

The *La Paz* hotel also has an excellent roof restaurant. Its atmosphere is far more formal, with dimmed lights and background music (sometimes a trifle loud). This is the ideal place for an intimate meal, with the romantic background of the city's twinkling lights. The restaurant's chef specializes in the famous dishes of the international cuisine, including several exceptional delicacies to satisfy the palate of the most fastidious gourmet. Recommended! The Plaza and La Paz restaurants also serve lunch, but evening is the best time to enjoy them.

There is a Swiss restaurant, *La Suissa*, opposite the La Paz. Even though its entrance is modest, you will soon discover that this is one of the town's best restaurants. Although it offers a variety of meat dishes, you should stick to their speciality — fondue. The restaurant's manager owns one of the best butcher shops in town, so this is definitely the place to order a meat fondue or "Mongolian hot pot" (a more delicate dish). Reservations are essential. The restaurant is closed on Sundays.

For lighter meals, go to *Elis* at Av. 16 de Julio 1497. This is a busy, noisy place, but the food is good and cheap. Not far from *Elis*, at the corner of Santa-Cruz and Colón, is the *Confitería Verona*, where you can have breakfast, sandwiches and the like, or simply relax with a cup of coffee and cake.

In the *Peña Naira* folklore club at Calle Sagarnaga 161 (the street leading to the market from the Plaza San Francisco) you will find a very good restaurant that serves an excellent and reasonably priced four-course lunch (*almuerzo*). Both lunch and dinner here are highly recommended.

In the markets you can get fairly satisfying meals at low prices, but for health's sake you should be extremely selective. Inexpensive restaurants can be found in every alley and street corner, but make doubly sure they are clean before eating in them.

Transportation
Urban: There is frequent minibus and regular bus service in the city. However, the buses are usually packed and the routes seem interminable.

The most comfortable way of traveling in the city is by taxi. They are unmarked and unmetered. Within the downtown area the fare is fixed, regardless of the distance traveled. The price, though, is per passenger and the driver is entitled to pick up other passengers on the way. The first passenger determines the destination, and the driver will take only passengers who are going in the same direction. The fare jumps by 50% at night. For short day excursions from the city, it is a good idea to organize a group to share a taxi. Conventional public transport (buses and trucks) is slow and unreliable, and will waste much precious time.

Interurban: Most buses depart from the central bus station or nearby. Tickets should be bought several days in advance. The journey to Cochabamba takes 12 hours, to Potosí 14 hours and to Sucre 24 hours.

Trains, which cover these routes several times a week, are far more comfortable. But by far the best way of traveling is the *ferrobus*, or express train service. If you are traveling to Villazón or Argentina, the train is your best bet.

LAB flies between La Paz and all the other cities in the country, and even to some far-flung villages in the Beni and Yungas regions. Bear in mind that there are frequent delays, and that some flights to the less popular places may be cancelled for lack of passengers or due to bad weather conditions. Reserve your seat well in advance, for your return flight too, since the planes are small and heavily-booked. The *LAB* offices are in Av. Camacho 1460, at the corner with Loayza (Tel. 36-7701).

To Peru: To reach Puno, the Peruvian town on the shore of Lake Titicaca, there are two options. The first is via a direct bus, which leaves La Paz several times a week and covers the distance in 10 hours. The second, which is cheaper, is to take one of the many local buses to Copacabana (4 hours) and then to cross the lake by ferry to Puno (see Copacabana).

Tourist services

Most tourist services are concentrated around the Prado, Av. Mariscal Santa Cruz. The blue booth of the **Tourist Information** is situated half-way down the street where it becomes Av. 16 de Julio. Maps, guides, tourist material, brochures and any other information you may require are all available, including material concerning other cities in Bolivia, excursions and treks.

The main office of the *Instituto Boliviano de Turismo* is in Mercadero 1328 (edificio Ballivan), 18th floor, and opens Monday to Friday, 8am to noon. The National Parks Authority is also represented here and will answer questions within its jurisdiction. The Military Geographical Institute (*Instituto Geográfico Militar*) on Av. Saavedra sells topographical maps of various areas which are especially useful for hiking.

Most travel agencies and airline companies are located on the Prado or on Calle Camacho (parallel to the Prado). The *Exprinter* travel agency, the largest in the city, has a large office on the Prado at the corner of Loayza. This company

LA PAZ

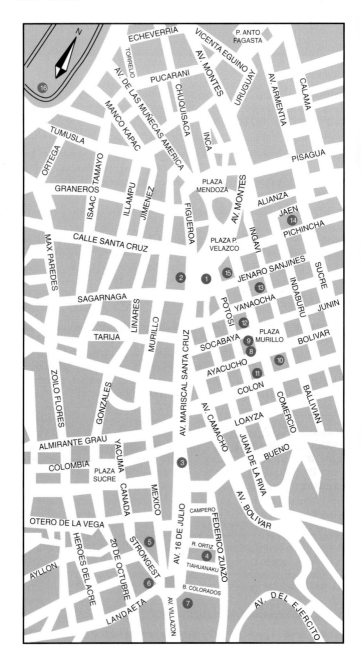

has branches throughout Latin America and also provides a package delivery and shipping service.

In the **Club Andino**, at México 1638, you can rent skiing and mountaineering equipment. They also have cars to Chacaltaya ski resort (see below) and you can get there good information about treking and mountaineering in Bolivia.

Car rental: There are several rental agencies in La Paz, which can supply passenger cars, jeeps and vans. Prices vary, but in all cases make sure that insurance, two spare tires, a repair kit, water and fuel containers are included.

The *Hertz* office is in the La Paz Hotel (Tel. 35-5592). *Kolla Motors* at Calle Rosendo Gutierrez 502 (Tel. 34-1660/35-1701) is recommended. They have a large fleet of reliable and well-maintained cars, are courteous and their rates are reasonable.

Tourist sites

La Paz's main·street changes its name several times, but is known as the **Prado** along its entire length. We will begin our tour at the western end of the Prado, Mariscal Santa Cruz, with one of the city's most important squares, **Plaza San Francisco**. The church and the convent in this square are of the largest buildings remaining from the colonial period, and are still, in spite of neglect, exceptionally beautiful. They were built in 1549 with stones, and rebuilt during the second half of the 18th century. The interior works were finished in 1753, while the facade of the temple in baroque style, quite unusual in South America, dates from 1790. The tower was added almost a century later, and it is clearly seen that it does not belong to the complex. On Saturday mornings, Indian weddings are conducted here and the blending of ancient traditions with Christian rites is especially interesting.

1. Plaza San Francisco
2. Iglesia de San Francisco
3. Tourist office
4. Tiahuanaku museum
5. National library
6. Immigration
7. University
8. Presidential Palace
9. Cathedral
10. Congress Palace
11. Central Post Office
12. National Art Museum
13. Museo Nacional de Etnografia
14. Casa de Murillo
15. Casa de la Cultura
16. Train station

Plaza San Francisco is at one edge of the large **Indian market**, which continues uphill and south on Calle Sagarnaga (see "Markets"). We will now turn southeast along the Prado, walking along the flagstone street whose narrow sidewalks overflow with pedestrians. To our left we will immediately catch sight of the lofty **Obelisk**, towering over the **Monument to the Unknown Soldier**. The Obelisk marks the beginning of **Calle Camacho**, which is a busy commercial street, more or less parallel to the Prado. Three blocks further down the Prado, in the middle of the road, is the Bolivian **Tourist Office** (*Instituto Boliviano de Turismo*) and alongside it the statue of **Simón Bolívar**.

At this point the Prado widens, and becomes Av. 16 de Julio. A pleasant **promenade** separates the traffic lanes. Adorned with decorative trees and statues, the promenade is usually crowded during the afternoon, evenings and on weekends.

The fourth street to the left is Calle Tiwanaku, with the **Tiwanaku Archaeological Museum** which houses most of the finds from this important archaeological site (see "Short trips around La Paz" below). The museum, founded in 1922 by initiative of the archaeologist Arturo Posnansky; it is at number 93, next to the corner with calle Federico Zuazo (open Tuesday and Saturday only, 9am-6.45pm; Tel. 39-2624), and is perhaps the most important of its kind in Bolivia. Notice the Bennett monolithe and other unique pieces of this still partially unrevealed culture.

A short way down the Prado is a large square dominated by a monument to the famous General **Sucre**. To the right of the square, at the corner of Calle Strongest, is the **National Library** building, and, to its left, the **University**. Its proximity to the university has earned the square the name of **Plaza del Estudiante** (Students Square), and it has been the starting point for many demonstrations and riots. Plaza del Estudiante marks the limits of the downtown area and beyond it extend attractive residential areas. We will, however, return to the city center, turning north this time, to Calle Comercio, Plaza Murillo, and their surroundings.

Climb from the Prado along **Calle Colón**. Its intersection with Calle Camacho is the main haunt of the black market moneychangers. The steep road leads us to the corner of Calle Comercio, where the **Banco Minero** houses the **Museo Mineralógico**, an interesting collection of minerals and ores (open Mon.-Fri. 10am-noon and 2-4pm; Tel. 32-6262).

A left turn onto Comercio will bring us to **Plaza Murillo**, named after one of the leaders of the 1809 uprising against Spain. The uprising failed and Murillo himself was executed. This pleasant square — one of the city's landmarks — is the seat of several of Bolivia's most important public institutions. The **Presidential Palace**, built 140 years ago, lies on the south side. Uniformed sentries guard its gates, and visitors are not allowed. Alongside the palace is the Municipal Cathedral, **Catedral de Nuestra Señora de La Paz**, recently renovated. In Socabaya 432, next to the Cathedral, there is a little but interesting Museum of Sacred Arts (open Tue.-Thur. 10am-noon and 2.30-6.30pm). In a chapel in the Cathedral lie the mortal rests of the national hero, the Mariscal Andrés de Santa Cruz. A small plaque opposite the palace bears testimony to the fact that President Villaroel was hanged here in 1946.

On the east side of the square stands the large **Congress Palace**. On the other side of the square, Calle Comercio becomes a **pedestrian mall** lined with shops and small restaurants. At the beginning of this mall, at the corner of Calle Socabaya, is the stately home of the *Condes de Arana*, which currently houses Bolivia's **National Art Museum** (*Museo Nacional de Arte*). The museum has a collection dating from colonial times, as well as the works of contemporary Bolivian artists. It is open Tues.-Sat. from 9.30am-noon and from 3-7pm; Sundays from 10.30am-6.30pm (Tel. 37-1177).

The Comercio pedestrian mall leads into Calle Sanjinés. Turn right at the top of the street to reach the **National Ethnographical and Folklore Museum** (*Museo Nacional de Etnografía y Folklore*). This interesting museum — which is housed in the Marquis de Villa Verde's residence — has a display of handicrafts, spun and woven fabrics, as well as exhibits of typical musical instruments (Ingavi 916, at the corner with Jenaro Sanjinés, open Mon.-Fri. 8.30am-noon and 2-6pm; Tel. 35-5889).

Not far off is **Calle Jaén**, a small alley closed to vehicles and sandwiched between Av. Sucre and Calle Indaburu. Redone in colonial style, this picturesque street has a number of boutiques, three museums and a folklore club (see Folklore). The most important museum on Calle Jaén is the **Casa de Murillo**, which has many late 18th and early 19th century exhibits, works of art, handicrafts, furniture, and more (Jaén 79, open Tues.-Sat. 9am-noon and 2-6pm; Tel. 37-5273). In front of it, at number 777 of the same street, is the **Museum of Precious Metals** (Museo de Metales Preciosos Precolombinos) with amazing aboriginal works, such as golden masks and other sacred tools (open Tues.-Fri. 9am-noon and 2-6.30pm. Sat. and Sun., 10am-1pm).

Moving away from the center, we come to **Plaza Arqueología** (Archaeology Square) in front of the **Municipal**

Plaza and church of San Francisco

Stadium. This square has an exact replica of the temple that was discovered at Tiwanaku, and some of the largest and most impressive statues that were uncovered there. Some distance from the center is the **Monticulo Observatory** (Mirador Montículo), which is located in a small, pleasant park in the heart of Sopacachi suburb. En route, you will pass through one of the city's most beautiful neighborhoods, contrasting harshly with

At the "Witches' Market"

other parts of La Paz. From the observation point you have a wonderful view of the city on your left, and a breathtaking view of Mount Illimani on your right.

In addition to the above, we have yet to visit the **Indian Market**, which is an attraction in its own right. Even if you have no intention of buying anything you should definitely not miss this. No doubt your resolution will weaken once you set foot in the market. (see "Markets" for further information).

Markets

La Paz has a superabundance of markets — so much so that it is virtually one immense market. No fashion shops or modern supermarkets here — La Paz is first and foremost an Indian market. A colorful, teeming market, offering everything from a cup of corn beer and charmed amulets to ward off the evil eye, to sweaters, ponchos, wood and metal ornaments, and jewelry.

The entire area southwest of Plaza San Francisco is in fact one giant market, which would take many days just to walk through. This is Bolivia's largest market — one of the largest in the world — and it lacks nothing.

We will start our tour of the market at Plaza San Francisco and work our way up Calle Sagarnaga. You will immediately notice the dozens of small shops on either side, packed with touristy trinkets. The goods in these stores are of extremely high quality, but their prices are commensurately high. Make a point of thoroughly checking the quality and type of product — and **bargaining**. Remember the iron rule here — always bargain!

You will not have to struggle uphill much longer. Only two blocks further, at the corner of Calle Linares, the market splits up into dozens of small alleys. However, before we come to this crossroad, turn right into a courtyard surrounded by shops on both levels! These offer a wide selection of knicknacks, jewelry, sweaters, and the like. Prices are relatively high, so, if you have the time, hunt around elsewhere. At the intersection, you can either carry straight on or turn right into Calle Linares, where the so-called **Witches' Market** (*Mercado de Hechicería*) begins. Take a good look at the strange objects on display: bottles with unidentified contents, statuettes, dry bones and even.... desiccated llama fetuses. Continuing along Calle Linares are some quality stores whose prices are marginally cheaper than those already mentioned.

A bit further on is Calle Santa Cruz (not to be confused with Av. Santa Cruz) which is one of the most beautiful streets in the market. *Punchay* is at Santa Cruz 156. It sells local arts and crafts and has an expensive music section which offers a wide selection of records and tapes. You can listen to them in the shop and ask the owner to record music for you.

A stone's throw from Linares down Santa Cruz and we are back in Plaza San Francisco. On our way to the square, on our left, is an enormous partially covered food market selling everything: fresh bread, fruit, vegetables, sugar, canned goods, and more. Turning left from Linares, up Calle Santa Cruz, a few meters further on, our path crosses a small alley. To the left, in a small cul-de-sac sells more magic wares are sold, while to the right a small lane leads into the very heart of the market. The center of the market is crammed full of stalls overflowing with goods — down the hill on the right and up it on the left. However alluring the descent may seem, and however unappealing the ascent, you will just have to grit your teeth and make your way through the stalls. At the top of the climb, you will notice that different types of goods are on display here — transistors, electrical goods and film. This section is known as the **Thieves' Market** (*Mercado Negro*) and for obvious reasons prices here are relatively cheap. Compare prices before buying anything, and make absolutely sure (!) that the goods you are buying are sound. When buying film, check the expiration date and make sure the manufacturer's seal has not been broken.

This is a good point from which to meander through the market.

On all sides you will be immersed in a crowd of shoppers, vendors, porters, or simply idlers, and it will be some time before you find your way out of the labyrinth of stalls, no doubt loaded with parcels...

Our tour has taken us through only a small section of this enormous market and there are many other places where you can shop. We have focused on this section because it represents far more than a mere shopping district or market. The customs and way of life of the local population are reflected in this unique quarter, and you will find hard to see such another place in the whole world.

An important market is held Sunday mornings in the Alto Lima neighborhood near the airport. From the early hours of the morning hundreds of Indians flock to this market with their wares: vegetables, fruit, sweaters and various artifacts. This large market spills out along the entire main street, and is so crowded that it is almost impossible to move. A unique experience, which should not be missed.

In conclusion, the inexhaustible richness and variety of the markets, and their attractive prices, make shopping here a truly delightful and worthwhile experience. La Paz is the ideal place for buying gifts and souvenirs.

Entertainment and folklore

If you are looking for nightlife, La Paz has little to offer. There are, it is true, a few discotheques, but these are exceptional landmarks in the town's cultural landscape. The best of these is at the La Paz Hotel. There are a few movie theaters showing mainly films with the original soundtrack and Spanish subtitles. The theaters along the Prado are modern and comfortable, but those farther out are old-fashioned, uncomfortable and with poor-quality projection equipment.

La Paz's main form of entertainment centers around local folklore and music — and not without reason. Although folklore clubs are a common feature in all large towns, those in La Paz are by far the best. Most of these clubs (known as *peñas*) have shows Wed.-Sun., beginning at 10pm. The program lasts about 3 hours, during which seven or eight groups perform Bolivian folk music. All the instrumentalists, singers and dancers wear traditional Indian costumes, down to woolen hats with earmuffs. The instruments are authentic and always include drums, various types of flutes and the *charango* — a South American mandolin whose sounding box is made of an armadillo shell.

The best peña is *Peña Naira*, which has already been mentioned regarding its restaurant (see "What to eat, where and when"). This peña is not far from Plaza San Francisco, in the direction of the market, at Calle Sagarnaga 161 (Tel. 32-5736). One of its owners, Ernesto Cavor, a virtuoso charangoist, sometimes performs for his patrons. The program is rich and varied, including songs, instrumental music and folk dancing. The audience is diverse, with local patrons as well as tourists. The cover charge is reasonable and includes the first drink. Although the show invariably begins late, you should be there early to be sure of getting a good seat.

Another excellent peña is *Marca Tambo* at Calle Jaén 710 (Tel. 34-0146). Here you can combine a meal with the show — ordering drinks or dinner before or during the performances. Although the place is attractive, the serving of meals during the performances does little to enhance the atmosphere.

The *City* restaurant on the Prado also has performances, but is unappealing, the program bill unreliable and prices inflated. Definitely not recommended.

Concerts of Indian folk music are also held in the **Casa de la Cultura** just off Plaza San Francisco. The performers are usually amateur or youth groups but of extremely high quality and well worth hearing. Tickets are subsidized and therefore inexpensive. For information about performances, you can check at the local newspapers or at Tel. 37-4668.

General information

Banks and currency exchange
Banks exchange dollars at the official rate — and with tiresome bureaucratic red tape. Official exchanges (*casas de cambio*) will occasionally cash travelers' checks into dollars for a commission. A reliable *cambio* is *Sudamer's* on Calle Colón near Av. Camacho.

The black market money changers are mostly to be found on Colón and Camacho. They are easily identified: men and women carrying attache cases will approach you with an offer to purchase dollars. Do not use their services even if the rates they offer are tempting, because the danger always exists that you have been approached by an undercover policeman. The black market is illegal in Bolivia; therefore, try to change your money in shops and businesses where you are bound to find someone who wants your cash dollars, and you can change money without running any risks. Before leaving La Paz for other areas, change as much money as you will be needing, since outside the three or four largest cities it is extremely difficult to change dollars, and even more other currencies.

Postal and telephone services

The Central Post Office is on Calle Ayacucho at the corner of Potosí, one block past Plaza Murillo. The usual stamps, postcards, envelopes and the like can be purchased here. At this branch, you can send letters by ordinary or registered mail and parcels weighing up to 1 kg. Everything should be sent by registered mail!

Parcels weighing over 1 kg have to pass customs control, and must be taken to the Customs Office, on Calle Potosí. Be prepared to wait. The parcel should be open when you bring it, with a detailed list of its contents. Only once it has been searched and officially approved may it be sealed. Parcels weighing more than 15 kg are not accepted. It must be wrapped in a bag, sewn shut and tied round with string. Delivery by sea mail can take months (sometimes over 6 months!) — so if you are sending clothes by sea, insert a few moth balls for good measure. The airlines also accept parcels and delivery takes only a few days. However, they are naturally far more expensive than the regular mail service.

International calls may be made from hotels, or at the Telephone Exchange in the *Entel* building on Calle Ayacucho. To some destinations there is no difference in price between a station-to-station and person-to-person call. Passports must be handed in when making international calls. There are 20 international call boxes along the hall and the wait is not usually very long. However, since this is also a domestic long-distance exchange, it is usually packed, especially at mid-day or in the afternoon, usually less so in the evening. It is open from 7am-9pm. On Sundays international calls are 25% cheaper. *Entel* also has a branch at the La Paz Hotel which is open till evening.

Note that regular calls from hotels sometimes involve waits of several hours and extra charges.

Books and periodicals in English

The large bookstore *Los Amigos del Libro* ("Friends of the Book") has two branches in La Paz and one in Cochabamba. The store, whose owners are also publishers, offers a wide selection of books in English on subjects relating to Bolivia and Peru, as well as guides, maps and the like. The larger of the two branches in La Paz is on Calle Mercado 1315, near Ayacucho, and the other on the Prado.

Photographical supplies

Film can be developed quickly and cheaply in La Paz, and the quality is good. The *Kodak* agency on Calle Potosí develops black-and-white and color film, as well as slides. *Photo Linares* on Calle Loayza develops film of high quality, quickly and cheaply. Film can also be bought in the Thieves Market (see "Markets").

Weather

Due to high altitude, temperatures are low throughout the year, even though the sun may be shining in a clear and cloudless sky. The average daytime temperature throughout the year is 10 degrees Centigrade (50 degrees Fahrenheit), but at sunset, or even in the shade, you will immediately perceive a drastic drop in temperature. Take warm clothes: you will almost certainly need them frequently.

The summer months, especially November-January, are very rainy, but sudden changes in the weather are likely to occur. Always bear this in mind as far as clothes are concerned, since even a clear spring day is likely to end in a heavy downpour.

The atmosphere is very dry, and you should use skin lotions and lip salve. The dryness may cause discomfort to contact-lens wearers.

Important addresses and telephone numbers

Emergencies: Tel. 118.
Ministry of Tourism: Mercadero 1328, Edificio Ballivan, 18th floor.

Consulates

U.S.A: Potosí 1285; Tel. 32-0494.
Great Britain: Av. Arce 2732, Esq. Campos; Tel. 32-9401.
Canada: Av. 20 de Octubre 2475; Tel. 37-5224.
Spain: Ed. Guanabara, first floor; Tel. 35-7203.
France: Av. Hernando Siles, corner with c. 8 (Obrajes); Tel. 78-6189.
Italy: Av. 6 de Agosto 2575; Tel. 32-7329.

Airlines

Air France: Plaza Venezuela-Ed. San Pablo; Tel. 39-0855.
Alitalia: Av. Camacho 1280, 3rd floor; Tel. 32-3494.
British Airways: Plaza del Estudiante 1920; Tel. 34-0831.
Iberia: Av. 16 de Julio 1616, 2nd floor; Tel. 35-8605.
Lufthansa: Ed. Hansa, 15th floor; Tel. 35-3176.
Swissair: Ayacucho 378, Tel. 37-5057.

Short trips around La Paz

The area around La Paz has a wealth of interesting sites that can be visited on day trips. Some can be reached only on foot, but they can be incorporated into visits to more distant places. The following is a description of some of the more important and famous places.

Diente del Diablo (Devil's Tooth)
This mountain, not far from La Paz, is known as the Devil's Tooth due to a huge rock similar in shape to an awesome tooth. The view from the top is simply dazzling.

To get there you should first travel by bus to Cotacota, cross over the ravine, and then make the several hours' climb to the summit on foot. The path is steep. Take it slowly and carefully to avoid a feeling of suffocation and lack of air. On the way to Cotacota, you will pass through some of La Paz's luxury neighborhoods.

Valle de la Luna (Moon Valley)
Millions of years of geological and karstic evolution have fashioned this wondrous valley in the heart of the Andes. The rocks, rifts and mounds have wierd shapes. Moon Valley is a good few hours' walk from the end of the bus line in Florida or Calacoto. While there, it is well-worth visiting the Río Abajo area, inhabited by a large Indian population who have been living in the same manner for centuries.

Chacaltaya and the Ice Cave
More than an hour drive north of La Paz is the Chacaltaya ski resort, which is the highest in the world. The start of the slope is about 5500 m above sea level! The ski season is between the months of October and March. Even off season it is worthwhile going up to the observation point to enjoy a wonderful view of La Paz. During off season one can only reach the site by taxi, or by car organized by Club Andino in La Paz (see "Tourist services"). Don't expect too much from skiing there — the slopes are bad and icy, and the resort is managed in Bolivian standards. Skiing equipment can be hired in the Club Andino, too.

The ice cave

Continue along the road which leads to **Ice Cave** (*Cueva de Hielo*) and to the foot of Huaina Potosí Mountain — recommended for mountain climbers. The cave is about an hour's walk from the main road. The path is steep, and in parts of it you walk along an aquaduct with a fantastic cliff to your left. The cave penetrates into a small glacier.

It is only possible to get here by taxi. If a number of travelers share the cost, and one bargains vigorously with the driver, the trip is cheap.

The road north to these mountains passes through the primitive Alto Lima Indian quarter. On Sunday mornings a large and colorful market is held here.

Tiwanaku
A small portion of the ancient city of **Tiwanaku** (sometimes spelled Tiahuanaku) was discovered here and is unquestionably Bolivia's most important archaeological site. It is a 1½ hour journey from La Paz (72 km).

B OLIVIA

The Moon Valley

Most researchers refer to Tiwanaku as South America's most ancient advanced civilization. There is still considerable controversy regarding its age. No one can say for certain when the Tiwanaku culture began to evolve, or when it reached its zenith. Nevertheless, the general assumption is that the roots go back to the Aymara civilization around 1600 BC, and reached a peak around 700 AD. The purpose of the city remains obscure, although the consensus is that Tiwanaku was originally intended as a port on Lake Titicaca. It began as a rural settlement and developed into a city and later into an empire. The reasons for the disappearance of so developed a civilization, which erected some of the largest stone structures in the Americas, are not very clear. Some theories point to a natural catastrophe, such as a flood or a plague. The generally accepted theory, however, is that social and economic decline in the kingdom led to famine and civil strife, after which the remaining inhabitants abandoned the site. Only a small portion of the town, less than 1% of its estimated area, has been uncovered. Nevertheless, this is unquestionably one of the world's most important archaeological sites. Visitors cannot fail to be impressed by the sophistication and technical expertise of this ancient civilization.

In any event, the Tiwanaku culture has remained a mystery to this day, and for every find discovered in the area, there are a number of theories to explain its meaning.

Literature: The bookstore *Los Amigosdel del Libro*, has a selection of books on Tiwanaku. *Discovering Tiwanaku* by Hugo Rojo has detailed information interspersed with photographs of the site and various other places in the area.

Transport: Many daily buses make the round trip to Tiwanaku. Buses of the *Ingavi* Company leave every two hours from the station in the intersection of C. P. Eyzaguirre and José M. Asin in the district of Challapaya. The return trip to La Paz leave from the central square in Tiwanaku, near the church. Groups may prefer to share the cost and hire a taxi to Tiwanaku, which will wait for you and then bring you back to La Paz. Tourist agencies in La Paz also operate organized tours to the site.

Visiting the site: As we enter this arid zone, the first thing we see is the hill looming up in front of us. Buried beneath this hill is the **Akapana Pyramid**, which was one of the largest structures in the city, and is further proof of the outstanding achievements of this ancient civilization. Open daily 9am-5pm.

To the right of the pyramid is the central part of the archaeological finds — the **Kalasasaya Temple**. Before entering this huge temple, take a look at the square "pool" slightly to its east. This is in fact the **Subterranean Temple**, some two meters deep. Many gargoyles peer out from its walls, but time has obscured their features. This subterranean temple was ingeniously designed to allow the rainwater to drain off. The monoliths that were found in the center of the temple now adorn the Archaeology Square next to La Paz's soccer stadium.

Six huge steps lead from the subterranean temple to a gate in the wide stone wall, through which we enter the area of the Kalasasaya Temple. Before us stands the large monolith, 3.04 m high. Careful scrutiny reveals that the figure is holding ritual vessels. The pictures on its feet are thought to represent a calendar.

At the farther end of the temple is the **Sun Gate** — the most famous find of the entire site. Its eastern side, which faces the sun, is richly adorned and scholars have various theories concerning their significance. Most are of the opinion that the three rows of figures on the upper section of the gate on either side of the **Sun Man** represent some sort of calendar. The Sun Man himself holds two eagle-tipped scepters, and rays ending in figures of birds or serpents radiate from his head.

At the other end of the temple is a smaller monolith, also adorned with interesting shops. The figure's belt has pictures of crabs which do not live in the nearby Lake Titicaca, and are therefore assumed to symbolize the distant ocean. The constrained features and appearance of the figure have earned it the name of **The Priest**.

Behind the temple is an unexposed area, divided into dig lots. This is **Putuni**, the western part of the temple. This area was excavated with extreme caution, and its finds transferred to the Museum of La Paz. Following the excavation, the area was once again covered over and further excavations left to future generations. From here we can return along the Temple's restored southern wall to marvel at its rainwater drainage system. Take a look at the drainpipes and tunnels that were carefully designed to prevent flooding. There are many South American cities that even today would envy such a drainage system...

Copacabana

This little town on the shore of Lake Titicaca is usually visited by tourists on their way to or from Peru. As well as being a transit point, the town also serves as a departure point for trips across the lake, in particular to the famous Sun Island. Its main square is dominated by a large, interesting church, and surrounded by shops, hotels, and inexpensive restaurants. Colorful celebrations are occasionally held here on weekends.

Lake Titicaca, at an altitude of 3810 m above sea level, is the highest navigated body of water in the world. It is almost 200 km long, about 70 km wide, with a maximum depth of some 300 m. You can travel across the lake in one of the large ships, or simply hire a boat. There are organized trips from La Paz, but these are rather expensive.

Sun Island itself, which is held by tradition to be the birthplace of the Inca dynasty, has a somewhat limited selection of archaeological finds, including the remains of a temple and a port. It too has an impressive sun gate, although less ornate than the one at Tiwanaku. The other islands on this side of the lake are inhabited by Indians living in tribal villages. Seeing their unique way of life is an interesting experience. However, the islands on the Peruvian side of the Lake seem to be more interesting (see "Peru — Puno").

Transport: Buses to Copacabana leave from La Paz twice a day (the *2 de Febrero* Bus Company runs at 8am and 3pm from José M. Aliaga 687; Tel. 37-7181 and the Manco Capac runs at 7am and 1pm, adding a bus on Sundays at 3pm; Tel. 35-0033). Tickets should be purchased in advance. Bear in mind that the ride is about three hours and the museum in Copacabana is open only on Sundays, 8am-noon.

On to Peru: From Copacabana you can cross over to Peru

Copacabana

at Yunguyo. You can take a taxi from the town center to the border point, have it wait while you arrange your permit, and then continue with it to the main square of the village, from where you can catch a bus to Puno. You may be required by the Peruvian Immigration officials to show an exit ticket from Peru before you can obtain an entry permit. An MCO ticket is not always considered satisfactory. A safe bet is to buy a cheap bus ticket in La Paz from any Peruvian border town to a town in a neighboring country.

Longer excursions from La Paz

Here too we select only a few of the dozens of possible trips, each of which lasts several days. The places chosen are the most beautiful, popular and accessible, and are sufficient to give the tourist an authentic, impressive picture of the country.

All the trips require physical fitness, since most incorporate hiking. Don't forget to take plenty of warm clothing, suitable camping equipment and sufficient food.

Lake Titicaca and the Northern Altiplano

One of Bolivia's most beautiful and lesser known areas is a large stretch of several hundred kilometers, north of La Paz. This area, characterized by enchanting lagoons and truly majestic scenery, is inhabited by Indians who are totally cut off from modern civilization. To tour this area you should preferably rent a four-wheel car or a jeep, have a good map, work tools, an extra spare tire and a reserve stock of gasoline, since there is no way of getting help if your car breaks down. The *Transportes Arles* Bus Company at Calle Tumusla 502 (Tel. 35-0506) runs buses to Sorata only and there is no public transport from here to the more remote and more interesting places.

The route north from La Paz passes through Alto Lima, and from there follows the paved road to Lake Titicaca. To get to the lake you take the dirt track as far as **Escoma**, which is the last refueling point on the way. En route to Escoma you will pass many tiny villages along the shores of the lake, and see the inhabitants busy fishing or freezing potatos. Incidentally, the method they use is the most ancient food freezing method in the world: the potatos are spread on the ground, trodden on to express their juice, and then left to freeze at night. After several days, the potatoes harden and can be kept for many months.

From Escoma on, the road is very bad, and you must drive with extreme caution. The road continues to the village of Villa General Pérez, more commonly known as **Charazani**, some 85 km from Escoma. The road is very steep and narrow, winding through an intoxicatingly beautiful scenery of mountains, valleys and streams, home to huge herds of llamas and alpacas (wild animals of the llama family).

The villages you will pass on the way are merely several rows of houses around the main square, inhabited by several dozen people only. Some of these villages are *pueblos*, i.e., villages in which each villager is responsible for himself. Others are known as *comunidades* — a sort of collective settlement, and the pride of the agrarian reform of 1952 which revolutionized agricultural settlements. The *comunidades* market their goods collectively. In the larger villages, market day is usually held once a month. These villages are one of the few places in the world where the barter system is still in use. Commerce is entirely in the hands of women, and the rituals of displaying wares, haggling and exchanging goods is truly exciting. To all this must of course be added the colorful costumes, unusual customs and strange language — which together make this an unforgettable experience.

Charazani

At Charazani the vehicular road ends. There are trucks taking passengers, supplies and food from La Paz to Charazani once or twice a week, but the journey is protracted and uncomfortable. The village itself has about 500 families and constitutes the center of the entire area. It has a health clinic that provides medical services for the local inhabitants, a small school and one policeman.

Not far from the village is a pool fed by hot springs, where you can enjoy a bath in almost boiling water. The main square has a few stores, but these offer a poor selection of goods. In the central plaza there are two cheap hostels (*Alojamiento*); the better one is to the right of the church. Its owners are friendly and are happy to help with advice and information.

Illiteracy is the norm — about 70% of the population can neither read nor write. Most of the population speaks Quechua, while others speak Aymara — both ancient Indian languages, and only a small percentage understand or speak Spanish. Charazani is the only village which has a power supply — only in the early evening. Although the past few years have seen the advent of transistor radios and tin roofs, the primitive isolation of this captivating area has remained unimpaired.

Charazani and its surrounding villages are well known for their exceptionally beautiful weaving. Pleasant paths through the mountains will take you across the considerable distances separating the villages. You will pass through areas cultivated

Agriculture in the Northern Altiplano

A flour-mill in Charazani

by methods familiar only from history museums. One of the most beautiful villages in the area is **Niño Corin**, a rural idyll of adobe houses with thatched roofs. This peaceful village has neither electricity nor running water and cooking is still done in earthenware pots over small wood fires. The village is famous for the hand woven fabric made by its women and is one of the most interesting villages in the area. **Cota** is another charming village, one hour's walk from Niño Corin.

At the end of July a number of fiestas are held in the villages in the Charazani area. These are authentic festivities in an area few tourists visit. The Indians wear their wonderful festive clothes, and drink and dance to the sounds of the local music. On the 25th July this type of fiesta is held every year in the **Calaya** village. The village is about 3-4 hours' walk from Charazani, but the effort is certainly worthwhile if you plan your trip to the area at this time of the year.

From Charazani you can return to the main road and continue north towards the Vicuña Reserve of Ulla Ulla, near the Peruvian border. The herds of roaming vicuña, the fantastic scenery, the beautiful lagoons and the ancient glaciers peering down from the surrounding ridges create a unique atmosphere. Make use of the information provided by the rangers at the entrance of the reserve. They can guide you through the meandering paths and tell you where to find concentrations of vicuñas and llamas.

Inca Trail (Camino del Inca)

The mighty Inca kingdom left behind impressive ruins, palaces, cities and temples. However, no less impressive are the sophisticated Inca roads. The Incas' technology for cutting roads through even seemingly impassable places was one of the factors that contributed to the power of this great empire. To witness this expertise first-hand, we thoroughly recommend a 2-4 day hike along one of the Inca roads near La Paz. These fascinating routes still bear signs of the original Inca paving.

Both suggested roads begin with an exhausting climb through an arid countryside of black granite rocks criss-crossed with valleys and streams, and end with a steep descent through a luxuriant jungle.

The first hike takes 2-3 days. It begins in the village of **Ventilla**, which can be reached by bus or truck from La Paz, or by hitchhiking from **Cotacota**. Take a map, food, camping equipment and extremely warm clothing. At night the temperature drops far below freezing. Take the path from the village to the San Francisco mines, near where you begin the ascent.

The first day is spent climbing to the pass, some 4700 m above sea level, along this splendid road, part of which is still covered with paving stones. Traces of hewn rock are still visible. On all sides, stark and rocky landscape soars towards the blue skies.

A few hours of climbing will bring you to the pass, beyond which the scenery is radically different. The slopes on this side are covered in greenery, at first scant and sparse, but gradually becoming thicker until without warning, it becomes a wild, luxuriant jungle. Two kilometers past the saddle is a small village, whose humble abodes will offer you shelter for the cold night.

The second day will be spent on the 2000 m descent, alternately above or beside the river, along a path meandering through wild forests and thick vegetation. If you walk fast you can reach the village of Chojilla on the same day. From this village, which lies on the slopes of a high hill, you can continue to La Paz, but you will not regret an extra day in the heart of nature. Although the road descends, it is by no means easy. The descent is steep, and you have to be careful all the time not to slip. If you are not in a rush, you can make camp amid the tiny villages spread along the road — each of which consists of no more than 3-4 houses — and spend another, much warmer (due to the lower altitude) night in the area. Then on the next day you can make the final steep ascent from the river to the village of Chojilla. There are several trucks a day from this village to La Paz.

This route is just one of several tracks which the Incas broke through in the La Paz area, and is known among travelers as the "short Inca trail". The "**long Inca trail**" is also very beautiful and popular, and the truck takes 4-5 days. It begins in **La Cumbre**, which can be reached by truck. The trucks leave La Paz at 9am every morning. La Cumbre is noted for its statue of Jesus, at 4650 m. One must alight from the truck at this point and climb to the saddle which is 4900 m above sea level. From the heights of the saddle one has a magnificent view of the immense snow capped peaks of the Andes, when suddenly the wide green valley between the mountains comes into view.

From here the road continues downhill through small and remote Indian villages to a height of 1000 m above sea level. On the third day the scenery changes to mountainous jungle — dense and exquisite. The route ends in the town of **Coroico** in the Yungas (see below), and it is worthwhile resting here in this pleasant green mountainous area. Buses leave 3-4 times a week for La Paz along a road which is astonishingly beautiful.

The Yungas
A few hours' journey from La Paz brings us into the heart of a real tropical jungle. The road winds through the mountains

Along the Inca Trail

Coroico

northeast of La Paz. After crossing the mountain ridge at an altitude of almost 5000 m, it descends to a warm, humid area, rich in vegetation but scantily populated.

The Yungas stretches over the eastern section of the Cordillera Real mountain range, between La Paz and Cochabamba. It is an extremely fertile agricultural area, but due to its isolation has no great economic significance. Nevertheless, the government policy of supporting the expansion of the transport infrastructure has contributed considerably to its development. There are signs of increased progress, and the cultivation of agricultural lands is evident.

Since the construction of the road to Trinidad in the late 1970s, the region has developed considerably, mainly because the inhabitants are now able to market their agricultural goods in La Paz. In spite of this, many villages have remained unchanged. When you visit them, you will have a glimpse of how they live in the heart of the jungle.

The regional capital is **Chulumani**, a small village some 130 km east of La Paz, and 1700 m above sea level. The village has a few hotels and is surrounded by many coffee plantations and orchards. It is also the center of cocoa cultivation in the Yungas. This crop, after suitable chemical processing, is marketed the world over.

The *Flota Yunguena* Bus Company on Av. de los Americas in La Paz (Tel. 31-2344) runs buses to Chulumani. The *San Bartolomé Motel* is centrally located, modern and not too expensive.

With Chulumani as your base, you can tour nearby villages or penetrate the jungle.

Another very pleasant Yungas town is **Coroico**, about 5 hours drive from La Paz (see above "Inca Trail"). The road to the town is exceptionaly beautiful (and dangerous); first passes the snow-capped great Andes, at hights of some 5,000 m, then descends to the splendid greenery of the Yungas. There are several buses a week and many trucks connecting Coroico to La Paz.

In Coroico you will find several cheap and simple hotels and some pleasant restaurants. The village, situated at the top of a green hill, has become a popular spot for travelers who wish to have some rest from the high altitude and the cold weather of the Andes, and it is certainly a good place for relaxation after the hike of the Inca Trail.

Sorata
Sorata is a pleasant town, at 2700 m above sea level, about 4 hours drive from La Paz. There are many hikes in this splendid vicinity. There are a few basic hotels and restaurants. Ask for the German; he owns the cheap and recommended *copacabana* hotel, and he has good information about hiking in the area. One recommended walk is to San Pedro Cave, 2 hours each way, which has a large underground lake.

Sorata is the starting point for the **Gold Digger's Trail**, a 7 days trek that ends at Guanay. From Sorata a dirt road goes up to a pass at 4900 m, and then the trail descends along the Rio Tipuani, in a beautiful scenery of mountains, rivers, lush vegetation and remote little villages. Along the way you'll meet the gold-diggers, who might try to sell some stones and gold.

The first days are very cold, and it gets hotter the lower the trail goes.

From Guanay one can either return to La Paz, or try to catch a boat to Rurrenabaque (see "El Beni and the Northern Lowlands"), a day trip downstream.

El Beni and the Northern Lowlands

If your heart is set on true jungle, and you are not deterred by the thought of heat, humidity, millions of irritating mosquitos, wild animals, boat trips and long hikes through dense tropical shrubs and vegetation, you will no doubt enjoy a trip to the Beni region of northeast Bolivia. The standard means of transport in the area are boat or ship. Dozens of these link the villages and Indian farms spread along the rivers and most take passengers. Take plenty of food, a mosquito net, mosquito repellent (!!!) and soothing ointment for when the mosquitoes are too hungry to mind the repellent. Most important, take water purification tablets and anti-malaria pills. The pills must be started at least a week before you enter the zone, and continued for six weeks after you leave it.

It is a good idea to come equipped with hunting bullets in order to give them to the local inhabitants who will gladly receive them as gifts, and sometimes even in lieu of cash payment. In La Paz they cost about one tenth of what they do in the jungle, where hunting bullets are a rare commodity in high demand. It is also a good idea to take modest gifts, such as candies, which you can distribute to the locals. This will assist in creating warm relations with them.

Trinidad
The regional capital is the friendly town of Trinidad, on the Río Mamoré, with 35,000 inhabitants. Trinidad can be reached from both La Paz and Cochabamba, so if you are planning to visit either of these two places, you should pass through this unusual area. *LAB* and *TAM* have daily flights from La Paz to Trinidad. Buses and trucks also cover the route, but are unreliable during the rainy season. Buses leave every morning from Cochabamba, (at the corner of Calle Lanza and Calle Brazil), for Puerto Villaroel. They cover the distance of 275 km in 6-7 hours. From Puerto Villaroel there are cargo ships to Trinidad, usually taking about a week (depending on the route, the depth of the river, the type of ship and the amount of cargo). A less adventurous but more comfortable mode of traveling is by plane — on the daily flight between the cities.

Trinidad has a few hotels and restaurants, but these are generally

Rio Beni

Rurrenabaque

more expensive than their counterparts in the rest of the country. This is only to be expected, since transporting provisions to towns in the heart of the jungle entails considerable effort and expense.

Trinidad offers countless possibilities for penetrating the depths of the jungle. Whether by boat, on foot (only a little way), or by plane, you can visit remote enclaves reached by a mere handful of people. Trinidad itself, and even more so the area north of it, is a primeval landscape where time, as it were, has stood still.

A day trip from Trinidad there is a **Biological Station** (Estacion Biologica), which is run by European scientists. They are very hospitable, and you might enjoy their explenations. You can camp at the station's yard.

Rurrenabaque

The charming village of Rurrenabaque is located in a lovely scenery. It is on the Río Beni, where the river cuts grin hills covered by dense jungle. Across the river is the village of San Buenaventura, where a fiesta takes place on July 16th. There is not much to do in Rurrenabaque. You can swim in a lovely small lake with a waterfall, which is found a short walk away. There are a few basic hotels and restaurants.

From La Paz there are flights of *Tam* and *Lab* once a week; other flights get to Reyes, a short drive away from Rurrenabaque. The bus drive from La Paz takes about 22 hours. You can also take a bus to **Caranavi** (a day trip), and continue the next day by boat to Rurrenabaque down the Río Beni. This boat trip offers nice jungle scenery. It stops in some places along the way, where you can meet locals and gold diggers.

In Rurrenabaque you can arrange a guide for exciting jungle trips. Usually they take 3-4 days along the Río Beni and its tributary, the Tuíchi, including wildlife watching, hunting and fishing.

There is an irregular boat that do the 7-10 days trip from Rurrenabaque down Río Beni to **Riberalta**, a short way from the Brazilian border. There are several flights weekly that connect Riberalta to La Paz and Cochabamba.

If you wish to continue to Brazil, take a bus (a few hours) to Guayaramerin, the town on the Bolivian side of Río Mamoré, where you should get the Bolivia departure stamp in your passport. Ferries cross the river to the Brazilian border town of Guajará Mirim, where you will receive an entry stamp. From here there are daily buses to the city of Porto Velho.

Southern Bolivia

Oruro

Oruro, about 200 km south of La Paz, has a population of approximately 175,000. The town, an important mining center, also serves as a main rail junction. In its center is a large market stretching on either side of the railway track, where Indian women sell their wares — mainly food brought from the many neighboring villages.

There is frequent bus service between Oruro and La Paz; the trip takes about 3 hours. Trains from Chile, Argentina, or the valleys of eastern Bolivia stop briefly at Oruro on their way to La Paz. The town has a large selection of hotels and cheap pensions.

Oruro is known particularly for its annual carnival, held in February. The three main figures of this carnival — devil, bear, and condor — symbolize the entire Bolivian tradition and are a constant motif throughout carnival week. The town's folklore groups are famous not only within Bolivia but also abroad.

Cochabamba

Cochabamba was founded in 1574. Since 1783, when it was officially declared a district town, it has served as the capital of a fertile and densely populated area. Although situated on the eastern slopes of the mountain range, its altitude of 2570 m endows it with an excellent climate, with moderate temperatures and lower humidity than in surrounding settlements. The city has about 400,000 inhabitants and is the commercial center for tens of thousands more who live in the nearby villages and small towns.

How to get there

Cochabamba's airport is one of Bolivia's most active and is used by *LAB* for flights to most domestic destinations, including La Paz, Santa Cruz, Sucre, Potosí and Trinidad.

Buses and trucks travel on the highways to the large cities, as well as to the numerous neighboring villages and settlements. The trip to Sucre takes 6-8 hours. There are several daily buses to Santa Cruz, a 10-12-hour journey over a paved road. There is a daily *ferrobus* train service to La Paz — the journey is far more comfortable, faster (8-10 hours) and expensive than bus or truck. The train station is at the western end of Calle 25 de Mayo, near the market.

Food and lodging
Portales: Av. Pando 1271; Tel. 4-8700. The best in town, away from the center.
Gran Hotel Ambassador: España 349; Tel. 4-8777. Central and recommended, moderate prices.
Hotel Bolívar: Av. San Martín S-0168; Tel. 2-2212. Right of the main square.
Florida: 25 de Mayo S-583; Tel. 2-7787. Inexpensive, very popular among young travelers.

Cheap pensions (*residenciales*) can be found near the main square and around the market and train station.

The *Confitería Zurich* on Calle San Martín, between Av. Heroínas and Calle Colombia, serves excellent cakes, and the *España*, on Av. Heroínas at the corner of Calle España (one block from the main square) serves good ice cream.

Tourist services
The **Tourist Office** is situated at the corner of Heroínas and Aguirre, and supplies maps and brochures on places of interest and transportation.

Postal and telephone service
The central post office is at the intersection of Ayacucho and Heroinas (Tel. 24479), and accepts regular letters, registered mail and parcels. Long-distance and international calls may be placed from the *Entel* Offices on Calle Gral. Acha. Both places are located two blocks from the main square.

Warning: There are reports about local people who introduce themselves to travelers as authorities at train and bus stations, and ask to accompany them for some reasons. Beware of them — they are probably thieves who are trying to take you to a quiet alley!

What to see
Downtown: The tranquil commercial center of the town is characterized by narrow streets lined with two-story buildings. The **main square** (*Plaza Principal*) is fairly modest, as is the Cathedral on its western side, dating from the first half of the 18th century. Near the church, one block south on Calle Sucre, is the **City Hall**, and to its east, on Calle 25 de Mayo, the **San Martín Church.** One block further along, at the corner of Calle Heroínas, is the **Cultural Institute.** Continuing along Calle

Punata

25 de Mayo, we come to the beginning of a promenade known as **El Prado**, which ends at the **Municipal Stadium.** As we walk along this promenade we will pass the **Tennis Club** on our right and, just behind it, the municipal **Archaeological Park.**

The Portales Palace: This palace, perhaps the most beautiful in the town, is situated south of the stadium, at the intersection of Calle Potosí and Calle Buenos Aires. The palace, built by Simón Portales, the "king of tin", between 1915 and 1922, is surrounded by 10 hectars of well-tended gardens, imitating those of Versailles, and a hall inspired by the Alhambra in

Granada. It is open to the public daily for one hour only, on weekdays in the afternoon, and on weekends in the morning.

The University and the Archaeological Museum: The University of San Simón is situated at the bottom of Calle Sucre. The pleasant campus is crowded with students who roam its attractive gardens, and many of the students speak English.

The Anthropological Research Institute has an entire wing devoted to the Archaeological Museum. The museum has exhibits from the locality as well as from all over Bolivia, including skeletons, pottery, work tools and a variety of ritual objects. The exhibits are well displayed and methodically documented. A visit to this museum is heartily recommended. You can obtain background material and explanatory pamphlets on ancient civilizations and the research conducted on them. The museum is open Mon.-Fri., 8:30am-noon and 2-6pm.

San Sebastian Hill: From the top of this hill — *Colina de San Sebastian* — south of the city center, there is a fantastic panorama. The hill has a monument commemorating the struggle for independence from Spain in 1812.

The market: Bustling commerce can be witnessed daily in Cochabamba's market area, within walking distance south of the main square, right next to the train station. Here various goods such as food, footwear, and housewares, to mention but a few, are sold. Market day is held twice a week, on Wednesdays and Saturdays. Indian men and women arrive from neighboring villages with their splendid handicrafts, renowned throughout the country. They are famous mainly for their marvelous wall hangings, which are woven and plaited from sheep, llama and alpaca wool. The sweaters, musical instruments and other typically Indian wares are also of outstanding design and artistry. Although La Paz market is the best place for shopping, Cochabamba is definitely recommended for buying wall hangings — not only are they cheaper here, but also more beautiful and unusual.

Excursions

Cochabamba is a good base for short trips in the area. Of most interest are those villages and small towns that excel in hand-made items of the type that are sold in the town's market. Below is a brief survey of some of the better known places:

Punata: This small picturesque town, 48 km from Cochabamba, is home to expert craftsmen specializing in a variety of handicrafts. When walking through the town, ask the inhabitants to direct you to their houses. There are buses to Punata from

Cochabamba every half-hour, from the corner of Calle 25 de Mayo and Honduras (not far from the train station).

Villa Rivero: Some 24 km beyond Punata is a small village whose inhabitants excel in woven wall hangings. Near the main square is a Weaving School, which is open to the public. The artists' work is quite impressive. In the small market held on Fridays you can purchase the local products at very low prices. There are buses from Cochabamba to Villa Rivero every 2 hours, leaving from the same corner as those for Punata.

Arani: The town of Arani, whose population consists almost exclusively of potters, is 55 km from Cochabamba. Here you will find pottery and ceramics of outstanding quality and beauty, at fairly low prices. The town is located at the further end of the Cochabamba valley, against a backdrop of mountains, lending the final touch to the special atmosphere and rare beauty of the place.

Jungle: Cochabamba is a good starting point for jungle trips, especially to El Beni. For details, see "Longer excursions from La Paz".

Santa Cruz

Santa Cruz de la Sierra, with a population of over 500,000, is the second largest city in Bolivia. It is some 700 km from the Brazilian border on the east and about the same distance from La Paz in the west. Santa Cruz was founded by the Spanish in 1561, but has only enjoyed a spurt of development and prosperity during the last few decades. This was largely due to the discovery of natural resources — particularly oil and natural gas — in the vicinity. A by-product has been the development of a transport network linking the town to other places. The weather is hot and disagreeable, but this is compensated by the small houses and peaceful streets, which create a pleasant atmosphere.

Over recent years, the population of the town and its suburbs has grown due to an influx of new settlers employed in the mineral exploitation industries. The city is surrounded by several large oil fields, interspersed among farms and orchards.

In the center is Plaza 24 de Setiembre, surrounded by some of the most important buildings, including the church and university.

Santa Cruz is a central crossroads for the eastern sector of Bolivia, with trains to Brazil and Argentina. There is a paved road to Cochabamba, used by both buses and trucks. The small and antiquated airport is used by *LAB* for domestic and international flights, and by several foreign airlines as an intermediate stop on the way to and from La Paz.

Warning: Because it is a central junction, the city has become the center for the Bolivian cocaine trade. Young travelers who sit down to relax in the central plaza will probably be given a "tempting" offer from one of the local cocaine traders. As a result of this situation, the attitude of police to young foreigners is much harsher here than elsewhere in Bolivia.

On to Brazil
The Santa Cruz-Puerto Suarez rail link is extremely antiquated. It is not for lack of good reason that the train on this line is known as the "death train": the monotonous journey has been interrupted more than once by sudden derailing... The train runs several times a week and the trip takes about 24 hours.

After passing through border checks, take a bus or taxi to nearby Corumba in Brazil, where your passport will be stamped. You can then continue by bus or train to São Paulo, Rio de Janeiro, or any other destination in southern Brazil.

Citizens of countries required to have visas to Brazil, should obtain them before reaching the border town.

Sucre
Although La Paz is Bolivia's de facto capital, Sucre remains the official one. It is home to some of the country's most important public institutions, notably the Supreme Court. Sucre was founded in September 1538 and for centuries has played an important and influential role in the development of the entire region.

During the pre-Independence era, when it was called Chuquisaca, its progressive outlook had a crucial influence on the character of the struggle against the Spanish. It was not by chance that independence was declared — on August 6, 1825 — in Sucre itself. In spite of a population of about 100,000, the city has preserved its provincial character. The narrow streets and white houses are a living memorial to the colonial era and make Sucre one of the most beautiful tourist centers in Bolivia.

Sucre is also known as "the town with the four names". In Pre-Columbian time this was the seat of the charca Indians, thus the Spanish conquerors gave it the name Charcas. Later on, in 1538, the name was changed to La Plata, since the town was chosen to be the collecting center for silver (*plata*) from the surroundings before it was sent to Lima. In 1776, after major

SUCRE

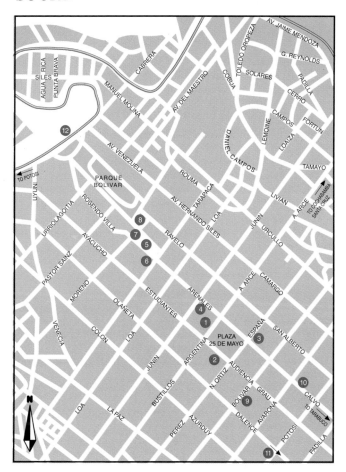

administrative changes, the name was once again replaced by Chuquisaca (now the name of the state), a deformation of the former Indian name, chokechaka. In 1825, the town was named after the independence national hero, Mariscal José Antonio de Sucre.

B *OLIVIA*

How to get there
The quickest way to travel to Sucre is by plane. *LAB* has daily flights between La Paz and Sucre, as well as several flights a week to Cochabamba, Santa Cruz, Tarija and Camiri. The *LAB* offices are at Calle Bustillos 121-127 (Tel. 21140 or 23479).

Trains from the Arce Train Station, behind Bolívar Park (Tel. 21114/5) leave for La Paz several times a week (18 hours), traveling via Potosí (6 hours) and Oruro. The *ferrobus*, a two-car express train, covers the distance in approximately two-thirds of that time — and in style! This is a recommended means of transport, but remember to purchase your ticket in advance.

Buses travel along dirt roads to Potosí and Tarija in the south, and to Cochabamba and Santa Cruz in the north. The northern route consists of 240 km of dirt track, which, although difficult to negotiate, takes you through breathtaking scenery as far as **Empizana**, which is located on the paved Cochabamba (128 km) — Santa Cruz (360 km) highway.

Food and lodging
Hostal Cruz de Popayán: Loa 881, Tel. 2-5156. Recommended, moderate prices, colonial atmosphere.
Municipal: Av. Venezuela 1052 (Tel. 21074), near the train station, moderate prices.
San Francisco: Arce 191; Tel. 22117. A pleasant inexpensive hotel, good location.
La Plata: Ravelo 26, Tel. 2-2102. One block from the Plaza 25 de Mayo. Lower prices than the former but not as pleasant.
There are many restaurants at the main square and in the neighboring streets. The *Plaza*, at Plaza 25 de Mayo 43, is recommended.

Weather
Due to its altitude of 2790 m above sea level, the weather here is pleasant and temperate, with an average annual temperature of 16°C (60°F).

Tourist services
The **Tourist Office** is on Calle Audiencia, one block from the main square (Tel. 25983). Maps and pamphlets can be obtained here.

Postal and telephone service: The main post office is half a block from the main square, on Calle Argentina. Long-distance and international calls can be made from the *Entel* Building at the top of Calle España, corner of Urcullo.

What to see

The town's main square, **Plaza 25 de Mayo**, is truly lovely. The trees and plants are interspersed with benches, where old and young rest from their afternoon stroll. Around the square are some of the city's most important buildings. Foremost among these is **Freedom House** (*Casa de la Libertad*), on the northeastern side of the square. This building, where Bolivian independence was declared, is both a national shrine and a historical museum. In addition to its **Independence Hall**, in which the declaration was signed, it has a collection of portraits, flags, shields and the like. It is open Mon.-Fri. 9am-noon and 2.30-6pm, and Sat. 10am-noon.

On the other side of the square is the **Cathedral**, built in 1559, and alongside it is the **Church Museum**, which, in addition to a mediocre art collection, has a selection of holy vessels and treasures dating from the 16th and 17th centuries. The church is open daily from 7:30-9:30am. The museum visiting hours are the same as for Freedom House. **The National Library and Archives** are on Calle España, northeast of the square, while the **Old University**, founded in 1624, is northwest of it. Next to the university, at the junction of Calles Junin and Arenales, is the **Church of San Miguel** (*Iglesia San Miguel*), which was built in 1621. The Church has been renovated tastefully and is today one of Bolivia's most beautiful churches.

A further collection of interesting sites can be found around **Plaza del Obelisco** (Obelisk Square). To the south are the large **Santa Barbara Church** and **Hospital**, and to the north, the imposing building of the municipal **Theater**. Behind the theater is the **Anatomical Museum** (*Museo Anatomia Humana*), maintained and operated by the University's Medical School, with human anatomical and pathological exhibits. It is open Mon-Fri. 8:30am-noon and 2-6pm.

North of the theater, towards **Bolívar Park**, is the contemporary building of the **Supreme Court** (*Corte Suprema*). This is Sucre's sole remaining government body of any significance and is regarded with due respect by the entire population.

University Museums: The university runs an excellent network of museums, including some of the country's best. The three main museums are housed in a renovated colonial building on Calle Bolívar, one block from the main square, and are open to the public Mon.-Fri. 8.30am-noon and 2-6pm, and from 9-12am on Sat. The **Colonial Museum**, founded in 1939, has nearly 1000 exhibits, including pictures, sculptures, general works of art and the like. The **Museum of Modern Art** has a collection of paintings and sculpture by Bolivian artists.

The most interesting and important of the three is the **Anthropological Museum**, founded in 1943. This museum is divided into three main sections: Archaeology, Ethnography, and Folklore. The Archaeology section has an impressive collection of skulls, mummies, pottery and ancient artifacts, which depict the evolution of the local civilizations. The Ethnography section, on the other hand, has contemporary exhibits, mostly from the jungle cultures in the country's eastern sector. The Folklore section has an admirable display of traditional Indian costumes, pottery, jewelry and ritual ornaments, with emphasis on the evolution of the local culture and its influence on dress and customs.

Other museums: The **Santa Clara Museum** at Calle Calvo 212, has a display of religious vessels and pictures, including silver objects, pottery and a church organ. The **La Recoleta Museum**, which is some distance from the city center, is housed in a 19th century colonial building, alongside the church of the same name. Next to the museum is an **observation point** from which you can see a fine view of the entire city.

Tarabuco's Market

One of the most beautiful Indian markets in South America is held on Sunday mornings in the Indian village of Tarabuco, two hours' journey east of Sucre. This small village, which on ordinary days is indistinguishable from the many other villages in the area, is transformed on Sundays into something quite unique. Market day is a cause for celebration. People dress up in their festive clothes, put on jewelry and hats and fill the streets of the town with their colorful stalls.

The large market teems with Indians walking around and selling ponchos, hats, and knitted and woven goods, among other things. These are all hand-made, in the original style characteristic of the region. Prices are usually high, but stubborn bargaining, especially towards closing time (early afternoon) is often rewarded with a considerable reduction. Bear in mind that there is no shortage of goods and that you, as a tourist, will be besieged on all sides, so you need to be in no hurry to buy. You are sure to find what you want — and if you persist, at a good price. There are stalls that sell coca leaves, spices, fruit and vegetables, knives, mousetraps and more. The colorful clothes, the popular music occasionally played in the streets and the splash of colors make a visit here a truly exhilarating experience.

Transportation from Sucre: Buses, taxis and trucks leave Sucre for Tarabuco starting at 6am, from the square at the end of Calle

Tarabuco

Sucre

Calvo, behind the San Lazaro Church. The dirt track leading to the village is extremely dusty, and if you are traveling by truck, by the time you reach the village your face will have assumed a chalky pallor and your hair will have turned white! It is worth trying to organize a group to share a taxi. The driver will wait for you in Tarabuco and take you back to Sucre.

Potosí

Potosí's Spanish founders had great hopes for the town when they laid the cornerstone in April 1545. They had just discovered the *Cerro Rico de Potosí* — the mountain rising to the west of the town, with its great silver and tin deposits waiting to be mined. For 200 years Potosí was the largest mining center in the Americas. With 200,000 inhabitants at the start of the 17th century, it was the largest town on the continent. However, the drop in world demand for silver and the discovery of other silver deposits led to the town's near total collapse. Only improved mining techniques, and a growing demand for tin, revived the town. Potosí is now reliving its glorious past, serving once more as an important center with considerable influence on the national cconomy.

Potosí, which is situated 3976 m above sea level, currently has a population of 100,000. The town, which was built alongside the largest, most important silver mine discovered by the Spanish, is notable for its unique architecture, which has resisted the march of time. The public buildings and numerous churches have been preserved with their magnificent facades, which bear witness to the town's golden era.

Transportation

There is *ferrobus* service several times a week to La Paz (10 hours) and Sucre (5 hours). This is the fastest and most comfortable overland means of traveling to these places. The train station is in the northern part of the town, not far from the central bus station (*terminal de bus*, Tel. 2-6075).

Several bus companies have daily service to La Paz — a journey of some 13 hours. There is also daily bus service to Sucre (6 hours), Oruro, Cochabamba, and Villazón (14 hours). Buses to Tarija leave several times a week.

LAB flies several times a week to Cochabamba and La Paz.

Food and lodging

Potosi's hotels and restaurants are nothing special. The best inexpensive hotel is the *4 Centenario*, on Plaza del Estudiante

(Tel. 2-2751). Here you can ask about Eduardo, a guide to the mines. Other cheap and pleasant hotels are the _El Turista_, at Calle Lanza 19 (Tel. 2-2492), and the _Alojamiento Ferrocarril_, at Av. Villazón 159 (Tel. 2-4292), opposite the train station.

Very few restaurants deserve special mention. The _Sky Room_ on Calle Bolívar (Tel. 2-6345) is centrally located and serves good lunches and dinners.

Tourist services
The **Tourist Office** is situated in a small building at the corner of the main square. Maps of the town and basic information are available here (Tel. 2-5288 or 2-6392).

Postal and telephone services
The central post office is at Calle Lanza 3. The Entel Building, for international calls, is at Calle Linares 15.

Weather
Potosí suffers from a harsh, cold climate throughout the year. Strong winds add to the feeling of oppression occasioned by the high altitudes and the open plains of the surrounding Altiplano. The average annual temperature is 8°C (46°F) — so take warm clothes with you. The lack of oxygen creates a feeling of asphyxion, especially during climbs or exertions in the Cerro Rico mining area.

What to see

Downtown
The town has an abundance of churches, which have seemingly remained unaltered since they were first built centuries ago. Here too the streets are fairly narrow and the houses seem to sprout out of the curb, leaving a tiny sidewalk for pedestrians.

The main square, **Plaza 10 de Noviembre**, a source of pride for the town's inhabitants and beautifully tended, has a refinement that is quite enchanting. On the north side of the square is the **Cathedral** (_Basílica Catedral_). One block further along to the left is one of Bolivia's most important buildings, the first **mint** (_Casa de la Moneda_) where, over the centuries, the silver mined from the mountain was transformed into legal tender. The museum can be visited Mon.-Sat., 9am-noon and 2-5pm; (Ayacucho 1, Tel. 2-2777); there you can see the tools and instruments used in the original mint and items related with the daily life in town during the colonial period.

The **Museo de Santa Teresa** behind the Casa de la Moneda, in the convent of Santa Teresa, houses art collections, mostly of religious nature (Chicas, at the corner with Ayacucho; Tel. 2-3847. Open Mon.-Sat., 4-5pm only).

The mines

The crowning experience is of course a visit to the Cerro Rico mines. The mountain has over 2000 mines, of which about 400 are active.

Thousands of workers are employed in extracting tin ore: some work with machines, others with picks, and others with their bare hands. Although for over 4 centuries the mountain's treasures have been plundered, the deposits have not yet been exhausted. Formerly, most of the mines were privately owned and the miners' working conditions and pay were nothing short of criminal exploitation. Basic safety devices, and medical and emergency services were lacking, and young children worked beside adults (who were old at 30). Constant exposure to dust and soot considerably shortened their life expectancy. The scarity of oxygen at the high altitudes (over 4000 m above sea level) was merely an added aggravation to their other hardships, such as the extreme cold most of the year round, occupational hazards and so on. Many met their death through illness, uncontrolled dynamite explosions, or the frequent collisions betwen the ore laden carts. The unprotected miners were forced to fight for their survival under intolerable conditions.

In recent years conditions have considerably improved. Although in some mines one is still reminded of Dickens' description of England's coal mines in the 19th century, many mines have been nationalized and reformed by the government in a truly remarkable manner.

There are guided tours to the Pailaviri mine Mon.-Sat. mornings, departing from the main square (Plaza 10 de Noviembre) in front of the Cathedral, 8am, with buses *ENTA* 100-200 or number 7. It can also be arranged through travel agents. There you will see modern mining and processing techniques and, to a lesser extent, the miners' working conditions. In hotel *4 Centenarios* you can ask about Eduardo, a recommended guide who will arrange your visit. To reach the mine, hire a taxi downtown or take a bus that will take you to the entrance of the mine or, alternatively, hitch a lift on one of the trucks taking the miners to work. Getting into one of the private mines for an unmediated glimpse of how they work is forbidden and complicated, but if you succeed you will have a shocking, never-to-be-forgotten experience.

Uyuni

From Potosí there is a rough road south-west to Uyuni, about

Salar de Uyuni

9 hours by bus. There's nothing special about this little Indian town, which is a railroad junction: the trains from La Paz to Villazón stop here, and a railroad goes from here south-west on to Chile. Yet, a good reason to come to this place is its surroundings.

From Uyuni there are 3-4 days highly-recommended excursions at this dry and deserted land. The trip takes you to the many attractions of the region: Salar de Uyuni, the greeny Laguna Verde, Laguna Colorada (famous for its flamingoes), geyzers and small and remote Indian villages.

There are a few tourist companies in Uyuni that organize such trips, and you can arrange small groups in order to share the price.

In Uyuni there are basic food and accommodation possibilities. *Avenida* is a clean and inexpensive hotel. A cheaper one but not as pleasant is the *Uyuni*.

Tarija

Tarija, 376 km south of Potosí, is the largest town in southern Bolivia, with a population of over 70,000. Situated at an altitude of 1866 m, it is the heart of an extremely fertile agricultural area. Its geographical isolation from most of the rest of the country is responsible for a commercial and professional structure based largely on self-sufficiency.

Tarija is the transportation hub of the south and has a number of hotels and restaurants. There are two main bus routes from the town: the first is to Villazón (7 hours) and La Paz (30 hours), and the second is to Sucre (15 hours), Potosí (13 hours) and on to Cochabamba and Santa Cruz.

LAB and *TAM* have numerous flights to La Paz, Cochabamba and other central towns. The Information Office on Calle Bolívar will give you up-to-date travel information, as well as recommended excursions around the town, in particular to the surrounding villages.

Villazón

This town on the Argentinian border is 3443 m above sea level and almost 1000 km south of La Paz. The town is small (pop. over 10,000), and fairly primitive — with unpaved streets, single-story adobe houses and a neglected and unattractive main square.

From Villazón there is a train almost every day to La Paz — a 24 hour journey over the dusty Altiplano. The train is unheated and extremely cold by night. It is generally packed and you should preferably travel first class. This is the fastest and most comfortable way of traveling to La Paz, since bus journeys are not only arduous, dusty and uncomfortable, but longer than those by train. There are buses to Tarija and Potosí almost every day, but the road winds continuously and the journey is unpleasant.

On to Argentina

The border crossing point to Argentina is on the outskirts of the town. You must already be in possession of an entry visa, since Villazón has no Argentinian consulate. The border point is closed daily for a two-hour siesta. The Bolivian border officials might ask for unexplained and inexplicable fees — especially on weekends.

_P_ _ERU_

Ever since the first Spaniards landed on its shores more than 460 years ago, Peru has been known as a fascinating country, and its charm has increased over the years. Apart from having so much to offer — fabulous scenery, rare archaeological sites, a wonderful culture — Peru bewitches visitors with her mystery, which is unlike that of any other country. Peru is a unique blend of sights and sounds, a treasure trove of experiences that words cannot easily express. It's an exotic, strange land, a land of yesterday and today, and to a certain extent of tomorrow, too.

It would take a tourist several months to really get to know Peru, to take in the numerous sites, even if only the most important and famous among them. However, in a short time — about a week or two — one can form deep impressions and get a taste of one of the world's most interesting countries, a "must" on the itinerary of anyone who wants to experience excitement and fascination. Since Peru's tourist infrastructure is rather limited (especially outside the major cities) visitors are forced to improvise tour routes, transportation — everything, in fact — and herein, perhaps, lies the secret of Peru's special charm, which attracts so many travellers.

History

Peru was the cradle of enlightened civilizations centuries before the Spaniards arrived. Remains discovered in Chavin, Paracas and Nazca date to 1000 BC and earlier. At the time of the Spanish conquest, until Francisco Pizarro overthrew their empire in the 1530's, the Incas dominated the entire region from Ecuador in the north to central Chile in the south (see "The Incas").

In the wake of Pizarro's takeover, Peru served as the principal foothold for the newly arrived Spaniards. In addition to the use of its ports, through which the treasures of South America were shipped to Spain, Peru became the starting point for the conquest and settlement parties who set out for neighboring lands. The Spanish viceroy established his seat in Lima and from there oversaw Imperial outposts throughout the continent.

*P*ERU

As the years passed and the other colonies developed and grew in strength, the viceroy's influence weakened until another viceroy had to be appointed for the Buenos Aires region.

As the King of Spain's largest and most important stronghold, Peru was one of the last colonies to respond when the call for independence rang throughout South America. Not only did Peru not declare its own independence, but it even dispatched armies to repress the revolutionaries in Argentina, Uruguay, Chile and Bolivia. Only when General Sucre defeated the Spanish forces at Ayacucho in 1824 was the struggle for independence brought to an effective resolution, and Peru, like neighboring Bolivia, won its freedom. Much of the credit was due to the intervention of the Argentinian General San Martín and Simón Bolívar of Venezuela, who led their armies to Peru's aid.

The Republic's first years were marked by power struggles between military and civilian forces for the leadership of the young country. Though a rather liberal constitution was adopted in 1828, General Augustín Gamarra seized power less than a year later, becoming, in effect, Peru's first military ruler. Economic and national interests led Peru to enter into a confederation with Bolivia, led by the Bolivian General Santa Cruz. But before the success of this pact could be tested, the two countries were forced into a war against Chile, who feared the consequences of such a union and therefore forced the partnership to disband. Spain, too, found it hard to accept the loss of Peru and only in 1869 did it officially recognize Peruvian independence, after a large Spanish naval force encountered spirited resistance and was forced to withdraw.

Around this time Peru began to develop its transportation and industrial infrastructure in order to fill the state coffers. But within ten years, in 1879, the war of the Pacific broke out with Chile fighting Bolivia and Peru over exploitation of the natural resources of the Atacama Desert, which was then Bolivian and Peruvian. The five-year conflict resulted in great losses of life and property. Chile's well-trained army won and took over the desert. Its soldiers reached the Peruvian capital of Lima, more than a thousand kilometers north of the battlefield, and imposed a humiliating treaty of capitulation.

The war's end found Peru on the verge of bankruptcy, but European economic aid, given in exchange for control of mines and other Peruvian production facilities, prevented a complete collapse and helped pull the nation out of its dire economic straits. This European involvement lasted into the 1920's, when the old problems again arose, chiefly concerning land ownership and the status of the Indian population. In the wake of the growing turmoil, the army again seized power. Social tension and economic pressures were greatly aggravated during the early 1930's, as a result of the Great Depression in the United States. Only some ten years later did a certain calm return, due to American economic aid, which must be understood in the context of Peru's unreserved support of the American policies during World War II.

Democracy was restored in 1945, but the hope for stability did not come in its wake. The 1950's and 1960's were characterized by political and economic unrest, with a rapid succession of presidents. Even so, much was done during these years to quiet the country, and attempts were made to solve painful fundamental problems. These included far-reaching reforms: land was allocated to the Indians, the irrigation system was improved, roads were paved, new schools were built, and more. Peru was plunged, however, into another economic crisis during the 1960's; the army rebelled in 1968, seized power once again, and implemented a tough nationalization policy involving not only domestic banks and financial institutions but foreign-owned — chiefly American — companies as well.

The military regime enacted far-reaching decrees with clear socialist overtones in the agricultural, mining and industrial fields. At the same time, Peru forged diplomatic ties with the Eastern Bloc and in 1974 became one of the first Latin American state to have Soviet advisors.

A severe earthquake struck Peru's coastal area in 1970, leaving fifty thousand dead and causing hundreds of millions of dollars of damage to the tottering economy. Only $500 million in credit received from the World Bank prevented total collapse. The quake and its consequences, in addition to the nation's economic straits, led the Army to apply sharp austerity measures in the mid-1970's. Leftist elements and students then initiated spirited anti-government activity, which was of decisive importance in restoring Peruvian democracy in 1980. In the middle of that year, free elections were held for President and Congress, and tranquility and order have since prevailed. A policy of economic restraint, along with encouragement of moderate social forces, has permitted orderly governmental procedures, though extreme leftist groups have been conducting a guerilla war, particularly in the mountain region, disrupting transportation and social life. Clashes between these forces and the army and police increased in 1983 and 1984, though not of an extent to undermine the overall stability of the democratic regime.

In 1985, Alan Gracía Pérez — then aged 35 — was elected president of the Republic. His election constituted a substantial change in Peruvian politics by virtue of his having moderate leftist tendencies. He enjoyed extensive public support during the first half of his period, and more so when he threatened not to pay the huge external debt to American banks. On other subjects, he intensified his struggle against the underground extremists, then very strong in the area of Ayacucho. In 1986 a rebellion of security prisoners was quelled with much cruelty when the army burst in and killed most of the prison inmates — more than 300 men.

He left his office in mid 1990, when his popularity was very low, accused of fraud and corruption, after the elections in which Alberto Fujimori, a second generation to Japanese immigrants, won over Mario Vargas Llosa, a very popular writer who turned from the left to the ultra-liberal right. In 1991 a cholera epidemic caused the death of almost 200,000 people.

Fujimori suspended the constitutional rights and dissolved the Congress in April 1992, in an unusual move. Six months later, in October, he won the general elections. In September of that year the leader and founder of the Sendero Luminoso ("Shining Path") maoist underground movement was captured, and was latter sentenced to lifetime.

Geography and climate

Peru, the third-largest country in South America, covers nearly 1.3 million square kilometers. Its range of geographical zones leads to variations from region to region. Peru can be divided into three geographical and climatic strips, each with its own characteristics.

The coastal strip: Peru's western section, between the Andes and the Pacific shore — covers about 10% of the country's total area. This fertile region is home to almost 50% of the population and is the center of most of Peru's political and economic activity. The cold Humboldt Current keeps rainfall scant and the climate arid, though temperatures are quite comfortable. The cool waters carry a wealth of fish, so that Peru ranks among the world's leaders in this important industry. The soil along the coast is fertile, and agriculture has blossomed as the irrigation system has expanded. All this, however, is disrupted every few years, when a hot current from Ecuador, *El Niño* — "The Boy", upsets the fragile desert equilibrium, bringing rain and flooding, and the death of fish, birds and other wildlife. This rather rare natural disaster usually occurs in September.

The Andes strip runs through central Peru, with a rather arid western slope (affected by the coastal region's desert climate) and a lush, wet eastern side. This area contains most of Peru's natural resources, and its mineral deposits account for about half of Peru's exports. The mountain range towers to more than 3000 meters above sea level, with many individual peaks reaching 6000 m and more. The northern peaks of the ridge have a tropical influence from neighboring Ecuador, but further south the weather turns cooler, more temperate. The Cuzco area is rather chilly, with noticeable day-night temperature differences. This region accounts for about one-fourth of Peru, as well as for some of its most splendid scenery. It has a comfortable climate, land suitable for agriculture and livestock and is home to more than 40% of Peru's population.

The remaining Peruvians are dispersed over the enormous **Amazon Basin**, which stretches over more than half the country's territory. The Andes' eastern slopes are, as said, blessed with lush vegetation, which grows more variegated and profuse as one journeys eastward, descending from the mountains into the broad valley. This vast region is covered throughout with thick tropical jungle carved by hundreds of rivers and streams — transportation arteries for local produce, which is comprised chiefly of wood products and the spoils of hunting. The region's economic potential has yet to be exploited. This is due to financing and development difficulties on the one hand, and to its geographical isolation from the rest of Peru on the other (almost no convenient land routes lead to the region's populated zones). Oil, however, has been discovered in commercial quantities in its northern sector, near the city of **Iquitos**, and an oil pipeline has been laid to the coastal region. As a result, the region's economic and settlement infrastructure is expected to expand which, it is hoped, will accelerate the development of the entire country.

Population, education and culture

Historical developments peculiar to Peru have given its population of 23 million a mixed and varied ancestry. Massive immigration, both from Europe, Africa and from the Far East, along with the tolerance shown the newcomers, created a colorful mixture in which Caucasians, Blacks, Chinese, Japanese and Indians intermarried freely.

Descendants of the pre-Columbian Indians account for about half of all Peruvians and some 70% of the mountain-dwellers. They have managed to preserve their traditions, dress and way of life, and even though most are baptized Catholics their religious practice is mixed with beliefs and rites from their remote politheistic past. The Indians generally speak their ancient languages, though some speak Spanish. They live in poverty and

PERU

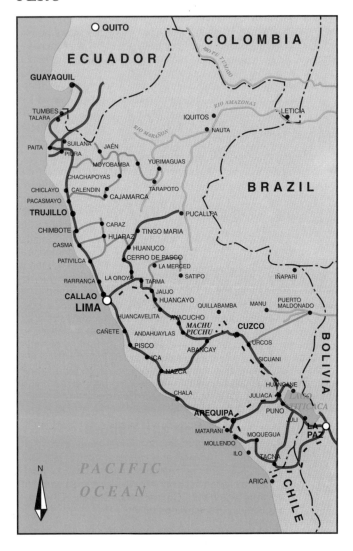

deprivation, in climatic zones where raising livestock agriculture are difficult. The day-to-day struggle for mere existence has thus far prevented their educational and technological development, and their way of life remains as primitive as ever. Illiteracy rates among the Indians exceed 60%; though education is compulsory from the age of 7-16, the government finds it hard to enforce such regulations among the Indians, due to the prevailing situation.

People of mixed Spanish-Indian descent called *mestizos* — the descendants of Spanish settlers who assimilated into the local population — constitute Peru's "nobility". The *mestizos* live chiefly along the coast and in the mountain cities, and control most of Peru's resources, industry, and economic and political institutions. Most senior army officers and government leaders are *mestizos*, and since it is they who determine the nation's mores and character, their imprint is discernible in everything. Most of them are well-educated and the illiteracy rate among them is low when compared with that of the rest of the population.

Children and teenagers account for about half of all Peruvians and many of them do not attend school. Nationwide illiteracy is about 20%, and in recent years the government has accorded education special priority. Peru has more than fifty universities of various types, but a severe shortage of jobs for university graduates, along with the low pay and low living standards, has caused a "brain drain". Migration from village to city has increased in recent decades, and the high rate of natural increase, by which the population doubles every twenty-five years, also creates severe problems in housing, jobs and education, problems especially fierce because only one-fourth of the population contribute to the productive sector of the economy.

Economy

Latin America's major affliction — deficits in the balance of payments and massive external debt — has not spared Peru. When the army seized power in the late 1960's, it introduced an economic policy based on socialist principles, by which national treasures would be exploited for the betterment of all. Accordingly, the government began nationalizing natural resources and production facilities on a slow and limited basis, while providing massive investments to encourage agricultural, industrial and power projects, giving export subsidies and enforcing severe restrictions on imports. At the same time, Peru strengthened its political and economic relations with the nations of the Eastern Bloc, thereby receiving easy credit while opening broad new export markets.

Peru's cultivated areas do not succeed in meeting the rising demand for agricultural products, because half the country is covered with forest. Though new areas are constantly being opened to cultivation, Peru must import basic foodstuffs — a heavy economic burden. Most agricultural activity takes place along the coast, with sugar, rice, cotton and coffee among its chief crops.

Fishing is undoubtedly Peru's most important agricultural sector. Until several years ago, Peru ranked first in the world in fish catches but this industry has declined significantly due to crisis and natural disasters that have afflicted it. Nevertheless, the government has expanded its investments in fisheries, which continue to occupy first place in Peruvian industry. About 2.5 million tons of fish products are produced in Peru each year, of which a large portion is exported.

Mountain agriculture is still rather primitive, with cultivation generally carried out using hand implements and with the aid of animals. Most of the produce is consumed locally and sold in regional markets; It has no importance in terms of the national economy. By contrast, wool shorn from mountain beasts, chiefly alpaca and vicuña, contributes to national production, with some being reserved for export.

Natural resources constitute Peru's major export. In recent years, since oil from the northern jungles near Iquitos has become Peru's most important export, the entire jungle has enjoyed tremendous development. The oil fields, once controlled by American companies, were nationalized in 1968 and the Peruvian National Oil Company has operated them since, pumping tens of millions of barrels each year from Iquitos to the coast, and from there abroad. The oil pipeline running from Iquitos to the coast, along with the roads pushed through the jungle, suggests that the tremendous potential of the Amazon jungle is about to be fulfilled.

The coastal and mountain regions yield more than one million tons of various minerals per year, including ores of zinc, copper, lead and silver. The mines, too, have been nationalized gradually since 1968, and their income flows into the national treasury. The mines were damaged in the 1970 earthquake, but were re-opened with assistance from the World Bank, and today produce more than ever.

About one-fourth of the gross national product is derived from the industry, centered primarily around the large coastal cities, with 50% in the vicinity of Lima. Accelerated urbanization has brought about extremely rapid development in industrial production, and chemical, petrochemical, steel, heavy and light industry and textile factories have been set up in the suburbs with funds supplied by the government and foreign investors. Most industrial production is intended for domestic consumption, and its main contribution to the national economy lies in reducing the need to import equivalent goods. Today there is a growing tendency to expand industry for export purposes as well, especially of fish products. The great concentration of industry in urban areas has led to ecological problems, but at present it appears that its supreme economic importance outweighs all other considerations.

Peru has been suffering from a spiraling inflation for a number of years, and it must accept the instructions of the World Bank and the IMF in order to get new loans. The situation worsened as a result of the cholera epidemics in 1991, not only because of the direct hit on the population, but also due to the sharp fall in incomes from tourism and exports such as fish. Since some movements of President Fujimori were unpredicted in the West, investors consider the Peruvian market as one of high risk.

General information

How to get there

By air: Peru is one of the cheapest destinations in South America. The visitor from Europe or the United States who wishes to take in the entire continent and has no special preference regarding the first stop, will undoubtedly find Peru the most suitable starting point price-wise. *AeroPerú* flies between Lima, Iquitos, Cuzco and other cities, and to many destinations in neighboring countries, as well as to the United States and Europe. The London-Lima and Miami-Lima routes are known for their low fares. There are daily flights from the United States — from New York, Miami and the large West Coast cities — operated by *AeroPerú*. *Faucett*, too, has very cheap flights from Miami. Most European airlines fly to Lima, including *Lufthansa*, *British Caledonian*, *Air France*, *Iberia* and *KLM*. The Russian *Aeroflot* also offers a cheap flight from Germany to Peru, with a stopover in Cuba. All the South American national airlines maintain daily service between their respective capitals and Peru's major cities, from where one can continue to other destinations the world over.

By land: Convenient bus lines link Peru with its neighbors. Direct lines run from the national capitals to Lima and Cuzco. If you have a private car you'll need to obtain customs documents from the *Auto Club*, along with an International Driver's License.

*P*ERU

Documents

When crossing into Peru, citizens of the United States and Western European countries (excluding France) must present a valid passport and fill out a tourist card, which must be carried at all times. Tourist cards are either issued by your airline or can be obtained at the border check-point. Visitors from certain countries need a visa, which is issued by a Peruvian consulate. A visa is usually good for one entry within one year of the date of issue. Both a visa and a tourist card allow a ninety-day stay. You can request a 30-day extension at the Ministry of the Interior in Lima.

When you enter Peru you will rarely be asked for proof of sufficient funds. However, the immigration clerks of frontier points usually demand to see your return ticket. A $150 MCO usually satisfies them, otherwise you would be well advised to buy and display a cheap bus ticket from a Peruvian border city to a neighboring town outside the country.

A valid Student Card, bearing your picture, will prove useful and cut expenses throughout Peru — in museums, institutions, public transportation, and elsewhere.

When to come; national holidays

Peru's weather is especially agreeable in winter, May through October, when only a little rain falls in the mountains and in the Cuzco area, where the Inca antiquities are situated. The rest of the year is rainier, though temperatures remain comfortable. Only in the mountains do temperatures fall below freezing point. The coastal area is very humid, especially between June and November.

The *Inti Raimi* Sun Festival, celebrated in accordance with ancient Inca traditions and considered one of the largest and most important of South American festivals, takes place in Cuzco at the end of June every year. Between June and September, Peru is swamped with European tourists who, exploring its treasures, create an overcrowded feeling at tourist sites, hotels, restaurants, transportation facilities — in fact, just about everywhere. You should take this into account, though it certainly should not put you off entirely.

National holidays during which Peru shuts down are January 1, May 1, June 29, July 28 (Independence Day), and December 25. In addition, a great many local festivals take place every month, offering a variety of folklore shows. For details about each month's events, consult *Peru — Where, When, How*, a tourist magazine distributed by the Tourist Office in Lima.

Fiesta in Taquile

Where to stay

There are plenty of good hotels, particularly in the large cities. Hotels are divided into four ranks: hotel, hostel, *residencial* and *pension*. The first two offer better service, higher prices and 20% taxes, plus 10% service on top of that. In *residenciales* and *pensiones* the rate already includes the tax, but the level of cleanliness and service are not of the highest. Camping is convenient and has become widespread, particularly outside the cities; but while it is a pleasant experience in the coastal region, mountain campers must consider the possibility of rain and equip themselves with extremely warm gear.

Wining and dining

Peruvians customarily eat a light breakfast and a moderate lunch (1-2:30pm), followed by a 5 o'clock break for tea, coffee, or alcoholic beverages. Only between 8 and 9pm do they sit down for the day's large meal, which usually includes soup, seafood and meat, and dessert, accompanied in elegant and intermediate restaurants by local wine.

Market places and city streets are strewn with countless kiosks serving various kinds of Chinese food, fruit juices, seafood, *empanadas*, and more, at very low prices. The national sweet tooth is satisfied by *churros* — a sort of doughnut filled with sweet cream and dipped in sugar; these too are sold in kiosks and are excellent when served hot. Try them!

As a rule, you must be very careful where you eat, for the level of hygiene is extremely low and visitors quite often suffer from intestinal upsets. The problem is especially acute in places where people are not strict about refrigeration, cleanliness in their tiny kitchens, washing their dishes, taking out the trash, etc.

Peru abounds in Chinese restaurants, which serve good food at low prices, and they are cleaner than the markets. These, like the *confiterias* (cafes) which serve cheap light meals — sandwiches and the like — are packed at lunchtime and during the late-afternoon tea break. Many Peruvian restaurants, called *chicherias* or *picanterias*, specialize in good and inexpensive national dishes.

The hundreds of *Criolla* restaurants, found everywhere, specialize in mixed Spanish and Indian cooking. You'll find lots of fish and seafood on this menu, as Peru's proximity to the coast and the well developed fishing industry are naturally reflected in the local diet. One famous dish is a combination of raw fish, lemon and onion called *cebiche de corvina*. Grilled chicken, another popular offering, is called *chicharrones de pollo*. Try it.

Take care to eat salads only in clean places, for raw vegetables are liable to cause disease. The soups are popular and extremely tasty.

Large cities offer an abundance of exclusive and intermediate restaurants, located in the large hotels, along the main streets, and around the central plazas. Here you will be served *menu fijo* (business lunch) according to a fixed menu; the tab will be lower than for a similar meal served at night, so that even a visitor on a tight budget can enjoy one. Taxes add 15%-20% to the bill.

One of the typical features of Peru are the outstanding cream cakes. In all the cities there are lots of coffee houses which serve such cakes which you certainly will not be able to resist.

Peru's "national drink" is *pisco*, a sort of brandy which is produced along the coast and serves as the basis for the *pisco sour*, served everywhere and downed with pleasure at any time. Tea, coffee and soft drinks are also found everywhere.

Domestic transportation

Buses and trucks reach almost every settlement accessible by any sort of land route. Most roads, especially outside the coastal region, are unpaved, and driving them is both difficult and tiring. Roads in the mountain region ascend to heights at which internal-combustion engines do not run smoothly and drivers would do well to seek out professional advice about suitable engine tuning. Rain or snow occasionally block roads, cutting off many places.

The large bus companies run modern, comfortable buses between major cities, although most other Peruvian buses are antiquated, noisy, uncomfortable, crowded and — above all — poorly maintained. Trucks operate mainly in the mountain region and link various places off the beaten path if they are close (at times a 20-hour trip is considered "close" ...). Travel at night requires **very** warm clothing (!!), a sleeping bag, and other means of protection from the cold. The trucks are crowded and their frequency unpredictable, but they are cheaper than the bus.

Trains operate in southern Peru, from the coast, via Arequipa and Puno, on the shore of Lake Titicaca, to Cuzco. From there a train sets out northward to Machu-Picchu. Another line links Lima to the nearby mountain cities. The trains are old, slow, very crowded and do not run on Sundays. Second-class is much cheaper, but finding a seat is difficult and your baggage is liable to be stolen (see "personal security").

AeroPerú and *Faucett* provide daily air service between all of Peru's large cities, and even to the remote jungle towns to which there is no overland access. Fares are moderate, but a 10% surtax is imposed on them. Because the planes, too, are very crowded, you must make reservations as early as possible and confirm them 24 hours before your flight. Take into account the possibility that your flight may be canceled, delayed, or disrupted in some other way, due to various and numerous breakdowns and unstable weather in the mountains and jungles. You should check that your flight is taking off as scheduled before you set out for the airport. Get to the airport early, since these airlines usually overbook! Keep a very watchful eye on your luggage during domestic flights, for the airlines generally treat it with great contempt, and their workers have a way of losing some en route. Once you reached town, buses or taxis will take you to a hotel or anywhere else. Taxi fares are determined between driver and passenger at the start of the trip, and one can (and should) bargain. Tipping is not customary.

Shopping
Artesanía — the range of artifacts and handicrafts is rich and varied. The southern region — Cuzco and Lake Titicaca — excel in woolen goods and sweaters, and this is also by far the cheapest place for these things. In the Huaraz region, too, the woolen goods are plentiful and are characteristically different from those in the south. Huancayo, situated on the mountains east of Lima, is famous for its painted gourds. These are gourds which are dried out in the sun or over a fire, and on which local artists engrave pictures depicting their daily lives.

In the north, particularly in the vicinity of Trujillo, you will find *chaguira*, a jewelry which is usually made with torquoise stones. One must not forget, of course, the popular wall carpets found here, as in other Andean countries.

Personal security
The problem of security in Peru has become much more serious in recent years, with a Maoist underground that calls itself *Sendero Luminoso* ("The Shining Path"). They operate in Lima and the mountains — laying explosive charges, clashing with the army and engaging in other forms of terrorism. Police in these areas act with great force and little manners, vis-a-vis tourists as well. Numerous roadblocks are scattered along the highways and searches are a common occurrence. Curfews at night are frequent in many areas, include Lima. Before setting to a trip to Peru, check very carefully the up-to-date situation in each region you attempt to visit. Some of the provinces are unsafe, others are permanently restricted by the authorities.

Another serious problem is thieves. Daring and sophisticated, they have bestowed upon almost everyone the "favor" of their attentions, sometimes successfully and sometimes not. The profusion of tourists on the one hand, and the helplessness of the police on the other, have created a convenient scene for their operation. Those who cross into Peru should consider the possibility of eventually leaving it without part of their gear. If

Artesanía

you wish, you can add it to your calculation of the total cost of the trip ...

Be doubly cautious in any public place, especially if it's crowded. A moving crowd is one of the best hunting-grounds for a thief. A wallet, camera, or even the contents of the inside pocket of your pants can vanish without your noticing it. The predators carry sharp knives and do not hesitate to cut open briefcases or trousers to get at the loot. You should therefore carry only the minimum of essentials and a little well-concealed money (an ordinary moneybelt isn't enough), and leave everything else in a closed bag which you **never carry on your back, but only in front of you and at chest height.** It's highly advisable to walk in groups, especially at night or upon reaching a new place with all your gear. Under no circumstances should you sport any sort of jewelry, or carry a camera openly. Attach metal chains to your camera and hook it to your belt, so that if someone cuts a strap you'll sense it immediately.

The thieves generally operate in groups; while several divert your attention by conversing with you or by "accidentally" knocking into you, their friends will finish the job. When you're on the train, secure your baggage to the shelf with a locked chain and hold all hand baggage firmly. Don't drowse or nod off, and try to bring along a flashlight which you'll turn on the moment your train enters an unlit tunnel. Unsupervised bags are liable to disappear in a few seconds of darkness! Both on the train and in the station, you should not move around alone; organize into the largest groups possible, walk as a group, and carry all equipment in front of you. Those who really want to do it right will wrap their gear (especially backpacks) in sacks or even metal netting to keep it from being cut open: the method may be cumbersome, but it works. Before getting off the train, wait until the platform is cleared of passengers. Crowds, as mentioned, are the natural habitat of thieves.

When traveling by bus, be sure to check at each and every stop that the baggage you placed on the roof or in the luggage compartment does not inadvertently "fall off" before you reached your destination. In taxis, too, remove your gear first and then get out; one often hears of drivers who take off immediately after their passengers have alighted, giving them no opportunity to remove their belongings.

Though all of this must sound odd if you haven't yet visited Peru, it won't take long to see that things are just so. Many visitors, of course, emerge unscathed, but many do fall victim to thieves. Remember that the thieves' great skill and brazen gall, and the minimal risk they face, have resulted in an "open season" on attractive tourist gear. The most extreme precautionary measures you can take are not excessive!

Those with the misfortune to have lost money or baggage to thieves must navigate an obstacle course in order to recover it (from the insurance company, that is). Go to the Tourist Police or to PIP — *Policia de Investigaciones del Peru* — after buying (!) the police documents necessary for filling out the report in the kiosk-like structures next to the police stations.

Health
Sanitation and hygiene standards in Peru do not begin to meet the expectations of a Western tourist. Visitors can contract

various diseases — most involving the digestive tract. We therefore recommend extreme caution concerning where and what you eat, especially in markets. In addition, it is imperative to be particularly careful about drinking water. As a rule, you should drink only bottled water, especially outside the cities. Water purification tablets will help, particularly on trips into the country where all sources of water will need them. Bear in mind that in 1991 Peru suffered from the cholera epidemic, so be double cautious. You should also bring a sufficient supply of medicines of various kinds, for those sold in Peru are costly and not always fresh and suitable for use. Anti-malaria pills are necessary only in the eastern jungles; take them for a week before entering the region and continue for six weeks after leaving. Elevation sickness becomes a problem in mountain regions; go slowly there (see "Introduction — Altitude — how to cope with thin air").

Currency

Peru's national currency is the *Nuevo sol* and its exchange rate varies due to inflation. Accordingly, change dollars only as you need to. Stock up on local currency before leaving the large cities for remote areas. Exchange rates are generally lower at border crossings; change only the minimum necessary to get into town. Occasionally it's best to buy *soles* in neighboring capitals (La Paz, Quito) where preferential rates sometimes prevail. Dispose of leftover *soles* before leaving Peru.

Official currency exchange takes place at banks and through moneychangers and travel agents. Some of the latter also sell dollars. *Casa de Cambio* (exchange offices) and moneychangers in the street will change your dollars according to the black market rate which is sometimes identical to the official rate at banks, but which can sometimes be much higher. When this happens the rate for travelers' checks is lower than for cash dollars. In any event, it is best to keep at least part of one's money in traveler's checks for fear of thieves.

International credit cards, too, are commonly used in the cities. *Diners' Club*, *Visa* and *American Express* are accepted in many shops, restaurants and hotels. Note, however, that cash advances against a credit card can be drawn in local currency only, therefore make every effort to cash only as much money as you will need during your stay in Peru.

Business hours

Shops and offices are open from 9am until 7pm, with an afternoon *siesta*. Banks and government offices are usually open in the mornings only. Most shops operate half day on Saturdays and are closed on Sundays. Restaurants are open from early morning hours until past midnight.

Measurements, electricity, and time

The metric system is used for weights and measures. Clothing is marked in European sizes.

Electricity: 220V. Peruvian time: GMT-5.

A suggested itinerary for touring Peru

Peru is rich in fascinating sites and you would need months to see them all. This chapter divides the country into three broad areas: the northern region, the central region and the southern region. These can of course be connected into one long trip or you can settle for a visit to parts of each separately, as your departure point and individual objectives dictate.

The northern region takes in the area north of Lima to the border with Ecuador in three strips: coastal, mountain and Amazon Basin.

The central region consists of the city of Lima and its immediate surroundings.

The southern region encompasses the areas south of the capital — the coast, the mountain ridge, Lake Titicaca and its surroundings, the jungles and, of course, the Incan capital of Cuzco and the nearby ruins.

The sites described in the sections on the northern and southern regions are surveyed in order of their distance from Lima, though the material is arranged so that it can also be useful to those coming from other directions. Possibilities for combining and merging touring routes are noted in every case. The two sections first survey attractions close to Lima which may be visited either on the way to or from the capital, or as a day trip from it.

PERU

Lima

Since 18th January 1535 — when Francisco Pizarro laid the cornerstone of Lima — and throughout the intervening four hundred fifty years, Peru's capital has been a major center for all of South America. In this foggy coastal city, covered on most days by a mantle of clouds, many of the historical processes that shaped the development of the entire continent were set in motion. Besides being the Spanish monarch's most established and reliable colony in South America, Lima was and remains an important focus of political, economic and social power. Then as now, it presents a blend of severe contradictions — wealth and poverty, beauty and ugliness. Only in recent decades, roughly from the end of World War II, has Lima undergone far-reaching changes, which have driven the city rapidly — sometimes too rapidly — into the 1990's. Its population has grown tenfold, and now approaches six million — about one-forth of the total population of Peru. With the growing trend of migration from rural and provincial areas to the city, a great many poor suburbs known as *pueblos jovenes* (young villages) have grown up, where "greeners" live in harsh conditions that are a hothouse for social unrest — expressed in criminal activity and extreme revolutionary politics.

Lima, built on the banks of Rio Rimac, takes its name from the mispronunciation of the river's Indian name. The eye-catching peaks of the Andes, only one hundred fifty kilometers away, loom to the east and the long beautiful seashore lies to its west. The port of Callao, one of South America's largest, was far from the new city when built, but the expansion of Peruvian industry (of which almost three-fourths are located in this area) has blurred the urban boundaries, creating a busy and crowded industrial zone. Downtown Lima is a mosaic of Colonial and modern architecture, centered about the Plaza de Armas. The suburbs, particularly the exclusive southern ones — Miraflores, San Isidro and Barranco — are no less effervescent, especially after dark.

Few tourists to South America skip a visit to Lima — either because it is the continent's major port of entry, with inexpensive flights from all over the world, or because it is a convenient starting point for all the captivating sites that Peru offers. Indeed, for all that it lacks beauty, charm and grace, and for all its squalor

PERU

and problems, Lima is among South America's most popular cities. Those who understand its spirit and come to know its ways, will find that it offers many interesting and extraordinary experiences.

How to get there
By air: Lima's modern Jorge Chávez Airport is located in Callao, fifteen kilometers from downtown. Flights arrive here from Europe, the United States, the Far East, and all South American countries. From the airport one can take a taxi, bus, or a minibus downtown; the latter is rather inexpensive and very convenient. Tickets are bought in the air terminal and you must specify your destination.

To get to the airport from the city, take a taxi, special minibus, or bus starting out from various locations downtown. Opposite Galeria Internacional, at Nicolas de Pierola 733, *colectivos* provide service to the airport from 6am-6pm. From Miraflores, a bus sets out from Palma 280 (Tel. 469-872). The trip takes thirty minutes. Those leaving Peru are subject to a $10 port tax — payable only in American dollars. The airport duty-free shop is one of Latin America's largest.

By land: Buses reach Lima from all parts of Peru and from neighboring capitals. Each bus company has its own terminal, from which you continue by taxi or local bus. The interurban and international service is convenient and dependable.

Where to stay
Lima has many hotels at a wide variety of levels. Most are decent and clean, but even here you must watch your luggage carefully and not leave valuables in the rooms. Service charges and tax add 15%-21% to the hotel's base rate; check carefully whether the prices you are quoted include this supplement.

If you want to spend a long time in Lima or want to keep down expenses without foregoing clean lodgings, you'll do well to stay at one of the many suburban pensions. These are usually private homes in which several rooms — immaculate, tidy and simply furnished — have been set aside for guests. Pension rates are far lower than those in hotels and sometimes include a Continental breakfast.

You'll find a great many hotels — some new — in Lima's central and southern areas (especially in Miraflores).

It's highly recommended to make reservations for most hotels and pensions, especially if you are planning to come during the tourist season.

*P*ERU

LIMA

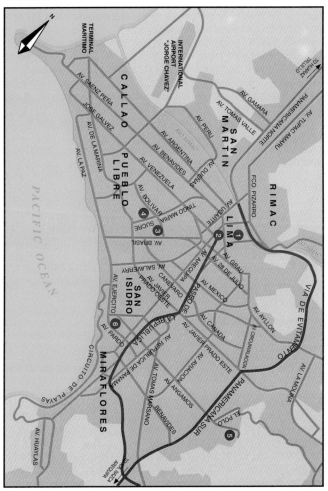

Index

Expensive hotels

Hotel Grand Bolívar. Unión 958, Tel. 27-6400. Just off Plaza San Martín, the very center of town, and the very top service and prices. Furnished in colonial style.

Lima Sheraton Hotel. Paseo de la República 170, Tel. 33-3320, fax 336-344. Quite new and modern, with a variety of sports facilities, shops, and the like. The view at the top is superb.

Miraflores César. Avenida La Paz at the corner with Avenida Diez Canseco, Tel. 44-1212. Far from downtown, but with all the luxury. Very expensive.

Crillón: Av. Colmena 589, Tel. 28-3290. Very central and large, the rooftop restaurant has a splendid view.

Moderately priced hotels

Savoy, Cailloma 224, Tel. 28-3520. Central, clean and comfortable, it is not cheap, but reasonably priced. Recommended.

El Plaza, Nicolás de Pierola 850, Tel. 28-6270. Modern and fair, try to avoid the rooms on the front, which are too noisy.

Riviera, Av. Inca G. de la Vega 981, Tel. 28-9460. Central, clean and comfortable.

Hostal Miraflores, Av. Petit Thouars 5444, Tel. 45-8745, fax 47-0116. Located in central Miraflores, spacious, pleasant and very comfortable, but far from downtown.

Inexpensive hotels

Hostal San Francisco, Jr. Ancash 340, Tel. 28-3643. Modern, just across the Plaza San Francisco.

Tight-budgeted travelers will find several cheap hotels in the vicinty of Plaza de Armas.

Young travelers will find several cheap hotels in the vicinity of Plaza de Armas. Among these *Hotel Damasco,* located one street away from the plaza at 199 Calle Ucagali, is recommended. *Hotel Europa* is popular among travelers, and is frequently fully booked during the high season. It is opposite the San Francisco Church on Calle Ancash in the San Francisco neighborhood. *Hotel Union,* although not recommended, is the cheapest and is situated near Plaza de Armas on the Union Pedestrian Mall.

Where to eat

Lima has thousands of restaurants offering a vast array of different cuisines. Though the tens of thousands of tourists who visit Lima each year appear to prefer the several dozen best-known restaurants, it seems that you would do well to let yourself experiment with gastronomic experiences at precisely those restaurants which do not generally appear in tourist guides or advertise extensively. The result will be much better and the food more interesting and much less expensive. You'll find a profusion of kiosks and stands around Plaza 2 de Mayo and along Calle Nicolás de Pierola, which links that square with Plaza San Martín. As you approach Plaza San Martín, you'll find restaurants and cafés replacing the kiosks, which become gradually more elegant and expensive.

Where the street meets the Plaza, you'll see the *Hotel Grand Bolívar* on one side and the large *Parrilladas Restaurant* across the way. *Parrilladas* specializes in superb Argentine-style steak in enormous portions and at moderate prices. Recommended. Along the side streets that branch off the plaza you'll find innumerable Creole and Chinese restaurants (*Chifa*) where you can eat your fill at prices anyone can afford.

Hotel Grand Bolívar and the other luxury hotels have excellent restaurants. Exceptional among them is the *Sky Room*, on the twentieth floor of *Hotel Crillón*, where a folklore troupe performs every evening.

Along calle Union there are countless coffee houses and inexpensive restaurants which serve "junk food". Do not miss out on the outstanding cream cakes in the coffee shops.

In Miraflores, Lima's rich suburb, one can find many Italian restaurants. This nightlife center is a good place for dinner.

A number of well-known restaurants are located downtown and are open mainly in the evening.

Las Trece Monedas, Jr. Ancash 536. Closed on Sundays. Peruvian and international cuisine in a beautiful building from colonial times.
La Costa Verde, Barranquito Beach (Barranco). Fish and seafood overlooking the Pacific, a bit expensive but worth. Open daily until midnight.
La Caleta, Dionisio Derteano 126, San Isidro. Also seafood specialities, very nice. Open from noon to 6pm.
L'Eau Vive, Ucayali 370. Run by French nuns, serving inexpensive French meals (fixed menu) or economic meals (*a la carte*). Open daily, noon-3pm and 8-10.15pm, when they start singing the Ave Maria. Profits go to the poor. Recommended.
Govinda's, Jr. Callao 480. Vegetarian restaurant and naturist drugstore. It also has a branch in San Isidro. *Natur*, Moquegua 132. Vegetarian.

Transportation
Urban: Buses, minibuses, *colectivos* and taxis will help you get

around Lima. **Bus** fare is cheap and service is frequent, though usually slow and crowded. Route numbers are clearly marked; bus stops are usually located on corners. **Minibuses** are really smaller buses that travel along the central routes. Because they charge slightly more than the bus, they are less crowded. They have no defined stops; drivers pull over for anyone who waves. **Colectivos** link downtown with the main suburbs, taking a number of passengers along fixed routes at fares double those of the equivalent trip by bus. This is the recommended way to get around Lima, since it's still quite cheap, and is quick and convenient.

A large fleet of regular **taxis**, too, fills Lima's streets. The fare is determined in advance between passenger and driver. Be sure to state your destination clearly, and bargain over the price. Try to pay drivers the exact amount, for they are likely to tell you they've got no change or put forth any number of other groundless claims designed only to empty your wallet. Tipping is not customary and it's enough to round off the price appearing on a meter — if one has been used at all!

Intercity: *Aero Perú* and *Faucett* (offices on Plaza San Martin) provide frequent and convenient air service throughout Peru. Reconfirm your flight twenty-four hours before the scheduled departure.

From Lima, **trains** set out only for the mountains, via La Oroya. They are very crowded and you must get to the station early because tickets can be purchased only one day in advance. The trains are slow, and though first class is comfortable and spacious, you still have to take every precaution against pickpockets and thieves. **Watch over your bags very carefully!** Lima's train station, **Desamparados**, is located behind the Government House; the ticket office is open 8.30am-noon and 1-4pm on weekdays, 7-11am on Saturdays. There is no Sunday train service in Peru, nor from January to March.

Excellent **bus** service links all of Peru's cities; a large number of companies have offices and terminals in Lima, most in the vicinity of Parque Universitario on the extension of Calle Pierola (La Colmena) southeast of Plaza San Martín. Because most roads between major cities are paved, travel is relatively fast and comfortable. For details, see the sections on the various destinations. Keep in mind that the area around bus terminals is infested with thieves. It is much better to take a taxi up to the bus. When you buy the ticket ask for the exact location of departure.

Tourist services
The central **Tourist Bureau** for Lima and the vicinity is at Jiron

de la Union (Belen) 1066, in the same building as the *Tambo de Oro* restaurant. Open 10am-7pm on weekdays and half-day on Saturdays, the Bureau offers explanatory material and maps along with a friendly staff who can give advice and guidelines about interesting sites, restaurants, hotels, transportation etc. The Ministry of Tourism has a branch office at the airport. On the whole, however, you won't find much material there, and it is mainly useful for making hotel reservations.

Topographic maps of areas you intend to visit on foot can be bought at *Instituto Geográfico Militar*, Avenida Aramburu 1190, San Isidro. Given the activities of terror groups in some parts of the country, several maps will not be sold to the public. Good road maps can be purchased at the *Touring y Automóvil Club Peruano*, Av. Vallejo 699, Lince (Tel. 40-3270). Here special counselors will advise you about travel routes and driving throughout the country. Discounts for members of similar associations in their countries.

Most travel agencies are located along Avenida Nicolás de Piérola and around Plaza San Martín. Airlines are either on Lima's center or in Miraflores and San Isidro. Most are open during weekdays 9am-5pm.

Car rental: Rent-a-car firms abound in Lima. *Avis*, *Hertz*, *Budget* and *National* have airport counters; *Avis* and *Hertz* have branches offices in Lima: *Avis* is at the *Sheraton Hotel* (Tel. 327-245) and *Hertz* is in San Isidro, Rivera Navarrete 550 (Tel. 42-1566).

Driving in Lima is difficult and we recommend that you use taxis in town.

South American Explorers Club is an American non-profit organization which provides very detailed and up-to-date information for travelers to South America. They also sell good maps and guidebooks and will provide information about unfrequented places like jungles and mountains. The Peruvian branch of the Club is in Lima, Avenida Republica de Portugal 146, Tel. 31-4480. The head office is at 126 Indian Creek Road, Ithaca, New York, U.S.A. (Tel. (607) 277-0448).

Tourist sites

Downtown
The bulk of Lima's commercial activity and most of its important tourist attractions are concentrated in an area demarcated by the city's four important plazas: 2 de Mayo, de Armas, Grau and Bolognesi. Square-shaped **Plaza San Martín** lies in their

epicenter and will serve as our point of departure to explore downtown.

At the heart of this huge plaza stands a statue of Argentine General José de San Martín, who helped Peru cast off the Spanish yoke. Surrounding the plaza are some of the city's grandest and most modern edifices, with the *Gran Hotel Bolivar* heading the list. Calle Piérola, lined with numerous shops, offices, restaurants and cafés, branches off to the northwest to **Plaza 2 de Mayo**, humming with hundreds of peddlers offering all kinds of food and other titbits. Around this square you can treat yourself to the strange foodstuffs sold in kiosks and get an impression of the daily lives of the Peruvians.

Calle Unión, Lima's main shopping street, crosses Plaza San Martín with its proliferation of shops offering souvenirs, clothing, jewelry, bric-a-brac and more. The quality here is superb even if relatively high-priced. Parts of the street are closed to vehicular traffic allowing pedestrians to meander freely in and out of the shops.

Turning northeast onto Calle Unión (to the right of *Gran Hotel Bolívar*) and proceeding about three blocks, we come to **Iglesia La Merced**, Lima's "Church of Mercy". Its interior decor is most impressive, as is its stone facade. The church is dedicated to the merciful Virgin who, according to tradition, defends Lima from siege and attack, serving as Marshal of the Peruvian Army. Her festival is celebrated each year on September 24, with the participation of the president of the Republic, army officers and public dignitaries.

Calle Unión ends at the lovely **Plaza de Armas,** Lima's most important square, with a fountain more than three centuries old in its center. It was here that Pizarro founded Lima — naming it Ciudad del Reyes (City of the Kings) — and where he built his home. **The Government Palace,** which took more than fifteen years to build, occupies the spot where Pizarro's home is believed to have stood. Here he was killed brutally on July 26, 1541 at the age of 63, by his old partner, Almagro, who was bitter that all glory and governorship was given to Pizarro. Since its completion in 1938, the Palace has served as the president's official residence, from which site state affairs are conducted. A red-uniformed honor guard patrols the front and the ceremonial changing of the guard takes place most days at 12:45pm (check at the Information Office). To have a guided tour of the Palace, you have to submit your passport at least 24 hours in advance (Mon.-Fri. at 12.30pm). To the left of the Palace is the **Central Post Office**, which houses a small **Postal Museum** (entrance free), open Mon.-Fri. 8am-1.30pm and 2-4pm, Sat. 8am-1.30pm,

Sun. 8am-noon. On the last Sunday's morning of each month stamp dealers meet here for trading.

Across Plaza de Armas we find the **Municipal Cathedral**. This impressive edifice, renovated a number of times, stands on the spot where Pizarro built Lima's first church, and in which he was buried. The cathedral houses a small museum of religious art (open daily 10am-1pm and 2-5pm). Beside it is the Archbishop's palace, built after World War I. Across the way is **City Hall**, constructed in 1945. It houses a small picture gallery (open Mon.-Fri. 8am-3pm), containing works of Peruvian artists. Rio Rimac flows behind the plaza and the train station is along its bank (on Calle Ancash). A short distance from there is **Iglesia San Francisco,** with **Casa Pilatos**, an impressive mansion which serves as the Municipal Cultural Center — opposite. The church, one of Lima's loveliest, was built in 1674 in Baroque style and features a collection of art, a decorative ceiling and a painstakingly constructed tile roof. The large church library numbers tens of thousands of volumes, some of them centuries old. The vaults beneath the church were discovered and opened to the public in the early 1950's, revealing a great many mysterious tombs. Visiting hours: 10am-1pm and 3-6pm.

Continuing down Calle Ancash and crossing Calle Abancay we come to Plaza Bolívar, site of the **Congressional Palace** and, to its right, the building of the **Spanish Inquisition.** The Inquisition was active in Peru from the late sixteenth century and was finally abolished only in 1820. A visit to this building, where the fate of hundreds and thousands of suspected heretics was decided, is highly recommended. The courtroom itself, where you will see the Inquisitors' thrones, inspires both fear and awe. The building is open Mon.-Fri. 9am-7pm, Sat. 9am-4.30pm. Part of the collection of the National Library is kept here.

Returning downtown, we walk two blocks down Calle Abancay and notice the **National Library** to our right. A right turn onto Calle Ucayali immediately brings us to **Iglesia San Pedro.** This church, also in Baroque style, was built by the Jesuits in the mid-seventeenth century and is considered one of the most beautiful in Lima. Directly across from it is the **Torre Tagle Palace**, currently the home of Peru's Foreign Ministry. The impressive building, dating from 1735, has recently been renovated and one can enjoy the beauty of its architecture, wood engravings and balconies as one strolls through its courtyard. Recommended. Open to visitors only on weekday afternoons.

Continuing along Calle Ucayali (which turns into Calle Ica after crossing Calle Union) we find **Iglesia San Agustín**. This church, two blocks from Plaza de Armas, dates from the eighteenth

LIMA — DOWNTOWN

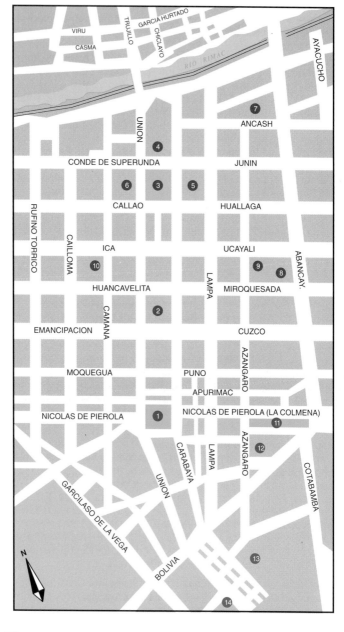

century, but was seriously damaged in an earthquake and only a small section of it may be visited. A famous wooden statue named *Death*, by an eighteenth-century Peruvian artist named Gavilan, is imbedded in the building's stone-chiseled facade, but cannot always be visited because it is in the damaged section of the church. One block further, we come upon the **Municipal Theater**, residence of Lima's most prestigious stage.

Returning to Plaza San Martín, we turn southeast and head down the Colmena (in the opposite direction from the *Gran Hotel Bolívar*). Four blocks down is a small, rather neglected park — **Parque Universitario**. Though best known as the departure point for most of the buses and minibuses that travel from Lima to its suburbs, the park boasts an additional importance, as well. In a corner of the park, teeming with peddlers and idlers, we find the national **Pantheon**, where a number of the most important figures of Peruvian history lie buried. The Pantheon was established in an eighteenth-century Jesuit church, converted to this use in the 1920's. Beside it is the **University of San Marcos**, South America's first, founded in the mid-sixteenth century. Damaged in successive earthquakes, the University building presently serves only for conventions and conferences. Across the park is the 22-story building of the **Peruvian Ministry of Education**, which was the tallest and grandest edifice in the country at the time of its construction in 1955.

A common occurence in Latin America, which will certainly revolt most Westerners is **cock fighting**. Two blood-thirsty fighting cocks, with small sharp blades attached to their legs, fight each other to the death. No less interesting than the cruel fight is the enthusiasm of the spectators, especially the gamblers among them. The amount of money involved in this betting is surprisingly high, particularly considering the poverty of the fans of this "sport". These fights are held several times weekly near the Parque Universitario at 150 Calle Sandia. The fights usually begin at 4pm and continue a few hours, but one only needs a short time to get the idea.

Retracing our steps, we head south from Plaza San Martín, down Calle Unión toward Paseo de la República (passing the Tourist Bureau). This broad promenade is lined with some of Lima's most important buildings, among them the **Civic Center** (first on the right), with the modern and luxurious *Sheraton* Hotel at its corner.

To the left we see the **Palacio de Justicia** — the Palace of Justice — with the **Museum of Italian Art** across the way. This museum, constructed in Renaissance style, has a collection of reproductions of Italian art in addition to changing exhibits of contemporary artists. Visiting hours: Tues.-Sat. 9am-7pm. The promenade itself, adorned with trees and greenery, is lined with benches and statues. At its end we come to the broad **Plaza Grau**, with **Avenida Colón** branching off from it. The **National Museum of Art**, one of Lima's most important, is located at the beginning of this avenue. It houses a large collection of paintings, sculptures, furniture, jewelry and more. The museum building was erected in 1868 for an international exposition held in Lima. Its spacious halls contain chronologically arranged exhibits of art dating from the first human settlement in Peru, about 4000 years ago, to our time. Highly recommended. Open Tues.-Sun. 9am-4.30pm.

Other sites

Many of Lima's most important and interesting sites are rather far from downtown, but can be reached quickly and easily by bus or taxi. A general survey follows:

Pueblo Libre

About five kilometers southwest of the city center is the Pueblo Libre Quarter (bus 7, 10, or 37 from downtown, or bus 21, 24, or 42 from Parque Universitario and many *colectivos* set out for Pueblo Libre from Plaza San Martín). Two of Lima's most important and interesting museums are located there, along with a large **artesanía** (handicrafts) market. Let's explore them one by one:

Museo de Arqueología y Etnografía — the Archaeological and Ethnographical Museum — located on Plaza Bolívar (not the one downtown), houses an impressive and highly important collection. In its many halls you will find handicrafts, textiles, ceramics, household implements, tools and sacred objects from all of Peru's pre-Columbian and pre-Incan civilizations. While the presentation is simple and uninspired, it is hard not to be impressed with the thousands of exhibits, the remnants of the Paracas, Chavin and other civilizations. The section devoted to the Incas presents a model of Machu-Picchu, while other wings contain mummies, skulls and more. A visit to this museum is a "must" for understanding Peruvian development. Open daily, 9am-5pm (Tel. 63-5070).

Nearby is the **Museum of History** and its collection of paintings, uniforms and other objects from the time of Peru's War of Independence. Open Sun.-Fri., 9am-5.30pm (Tel. 63-2009).

Fascinating **Museo Herrera**, Avenida Bolívar 1515 — a fifteen-minute walk from the Archaeological Museum — contains a tremendous private collection of pottery — chiefly jugs hundreds or thousands of years old, which have been collected from all over Peru and faithfully represent the various civilizations and periods. The main building houses the ceramics exhibit, alongside a number of excellently preserved mummies, a splendid display of gold and silver jewelry (in what is, in fact, a giant vault), an exhibit of textiles and more. A separate building one story lower contains a special hall with hundreds of statuettes in various erotic positions. This hall, to which only adults are admitted, has given the entire museum a glorious reputation; a visit there is highly recommended. Even the most worldly of visitors can certainly learn something here... or at least come to realize there's nothing new under the sun. Open Mon.-Sat. 9am-1pm and 3-6pm; Sun. and holidays 9am-1pm (Tel. 61-1312).

Feria Artesanal — the artisans' market — is also located in this neighborhood, on Avenida La Marina. Here a number of large stores offer a wide variety of handicrafts and folk art, made of cloth, wood, ceramics and metal. Here is Lima's largest concentration of souvenirs of this sort with a large selection at affordable prices. We highly recommend that you stop here, compare prices — and bargain!

Museo de Oro

Ancient gold objects are undoubtedly among the most fascinating remnants of the ancient Peruvian civilizations. Since gold was abundant, easily mined and easy to process, much of the nobility's jewelry and other artifacts were made of the precious metal. Apart from their artistic value, it's hard to overlook their monetary value — more than worth their weight in gold! Most of the treasure was plundered by the Spanish *conquistadores*; the tiny remnant that has survived is displayed today in a number of museums, of which the important ones are the "gold museums" — *Museos de Oro* — in Bogota (Colombia) and Lima.

Lima's **Museo de Oro** allows visitors a close-up view of the artistry of the ancient craftsmen, who created stunning jewelry and ritual objects, many embedded with gems. The well-kept

Plaza San Martin

museum feature a tasteful exhibit of some of the most important displays that have survived. Part of the collection is displayed in major museums throughout the world.

The "golden" section is in the basement which is actually a safe. On the entrance level there is a large exhibit of arms from different periods and places throughout the world.

The museum is far from downtown, and getting there is a problem. A taxi will convey you swiftly and with no difficulty, but it's expensive. You can take the No. 2 bus from Plaza San Martin to the junction of Avenidas Arequipa and Angamos, and from there transfer to one of the *colectivos*, which go as far as

Av. Primavera to the museum. The entire trip takes about an hour. The museum is open daily noon-7pm (Tel. 35-2917).

Miraflores

The Miraflores quarter, undoubtedly Lima's most beautiful and important suburb, is situated along the Pacific coast. Here reside the city's aristocrats and dignitaries, amid some of Lima's best hotels, movie theaters, restaurants and shopping centers. A tranquil walk down its streets will reveal the exclusive character of this neighborhood. Alongside modern high-rises there are grand estates that serve as residences for diplomats, government officials, businessmen, and so on. It is not a good idea to stay here, as it is far from downtown. A visit, however, is definitly worth your while, to get an impression of a Lima quite different from the one we've known thus far — the bustling, somewhat antiquated and faded city center. Here greenery dominates, and the broad avenues radiate a modern familiar atmosphere. Though Miraflores has no special sites, it reflects, perhaps more than anything else, the social, economic and class polarization which characterizes Peru. A visit here helps one to appreciate the severity and extent of the problem.

Colectivos leave for Miraflores from the south-western corner of Plaza San Martín every few minutes, and the trip takes less than half an hour.

Miraflores is home to the small and interesting **Museo Amano** (Retiro 160). This private owned museum features an excellent collection of pre-Columbian and pre-Incan embroidery and ceramics from various regions of Peru. It can be visited only in small groups, with guided tours by appointment (Tel. 412-909) Mon.-Fri. 2-5pm, every hour. Admission is free. Take Minibus No. 13 as far as Avenida Santa Cruz, and then walk on for another block.

Shopping

Lima's major shopping street is Calle Unión between Plaza San Martín and Plaza de Armas. Here you'll find anything your heart desires — from colorful buttons to elegant clothing to gold jewelry and diamonds. Dozens of shops line the street, and this is where most tourists find their souvenirs. Calle Piérola, between Plazas 2 de Mayo and San Martín, also has an abundance of stores, which specialize more in popular souvenirs, local works of art and the like. Though prices are rather high in this area the goods are usually exclusive and of superb quality. Those interested in handicrafts will certainly find a broader selection and far lower prices in the Pueblo Libre artesanía market (see "Tourist sites" above).

There are a number of shopping centers in the very center of town, one of which shares a building with the *Tambo de Oro* restaurant and the Tourist Bureau. Here and in the vicinity, along Calle Unión, there are many shops that sell tourist souvenirs at reasonable prices. Another small shopping center, with slightly lower prices, is located at Calle Unión 1030.

Miraflores, where the most important shopping centers are located, is the best place for clothing and footwear. Here one pays steep prices for imported goods just off the boat from exclusive manufacturers in New York or Paris.

Simple jewelry of gold or silver is extremely popular, as are woodcrafts and lovely gourd carvings produced mainly by artists from Huancayo. High-quality sweaters, ponchos, hats and wall carpets, all hand woven, are also sold throughout Lima. Most woolen products are made of lamb or llama wool. A small quantity of such goods, softer to the touch, are of the superior alpaca.

If you travel elsewhere in the country, you'll find that though prices are higher in the capital than in the periphery, there are significant differences in quality in favor of Lima-produced goods, and this must be taken into account.

Most stores in Lima close for *siesta* between 1-3:30pm.

Entertainment and cultural events

Although Lima is an effervescent and bustling city both day and night, it is not noted for a wide range of quality entertainment. The city center has a great many cinemas (some right on Plaza San Martín), as do the new neighborhoods which screen relatively recent films, in the original languages, with Spanish subtitles. If you want to take in an evening show, buy your tickets several hours in advance.

There are performances at the Municipal Theater, private theaters and concert halls almost every evening. Tickets can usually be obtained without difficulty, and prices are not high. The Lima Symphony Orchestra, though not of a standard for discerning music lovers, performs several times a week, usually in the Miraflores concert hall.

We especially recommend that you take in a folklore performance, offered almost every evening in a *peña* (folklore club) or theater (the Municipal Theater on Mondays and the La Cabaña Theater on Tuesdays). The *Sky Room*, on top of Hotel Crillon, features nightly folklore performances. The *Peña Hatuchay* offers especially enjoyable folklore performances on weekends, with instrumental music and singing and dancing with audience participation. The club is at Trujillo 228, on the other side of the Río Rimac, behind the Central Post Office. Prices are certainly reasonable.

Nightclubs and discotheques abound in the large downtown hotels or the southern neighborhoods, especially San Isidro and Miraflores. They are open on weekends and they charge rather stiff entrance fees. This is where a great many Peruvian youths and students, etc. spend their evenings.

General Information

Banks and currency exchange

The national bank, *Banco de la Nación* (open only in the mornings) has numerous branches throughout Lima where you can carry out any conventional banking transaction, including moneychanging and receiving international transfers, letters of credit, documents, etc. American and British banks also have offices in Lima, and transferring money to them is simpler. You will be paid only in local currency however, as is the case when you make cash withdrawals against international credit cards.

In the vicinity of Plaza San Martín — especially along Calle Nicolás de Piérola — there are a large number of travel agents who will change foreign currency into Peruvian *soles* at rates similar to the banks.

On the end of Calle Union and along the length of Calle Ocona, which turns right from Union at Plaza San Martin, there are a number of *cambio* (exchange) offices and many street moneychangers. Compare rates before changing your money. The black market rate in Lima is the highest in the country, so change enough local currency there before setting out for the provincial towns.

Postal and telephone services

It is highly recommended that you send everything by registered air mail. The Central Post Office (*Correo Central*), near Plaza de Armas, is open Mon.-Fri. 8am-6pm and on Sat. and Sun. till noon. Parcels weighing more than one kilogram must undergo a customs inspection before you send them — a time-consuming, bothersome and exhausting bureaucratic nuisance. A centrally located post office is off Plaza San Martín, on Colmena, across from *Hotel Crillón*, and is open Mon.-Fri 8am-8pm and on Sat. mornings only.

International phone calls are made from *Entel*, in the post office located off Plaza San Martín. You must deposit a passport or sum of money when you place your call, which is made from one of the many booths lining the hall. At times there is a long wait until the call goes through, and you'll have to listen for your name to know that your turn has come. International phone calls are very costly and collect calls are possible only to the United States and a number of Western European countries.

Books and periodicals in English

Many books are published in Peru about its culture, archaeology, history and the like, and English translations are often available in many shops, primarily downtown. Bookstores abound along Calles Unión and Piérola, especially in the vicinity of Plaza San Martín. They offer an adequate selection of foreign newspapers and literature — including imported books — on various topics.

Several bookstores in Miraflores and San Isidro stock mainly foreign newspapers. The local English-language weekly *Lima Times* is available at most stands in town.

Photographic supplies

If you're going to travel throughout Peru, it's best to stock up on film before leaving the capital. It is difficult, if not impossible, to find film in outlying villages and towns, and that which is available has not necessarily been kept in conditions which ensure its freshness. Developing film in Peru is not especially expensive and is done relatively quickly and well.

Weather

Though Lima is relatively close to the equator, its climate is temperate. The Humboldt Current cools the air a little, but the humidity is very high, exceeding 90% in winter (May to October). Skies are usually heavily overcast. It is a little warmer between November and April, but that should present no problem for the visitor because the humidity is lower and the skies are clear. It hardly rains and the infrequent showers do not last long.

Important addresses

Peruvian Tourist Ministry: Unión (Belén) 1066, Tel. 323-559.
Tourist Police: Salaverry 1158, Jesús María, Tel. 714-579.
Clínica Anglo-Americana: Avenida Salazar, San Isidro, Tel. 403-570.
Clínica Internacional: Washington 1475, Tel. 288-060.
Visa Extension: Paseo de la República 585, Tel. 276-927.
Auto Club: Avenida César Vallejo 699, Tel. 403-270.

Consulates

Great Britain: Natalio Sánchez 125, Plaza Washington, Tel. 335-032.

Canada: Libertad 130, Miraflores, Tel. 444-015.
France: Av. Arequipa 3415, San Isidro, Tel. 704968.
Germany: Av. Arequipa 4210, Miraflores, Tel. 457-033.
Italy: Gregorio Escobedo 298, Jesús María, Tel. 632-727.
Spain: Jorge Basadre 498, San Isidro, Tel. 705-600.
Switzerland: Av. Salaverry 3240, San Isidro, Tel. 624-090.
U.S.A.: Grimaldo del Solar 346, Miraflores, Tel. 443-621.

Airlines
AeroPerú: Plaza San Martín, Tel. 285-721.
Faucett: Inca G. de la Vega 865, Tel. 336-364.
AeroCondor: Juan de Arona 781, San Isidro, Tel. 425-663.
Aeroflot: Paseo de la República 144 (Of. 116), 321-377.
Air France: Juan de Arona 830, San Isidro, Tel. 704-870.
Alitalia: Camino Real 497, San Isidro, Tel. 428-507.
British Airways: Andalucía 174, Miraflores, Tel. 469-777.
Iberia: Nicolás de Piérola 820, Tel. 283-833.

North of Lima

In this section we will survey the sites and routes north of Lima, to the Ecuadorian border — in the mountains, along the coast and in the depths of the eastern jungles. Some sites, especially those in the vicinity of Huaraz, can be included on a tour beginning and ending in Lima, while others are best visited en route from Lima to Ecuador or vice versa. Various possibilities have been noted. Since the coastal axis between Lima and Trujillo offers no sites of special interest, the mountain route is recommended, with stops in Huaraz and the vicinity on the way.

Transportation
Many companies provide comfortable, dependable and rapid bus service to all the destinations surveyed here. *Roggero* (La Colmena 733, Tel. 282-044) and *Tepsa* (Paseo de la República 119, Tel. 731-233) are among those we recommend.

Huaraz
Huaraz, 408 km northeast of Lima, is a national and international center for hikers and mountain climbers who enjoy roaming through the gorgeous expanses of mountain landscape. Of Huaraz's 80,000 people, a significant number make a living by catering to the tens of thousands of tourists who throng to the town, especially from June through October, when comfortable weather and the European vacation season coincide. Though Huaraz is situated 3090 meters above sea level, it is in the middle of a valley — the Santa Valley, split from north to south by the Rio Santa and hemmed in on both east and west by tall mountain chains whose peaks soar thousands of meters farther into the sky.

The range of mountains in the west are known as *Cordillera Negra* (black range) because it is free of snow in summer and the soil is dark. The eastern Cordillera is the immense *Cordillera Blanca* (white range). Its peaks are covered in snow and glaciers and most reach heights of 6000 m above sea level. The highest in the Cordillera Blanca range is Mt. Huazcarán, which is 6768 m high. Another range to the south of Cordillera Blanca is Huayhuash.

Huaraz, like many of its neighbors in this part of Peru, was severely damaged in the earthquake of May 1970, and large areas have since been rebuilt. Today it serves as a mountain climbing center and a point of departure or return for dozens of fascinating outings, some on foot, others on donkeys or horseback.

Transportation

Bus service from Lima to Huaraz is frequent, comfortable, fast, dependable and inexpensive. *Rodríguez, Expreso Ancash* and *Arellano Intersa* are a few recommended companies of the many that provide service on this line. The trip takes about seven hours over a good, paved road. The buses set out at all hours of the day and it is best to buy tickets in advance. Travelers who reach Huaraz before sunrise (if traveling by night) may spend several hours — extremely cold ones — unable to find a hotel room, for most hotels are closed and shuttered at night.

Convenient public transportation links Huaraz with all the sites in the vicinity and with villages and towns that are attractions in their own right or serve as starting points for hikes. Buses set out several times daily for Trujillo and Chimbote, along the coast, and from there you can proceed northward in the direction of Ecuador.

Huaraz is very easy to reach by car, but bear in mind that relying on a private car is a problem for hikers, who must then forego the option of starting from one place and winding up in another. It is better to park your car in town and tour the area by public transportation.

AeroPerú flies from Lima to Anta several times a week. It is not worth the bother, for it takes quite a while to reach the airport and then more time is lost getting from Anta to Huaraz.

Where to stay

As a tourist center, Huaraz naturally has many hotels, suited to all budgets and tastes.

Hotel de Turistas, Av. Centenario, 10th block, Tel. 721-709. Part of the state-owned chain, in the center; recommended.
Marañón, in the center of the market. Pleasant and comfortable.
Alpamayo, Las Américas, Tel. 721-333. Opposite the soccer stadium which lies on Confraternidad Oeste. Inexpensive and a good meeting point for climbers, displays useful information.
Pensión de la señora Mariela, near the Alpamayo hotel, basic.

Owners of other *pensiones* wait for the buses to arrive in order to

PERU

HUARAZ AND VICINITY

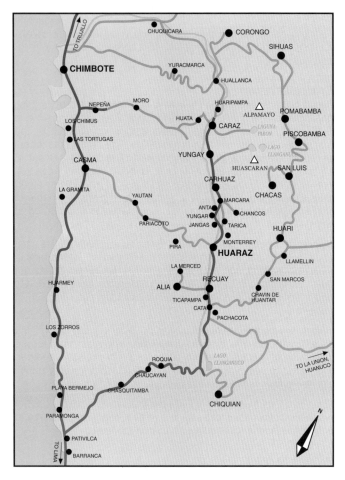

"enlist" tourists. Take your time and compare until you find the one that suits you. At all the listed places you can leave your unnecessary gear when you go on hikes in the area.

Where to eat
The local market, shops and restaurants all meet our gastronomic needs satisfactorily. Although Huaraz is not a

Cordillera Blanca

Mecca for fussy eaters, you can certainly find plenty to eat. Here, too, like everywhere in Peru, there are lots of Chinese restaurants, along with others serving local fare. Most restaurants are downtown, near Plaza de Armas and along Av. Luzuriaga which branches off from it. One street below the avenue (boulevard), there is a popular restaurant patronized by the locals which serves large and tasty portions at low prices. Try the excellent *criolla* soup.

Fresh and canned foods which are essential supplies for your hikes in the vicinity are available in the market and shops.

Tourist services

The municipal **Tourist Bureau** is on the ground floor of the Municipality building on Plaza de Armas (Tel. 721-031). It offers material concerning outings in the vicinity, shops where you can stock up on supplies, transportation and the like. Buy maps in Lima, for the ones on sale in Huaraz are nowhere near as good.

The Peruvian *Auto Club* has a branch at Luzuriaga 866 (Tel. 2590). *Club Andino*, Barron 582, will advise you about mountain trails.

Travel and tourist agencies abound as well, most are located along Avenida Luzuriaga. They offer guided tours of the area, some involving hikes of several days' duration. Though this is the quickest and most convenient way to cover the area's interesting and special sites (see below) without wasting precious time hitching rides or waiting for irregular buses, it comes at a price.

Food should be purchased in town for the entire duration of hikes, plus a reserve, for it is almost unobtainable on the road. Take nourishing and filling food that will not spoil, which does not weigh much and is easy to prepare (rice, beans, etc.).

General Information

Currency exchange

Dollars can be converted at the *Banco de la Nación*. As long lines and bureaucracy are almost inevitable, you must simply grin and bear it. Businesses and certain travel agencies change money according to black market rates, but in Lima the rate is a bit higher.

Postal and telephone services

From the post office on Plaza de Armas you can send letters and small parcels by air or sea. For international calls go to *Entel*, across from the post office.

Camping and photographical supplies
Many shops in Huaraz sell or rent camping equipment of various types — everything from sleeping bags to tents to gas burners. Check the condition and quality of the equipment when you rent it and do not leave an excessive deposit. Gas cylinders, rather rare in South America, can be bought here, though at high prices. Photography shops in town stock film, but only the most common types. Be sure to check expiration dates.

Weather, elevation and mountain climbing guidelines
The weather around Huaraz is rather pleasant, though temperatures drop at night and the chill can be quite painful. Be very sure to bring along the best camping gear, for nights under the stars are liable to be unbearably cold without it. A two-layer tent is important for keeping out the rain, and be sure to have enough warm and comfortable clothing. When hiking in the mountains, be sure to choose protected places sheltered from the wind for your campsite at night.

Because of the high altitude — in town, and all the more so in the surrounding mountains — you must observe certain essential safety rules. The physical consequences of thin air must be taken into account when planning any outing (see "Introduction"). In Huaraz itself the average temperature is 15°C (60°F), and it tends to drop as you ascend. During the rainy season, January through April, mountain climbing is very difficult. We recommend that you try to schedule your visit between May and October, the dry season.

Most trails require three to seven days of hiking at altitudes of up to 5000 m. This demands superb physical condition and sufficient acclimatization to the area's conditions. You should therefore come to Huaraz **at least** two or three days before you begin your hike. On certain routes you can hire a guide with donkey (*burro*) to haul your gear, and this seems very worthwhile despite the expense. At high altitudes all climbers, however fit, will find it difficult to bear even their own weight, and the benefits of moving about without gear are worth their "weight" in gold.

Trails and sites in the vicinity

Laguna Churup
This enchanting lake lies 4600 m above sea level. It is almost surrounded by straight cliffs, and the color of the water is turquoise. It is located about 35 km away from Huaraz and a

Morning in the Cordillera

good portion of the trip can be done by car. One can do a day trip to the lake, or perhaps spend a night out camping. There is an area suitable for camping not far from the lake.

The taxi will bring you to the village **Pitek**, and from here there is a difficult 2-3 hour climb to the lake. A glacier descends to the lake from the mighty snow-capped peak which rises above.

You can ask the taxi driver to wait for you in Pitek to return to Huaraz, or otherwise take a three hour walk back, passing Indian villages on the way.

Another alternative is to combine this trip with visits to other lakes in the vicinity, using Pitek as a base, and setting up camp there. One can also ask to sleep in one of the village huts.

Llanganuco Santa Cruz
Though dozens of mountain trails wind around Huaraz and the vicinity, the Llanganuco Santa Cruz is by far the most popular. This pleasant hike lasts four to five days and reaches heights of up to 4800 m. Here, too, it is important to adjust to the elevation slowly and to pack camping gear, warm clothing and food for the trip.

The trail begins in the village of Yungay (elev. 2585 m), 56

The pyramid of Mt. Alpamayo

km north of Huaraz. Here you can get organized, load up on last-minute food items, and leave behind unnecessary gear.

From Yungay set out, preferably by car, on the dirt road leading to Lake Llanganuco. It is a lovely short trip by itself for those who wish to enjoy the great view of the Huascarán. From there begins the exhausting climb to the first ridge, 4700 m high, with an enchanting backdrop of glaciers and mountain peaks. Below the ridge are some sheepfolds where you can spend the night. The next day begins the descent, which continues the following day as well, until the village of Vilcabamba. Then there is a climb again from 2200 m to 4800 m. You should sleep on the way before crossing this ridge. You can rent donkeys to carry your gear — which is important and useful. The next day, the ridge summit will afford a splendid view of Punta Unión, with a glacier on one side and a fertile agricultural valley on the other. Then begins the descent again — as far as the village of Caspampa, from which you can go on to beautiful **Laguna Parón**, 32 km away, or to Caraz and then back to Huaraz. In the central plaza in Caraz you can rent a car and drive to Laguna Paron.

Alpamayo

Mt. Alpamayo is considered to be one of the most beautiful mountains in the world. It is shaped like a perfect pyramid with four facets, and is covered with snow. The summit is about 6300 m high and is a difficult challenge for mountain climbers. Hikers can reach the base of the summit. This trip, there and back, takes five to six days, while the truly enthusiastic may choose to continue from the mountain and cross the Cordillera — a difficult hike which demands good orientation skills. If one chooses this option the trip lasts 6-7 days.

The hike begins in the small village of Cochapampa, which can be reached with one of the *camionetas* (pick-up trucks) which leave from the market in Caraz. From the village, a long and exhausting climb lies ahead to reach the magnificent Laguna Collicocha, and the mountain saddle, which is 4900 m high. From the saddle there is a steep descent to the wide valley, Quebrada Alpamayo. Several hours along the slopes of the valley brings you to the magnificent foothills of Mt. Alpamayo. You can hire a donkey at Cochapampa to carry the gear up to this point, but here you separate from the muleteer, and must pay for the number of days it takes him to return to his village (unless you wish to return on the same route). The remainder of the trip takes about three days, and includes the crossing of some difficult mountain passes, the highest of which is 5000 m high. The views are breathtaking, the lakes are magnificent (especially Lagunas Safuna), and it is worthwhile spending some time walking around them.

The route ends in the pleasant town **Pomabamba**, from which buses depart a few times a week to Huaraz. The return trip to Huaraz by truck is certainly an exceptional experience, although it lasts at least 12 hours and is exhausting. Before you leave Pomabamba, you can enjoy the hot springs which are situated a few minutes walking distance from the central plaza.

Huayhuash

One of the most difficult trails in the Huaraz area circles the Huayhuash (pronounced Wai-wash) mountain range. This is a beautiful route, winding among deep blue lakes and gigantic glaciers which descend to them from the mountain tops. Many sections of the trail climb to more than 4000 m, so you must make appropriate arrangements. You need ten days to complete the full "circle route", though you can scale it down by foregoing some stretches and settling for a route which is shorter, though no less impressive and enjoyable.

Pack plenty of food and excellent camping gear. Physical fitness is a prime condition before setting out, as is slow and easy adjustment to the elevation. Part of the way you may wish to avail yourself of the services of the locals, who will be glad to accompany you and load your gear on the backs of their donkeys and mules — a real help along this route.

Take the daily bus from Huaraz to Chiquian, 110 km to the south. This charming little village has a modest market where you can stock up on last-minute items. The hike begins here, first along the river and then atop the soaring mountain ridge. Llamac is the last village pass before ascending the first ridge of mountains — beyond which there is a stunning view of the glaciers. From here on, the trail leads around deep blue lakes to mighty glaciers, amidst green flora and brown hamlets, offering the hiker several days of quiet tranquility.

The lengthy trail ends in the town of Cajatambo, from which regular transportation will bring you to the coastal road and to Lima.

Yungay

In 1970 an earthquake devastated the Cordillera Blanca area. This caused a huge piece of the glacier from Mt. Huazcarán to break off and descend at high speed, destroying everything in its path. All 18,000 inhabitants of Yungay were killed, except a few who were elsewhere at the time. Not a single house was left standing.

Four date palms mark the spot of Plaza de Armas. While walking along the plain, which a short while ago had been a vibrant town, you will discern a few pathetic remnants of the daily life that used to exist here; a piece of a wrecked bus, or bits of half buried furniture. From the monument built on the hill, one can clearly see Mt. Huazcarán and the glacier which caused the disaster.

A short time after the disaster, a new town of Yanguy was established not far from the former town, and today it has a similar number of inhabitants — about 20,000. It's less than an hour's ride away from Huaraz, and the buses which depart frequently for Caraz, pass through the ruins of Yungay.

Chavín de Huantar

The ruins of a temple some 3000 years old are located 110 km southeast of Huaraz. Due to damage in the 1970 earthquake, parts of it are closed to the public. The site features wonderful stone carvings, an impressive building and the remains of statues. The figures of condors and pumas, etched in precise detail on the temple walls, are especially beautiful, as are the remains of gargoyles protruding from the walls. Do not miss the temple's underground vaults, from which you can form an impression of its construction and design.

Getting to Chavin involves about five hours of difficult travel on an annoying dirt road, and only its scenic wonders make it bearable. Daily buses from Huaraz (morning and afternoon) reach the village of **Catac** quickly and with no difficulty along a paved road which extends the full length of the Santa Cruz Valley. Here you turn eastward and continue another eighty kilometers to Chavin on a rough trail. Hitchhiking is very difficult once you've passed Catac, while a similar route on foot is complicated, difficult, and not worth the effort since it offers no special attractions. Tour companies in Huaraz organize round trip excursions to Chavin, and you would do well to consider joining one. There is daily bus service between Chavin and Lima, but the route is circuitous and tiring, passing through innumerable towns and villages. We recommend that you use Huaraz's bus services instead. (The site is open 8am-4pm, weekends and holidays — 10am-4pm.)

Trujillo

Francisco Pizarro founded Trujillo in 1536 next to the ancient adobe city of Chan Chan and named it after the city of his birth in Spain. Though rich in modern buildings, Trujillo (pop. over 750,000) seems to have retained its colonial charm. Buildings and churches dating from the sixteenth to the eighteenth centuries create a special atmosphere, dominated by Spanish architecture and imported building styles which few other cities preserve so well and so beautifully. Trujillo has many magnificent estates, which once belonged to the city's aristocratic and wealthy families. Most have been expropriated by the government. While some have been turned into office buildings and corporate headquarters, others are put to social uses and are usually not open to the public.

The excellent weather (average temperatures are 25°C in summer and 15°C in winter) goes far in explaining the attraction the Spanish felt for the city and the dryness explains the wonderful preservation of archaeological ruins in the vicinity.

*P*ERU

Trujillo — Plaza de Armas

Transportation

Frequent and convenient buses connect Trujillo with Lima and the Ecuadorian border. The highway from Huaraz to the coast goes via **Casma** (pop. 20,000). Not far from Casma there are numerous temples and antiquities, the most impressive of these — **Sechin** — is some six kilometers up the hill from Casma in the direction of Huaraz.

From Casma the road leads northward to **Chimbote** (pop. approximately 300,000), which until recently was the center of the Peruvian fishing industry. The only two things worthy of mention here are the stench of fish which permeates the city and the many thieves. Another 135 km brings us to Trujillo.

It's about ten hours from Huaraz or Lima to Trujillo and up to eleven hours from Tumbes, close to the Ecuadorian border. *Roggero* and *Tepsa* buses are recommended. The lines from Lima and back are very crowded! Make reservations. If all buses are booked for the forseeable future, you can make the trip in stages.

AeroPerú and *Faucett* fly daily between Trujillo and Lima and thence to Peru's other cities. *Faucett* flies to Tumbes and stops over in Trujillo on the way to Iquitos.

Where to stay
Hotel de Turistas, Plaza de Armas (Tel. 232-741) is a nice colonial building on the very center. One of the best in town.
Hotel Americano, Pizarro 792, is basic, noisy and inexpensive, though at first glance it seems luxurious.

On Calle Ayacucho, a few blocks from Plaza de Armas, there are a few inexpensive hotels. The most recommended (and least cheap), is the *Hostal Vogi*. One block away is the *Hostal Lima*, very cheap and basic, where many young travelers stay and meet.

Tourist services
There are Tourist Bureaus at the airport and at Calle Independencia 628, Tel. 241-936. Their staff will be happy to advise and guide you concerning accommodation, transportation and places to visit (especially important if you're interested in the colonial estates where visiting hours are irregular). For maps and road information, visit the Auto Club (*T.A.C.P.*), Calle Almagro 707.

Currency exchange
Banks on Plaza de Armas will exchange money at the official rate and without excessive commission. If you are going on to Ecuador you can buy *sucres* (Ecuador's currency) farther north.

What to see
The pleasant **Plaza de Armas** lies in the heart of town, with a fountain at its center and surrounded by statues of national Independence heroes and palm trees. Surrounding the square you'll find the **Municipal Cathedral**, the **City Hall**, public buildings and the **Iturregui House**, one of the remaining grand estates from Colonial days, which today serves as a social club and Chamber of Commerce.

Dozens of churches and impressive buildings have survived from the pre-Independence period, when all Peru was under Spanish influence. Though some were damaged in the many earthquakes that have struck the coastal area, many have survived, and these convey the former character and style of the city. Most of the churches feature impressive stone and wood contruction and some are graced with gold and silver ornaments. **Iglesia Carmen**, next to Plaza de Armas, is an example of religious art at its best, and though it is closed in part (due to earthquake damage), you'll be impressed with its facade, balconies and spires. **Iglesias San Francisco and Santo Domingo** are also worth visiting.

The interesting **archaeological museum** (Pizarro 349) at the University of Trujillo contains a collection of pre-Columbian art. Open Mon.-Fri. 9am-noon and 4-5pm. A private museum of pottery from all over Peru, particularly that of the Chimu civilization, is located in the **Cassinelli House**, Pierola 601. Open Mon.-Sat. 9am-1pm, and 3-5pm.

Around Trujillo

Chan Chán and other archaeological sites

One of Peru's most interesting archaeological sites — the remains of the "mud city" of Chan Chán — should certainly be visited. (It is five kilometers north of Trujillo.) This city, whose buildings, temples and walls are made of adobe bricks, was the capital of the Chimu kingdom, which extended from Guayaquil (Ecuador) in the north to Paramonga (north of Lima) in the south. The Chimu existed from the 10th-15th centuries, and their capital, Chan Chán, was built at the 13th century. Chan Chán knew many kings, each of whom built and glorified the city by adding more giant walls (more than twelve meters high), mighty fortresses and magnificent temples.

The city's streets, lined with stores and workshops, once bustled with life. The plazas served as religious and social centers. In the middle there where well-tended gardens, canals and pools, granaries and warehouses filled with jewelry and treasures. The Incas conquered Chan Chán in the fifteenth century, and ruled until the arrival of the Spanish, who destroyed and plundered it.

The dry climate has helped to preserve Chan Chán, and visitors can still get an idea of its beauty and special glory despite the ravages of time. Chan Chán can be reached by bus or taxi from Trujillo; allow yourself several hours to explore.

Besides Chan Chán there are other ruins of *huacas* (temples) scattered around Trujillo, the most beautiful of which is **Huaca Arco Iris**, also known as Huaca del Dragon. The Chimu building is well preserved, as are the many engravings on the walls. Buses which reach the temple, 5 km northwest of Trujillo's center, pass the corner of Avenidas España and Mansiche near the stadium every 15 minutes. Open 8.30am-4pm.

About 10 km southeast of Trujillo are the **Huaca del Sol** (Temple of the Sun) and **Huaca de la Luna** (Temple of the moon), the largest and most important remains of the Moche, a culture which flourished in the region around the 1st-7th centuries AD. These excellent craftsmen (especially pottery), architects and fishermen lived mostly in small villages, and they built a few warship centers. The two *huacas*, the Temples of the Sun and

Chan chán

Huanchaco

Arco Iris

the Moon, are two pyramides less than a kilometer away from each other, and are dated from around the 6th century. The Sun pyramide is the largest pre-Columbian structure in Peru, but don't expect much from the site — it is badly preserved and partly covered with sand. You can get there by taxi or by bus marked El Alto from the market. The site has no fences and always open, but come in the morning, before the wind blows up the sand.

Huanchaco
This tranquil fishing village lies a few kilometers from Trujillo along the coast, and is a holiday spot for inhabitants in the area. Those who have been traveling for a long time will find this a good place to renew their strength, and surfers will find the beaches very good for surfing. It's worthwhile going down to the beach in the morning or afternoon when the fishermen go out to sea. Their boats are similar to the famous straw boats on Lake Titicaca.

Hotel Bracamonte is very good and cheap, and the owners are very congenial. One can sleep there in a sleeping bag for a token payment. In the house of *Señiora Violeta* one can eat decent meals for low prices.

The typical *artesania* of the region are necklaces made with turquoise stones called *chaguira*. The local youngsters will certainly try to sell them to you. They ask for high prices, but bargaining will bring them down.

Cajamarca

It was in the mountain city of Cajamarca (elev. 2750 m), northeast of Trujillo, that Pizarro killed the last Incan king, Atahualpa, thus gaining his control of Peru. In this agreeable city of 100,000 people, 300 km from Trujillo, houses and streets seem to have preserved their character and have not allowed time to leave its mark. Buses from Trujillo (6 hours), Lima and Pacasmayo arrive frequently, most at the terminal on Calle Ayacucho. *AeroPerú* also flies in from Lima and Trujillo.

The most interesting place in town is the room where the Incan ruler was held captive and to which the gold for his supposed ransom was brought. This room, next to **Iglesia Belen**, was recently opened to visitors after centuries of being locked. Once you've seen the prison and church (closed on Tuesdays), you can visit the square where Atahualpa was taken captive, and thereafter the many churches which grace the city.

Two museums — one of archaeology (at the University) and another of Colonial art — house interesting displays of the city and its surroundings, and are recommended. There are hot springs — the **Baños del Inca**, or the Incan Baths — near town. Those with wanderlust for unknown parts can hop aboard a truck for the difficult five-hour trip through wonderful scenery, to the tiny mining town of Hualgayoc, ninety kilometers north, at a height of 4000 m. It is not worth your while to go onward, and you should return by the same route.

Tumbes

Peru's northern border town (pop. app. 35,000), 1320 km north of Lima, doesn't have much worthy of mention, and serves primarily as a crossing point to and from Ecuador. Here Pizarro landed with 180 man in 1532.

If you have to spend the day or night waiting for transport, you better do so at **Puerto Pizarro**, a small fishing beach a few kilometers away. There is a fine beach with basic accommodation and seafood restaurants, and you can take a boat to see the mangroves.

Transportation

Tumbes is linked with Lima by plane, bus and *colectivos*. Modern, comfortable buses ply the coastal route to Lima in about sixteen hours. If you wish to use Tumbes as a point of departure for your tour of Peru, you can get off at any of the coastal cities (Trujillo, for example) and proceed from there to the mountains.

On to Ecuador

The border crossing may be reached by bus (a thirty-minute trip) or by taxi. Border crossing procedures include a routine inspection of passport and bags, though painstaking searches of travelers' luggage have been known to occur every so often.

From the Ecuadorian border town there are direct buses to Quito (12 hours) and Guayaquil several times a day. The Peruvian border station, located in Aguas Verdes, is open from 8am-6pm, but occasionally closes for siesta, when you'll have no choice but to wait.

Crossing the border in either direction in a private car requires an International Driver's License and certificate from the Auto Club (which has an office in the central plaza in Tumbes).

Currency exchange

Change money at the branch office of *Banco de Crédito* or *Banco Popular*, both at the main square. Dealing with street moneychangers is strictly forbidden and the authorities have been known to deal harshly with offenders. The bank on the Ecuadorian side, in the town of Huaquillas, is open only until noon.

The Amazon Basin

One of the most exceptional experiences awaiting a tourist in South America is a visit to its thick jungles, where wild and unconquered nature rules supreme. The slight progress that has penetrated the jungles — be it electricity (generators), motor vehicles (rarely more than noisy crates), or roads (twisting, narrow trails passable only during the dry season) — has not managed to hide the fact that only in recent decades has the white man been able to establish a permanent foothold in this corner of the world and begun to make substantial use of its resources. Not for nothing has the Amazon captured the imagination of tourist and scientist, adventurer and philosopher. Its mysterious green mantle conceals fascinating oddities, wild animals, a special type of people and unknown Indian tribes. The dense jungle, fed by the limitless waters of the Amazon, summons visitors to one of the most stunning experiences which man can undergo. It's an ordeal involving effort and risk, and one must prepare for it carefully. A tourist who wishes to explore this corner of the world must behave with caution and patience, freeing himself as best he can of Western prejudices, ways of thought and behavior which do not fit in here. Here one must totally submit to the laws of the area and attempt to integrate into the local way of life, where time is meaningless, cleanliness and hygiene unimportant, and safety (on the roads, for example) unworthy of attention. Here it's jungle law, do-as-you-please: cars that travel without lights; buses that either set out or don't; boats that stop for a week in mid-stream with no forewarning and any number of similar wonders liable to bring the most stable of souls to the verge of total nervous collapse. Remember that a journey into this region involves the likelihood of all sorts of difficulties, and all the preparation in the world will not serve even as a basis for the changes you will have to accept in your plans. Even your destination can be predetermined only along very, very general lines.

Where to go
A certain number of jungle routes have been opened to adventurous tourists in recent years, mainly in Brazil, Ecuador and Peru (Bolivia's jungle tours are entirely different in nature). Many tourists prefer to penetrate the depths of the jungle from

Ecuador, from where it is relatively easier to reach and where the scarcity of visitors and restricted contact with modern civilization have left things much as they always were.

While most excursions in Brazil focus on the vicinity of Manaus, in this chapter we will focus on its Peruvian counterpart, Iquitos.

Peru offers the tourist two main possibilities: a jungle route northward from Lima to Iquitos and a southward route from Cuzco to Río Madre de Dios — Manú Park and the jungle town of Puerto Maldonado (see "Extended Tours in the Cuzco Area").

Equipment
It's very important to equip yourself properly before you set out for the jungles. In addition to malaria pills, pack water purification tablets, canned food and more as hygienic conditions are exceptionally poor. Mosquito repellent is essential, for these pests abound in countless numbers. You won't be able to sleep without a hammock and **mosquito netting**, whether you are under the stars or on boat. You will also need a sleeping bag, a good tent (a two-layered model to keep out the rain) and a cooking stove. Warm clothing is essential, particularly for the mountain sections of the trip, where temperatures plunge to bone-freezing lows at night. Locks and other devices for safeguarding your gear are as necessary here as they are elsewhere, and always keep a watchful eye on your jackets and packs. For the jungles we recommend light clothing — so long as it keeps you covered. Despite the heat, do not go about exposed, and be sure to keep your shoes laced at all times.

When to visit
The tropical climate guarantees high temperatures, high humidity and lots of rain most of the year. It's rainiest in the summer, between January and May, while the driest months are August and September. During the rainy season many roads are flooded, and moving from place to place is liable to take twice as long as it would normally. For animal watching the better time is the dry season, as the animals gather at the river banks for water.

The journey to Iquitos
There are two ways to get to Iquitos, the "rubber city" of the late nineteenth century. The faster, more convenient and more dependable method is by air: *AeroPerú* and *Faucett* fly there every day from Lima, Trujillo, Pucallpa and other cities. The second and increasingly popular way combines an overland trip with a river cruise. Though a long and exhausting trip, it passes through fascinating scenery and isolated settlements in parts that few people visit.

The land route ends in Pucallpa, 782 km from Lima, which you can reach by bus, truck, or rented car. Despite the hardships of the route — or perhaps because of them — it seems best to avail yourself of public transportation, which will take the **Carretera Central** (the "central throughway"), parallel to the wonderful railroad to La Oroya (see "The road to Huancayo") and then head for **Cerro de Pasco** (pop. 30,000), a mining town 4300 m above sea level. (Beware of breathing difficulties). The train is the most convenient way of reaching this point. It sets out from Lima for Huancayo, and you must change trains in La Oroya (where you can head eastward through lovely agricultural districts on outings to the towns of Tarma, Palca, San Ramon and La Merced). The route to Cerro de Pasco passes through a town called **Junin** and a plain of the same name. Here Bolívar's army defeated Spanish loyalists in August 1824, the first of many victories that led to Peruvian independence.

From Cerro de Pasco the road continues another 110 km, as far as the town of **Huanuco** (pop. 75,000). It's a steep climb all the way, and buses and passenger trucks crawl along. Frequent buses link Huanuco with Cerro de Pasco, La Oroya, Lima and Huancayo to the south, and with Tingo Maria to the north. Several buses per week travel the difficult route between La Union, Catac and Huaraz to the west to Huanuco. That city is surrounded by Incan and pre-Incan ruins, including a temple and fortress.

Another 135 km brings us to the outskirts of the jungle town of **Tingo Maria** (pop. 20,000). The area is lush in natural and cultivated flora, and the combination of mountains and the beginnings of the jungle makes for exceptional scenery. From Tinga Maria there is frequent bus service to Pucallpa (5-8 hours) and Lima. In addition, *AeroPerú* and *Faucett* flights to Pucallpa and Lima touch down there almost every day.

From here the road divides: while its western branch reaches Mayobamba, about 600 km north (from which you can return to the Pacific coast), its eastern branch continues another 300 km or so to·**Pucallpa**. At this jungle town, on the western bank of Rio Ucayali, the land route ends. The 75,000 mixed Indian-Spanish people of Pucallpa engage in river sailing, industry and commerce. In recent years the city has attracted renewed attention with hopes of finding oil in the vicinity.

Pucallpa has hotels and restaurants, though of no great quality and, like their counterparts in all the jungle towns, rather expensive. *Faucett, AeroPerú* and local airlines link the town with Lima and Iquitos. Buses set out for Lima many times each day. There's a Tourist Bureau on Calle 2 de Mayo.

In the Pucallpa area one can visit Indian villages to watch the fishermen and bustling marketplace. The Albert Schweitzer Hospital, established to care for the children, is located on the shore of Lake Yarinacocha, about ten kilometers out of town. There are a number of interesting institutions and villages worth visiting in the area. You can rent a boat and go upstream or downstream for a few days, visiting Indian tribes and getting an impression of a way of life which has hardly changed in centuries.

Frequent river transportation links Pucallpa with Iquitos, along Rio Ucayali. Numerous sailing craft, both for freight and passengers, make the trip in three to eight days depending on the season and the type of craft (the best time is from April to October, when the water level rises and ships sail at night as well). Be sure to bring food, water-purification tablets (don't drink the river water!) and mosquito repellent. The voyage is interesting at first, but soon begins to get monotonous. With this in mind, try to select the fastest and most comfortable boat you can find. As for prices — bargain with the captain, and make sure you know his route and various stops.

Iquitos

This legendary port, Peru's outlet to the Atlantic ocean, grew out of a mid-eighteenth century missionary settlement built on the western bank of the Amazon. It was only in the 1880's, when the world demand for rubber (produced from trees that flourish in the Amazon region) increased, that the little village, 3100 km from the Atlantic, turned almost overnight into a center of world importance, with European and American commercial and diplomatic offices. Iquitos, like Manaus in Brazil (halfway to the ocean), experienced the kind of boom few cities in the world have known.

As Iquitos prospered, magnificent buildings — veritable palaces — were built, and a life of culture and luxury took root. Its people enjoyed imported food and drink, attended Parisian opera and saw the best of Europe's performing troupes. But all that ostentatious prosperity vanished in a flash, when seeds of the rubber tree were stolen and planted in Asia. The rubber monopoly was over, and it took only a few months for Iquitos to fall into absolute economic collapse.

Today's Iquitos is no more than a grey, dilapidated port city whose population of 270,000 labors unstintingly for their sustenance, finding it hard to imagine those remote days. Even the magnificent port, the adjacent promenade, the Plaza de Armas with its grand buildings, and the rubber barons' well-kept estates are no more than neglected remnants of a glorious past.

Iquitos is isolated; save for visiting planes and ships no one comes and no one goes. The new neighborhoods which have gone up recently, especially since oil was found nearby, haven't broken through the barrier of isolation, and the sense of being cut off is apparent everywhere.

Transportation to Peru and neighboring countries

AeroPerú and *Faucett* land at Iquitos' international airport several times daily on flights from Lima and Peru's other major cities. *Faucett* flies several times a week to Miami. *Varig* and *Cruzeiro del Sol* serve the area, flying to Manaus (Brazil), Leticia (Colombia) and other destinations. Since most flights in this region are fully booked, you must make reservations well in advance and confirm them the moment you arrive in town. There are no flights between Iquitos and Ecuador, an expression of an unresolved border dispute.

Propeller-driven planes fly to villages and towns in the Iquitos area, where Indians live in ancient tribal dwellings. Ships ply the Amazon and its tributaries, though most are decrepit cargo vessels that chug along slowly and are often delayed in mid-journey. Stock up on mosquito netting, a hammock, canned food, water-purification tablets and mosquito repellent before you board one of them!

Ships set out for Brazil and Colombia at irregular intervals; make inquiries at the harbor. The river route to Leticia goes via Ramon Castilla, where immigration procedures are arranged. The fastest way to Brazil is via Leticia, and on to Benjamin Constant and Manaus.

Food and lodging

Amazonas: (ex-Holiday Inn), Abelardo Quiñónez, Tel. 231-091, is about 3 km from downtown, and rather expensive. Good for those who want to spoil themselves after the exhausting shipboard voyage.
Hotel de Turistas: Malecón Tarapacá, Tel. 231-684. Part of the government hotel chain, centrally located, comfortable.
El Dorado: Calle Napo. A few steps from the Municipal Palace, at the very center of town, medium-priced and recommended. Extras at the bar can be very expensive.

A large number of pensions (*residenciales*) offer cheap rooms. In most of the second and third class hotels you can have a cheaper rate by selecting a room without air-conditioning or showers.

Iquitos' best restaurants can be found near the plaza 28 de Julio, at the southern part of the town. They offer a variety of dishes, but nearly all — especially the cheaper ones — concentrate on fish. Tropical fruit is plentiful and cheap in the local market, and you should stock up before heading for outlying areas. Remember that as a rule prices in Iquitos, as in all the jungle cities, are considerably higher than those in central Peru, essentially because of the added cost of transport.

What to see

Little remains of the Iquitos of long ago. Man's neglect combined with the jungle's predatory tendency have taken their toll on the ruins of that turn-of-the-century grandeur. True, the city center — Plaza de Armas — is surrounded with public buildings from that era, but their sorry appearance doesn't compare with the glory they once knew. Even the Church of Santa Ana and the Municipality building on Plaza de Armas (with a Tourist Bureau in one corner, open only till noon) preserve but a trace of the spirit of that time.

The floating slums of Belen are perhaps more indicative than anything else of Iquitos' current condition. This suburb, in which more than ten thousand impoverished people are crowded into miserable boats, is exceptional even in terms of South American poverty. Children roam about in the mud between the boats as adults attempt to find their place in the terrible press. At high tide, when the water level rises several meters and tiny craft sail among the boats offering various goods for sale, the entire quarter looks like a huge floating market.

Near Iquitos is Lake Quistacocha, with a small and interesting zoo on its shore. Some of the water creatures common to the area can be seen at the Municipal Aquarium on Calle Huitado. A small museum in town displays local artwork, a few archaeological remains and samples of local flora.

Excursions

The major reason that makes the exhausting trek to Iquitos worthwile is the visit to the Indian villages in the area.

Many tour companies organize guided tours of one to three days' duration, which include a river voyage and hike through the thick of the jungle (the *selva*). Some of these companies have branch offices or agents in Lima where you can make reservations and pay accordingly; others have offices in downtown Iquitos, near Plaza de Armas or on Calle Putumayo. Bear in mind that penetrating the jungle is both complicated and difficult. We therefore recommend that you utilize the services of a reliable company with a staff that is familiar with everything liable to be encountered along the way.

The Indians in the Iquitos area are in constant contact with the modern world, to the great detriment — from the tourist's viewpoint, of course — of their traditional way of life. It's become rather unusual to see colorfully painted Indians hunting with blowguns and fishing with harpoons. Wild animals, too, annoyed at the disturbance, have wandered off deeper into the bush and very few tours penetrate deeply enough to encounter them.

Iquitos is therefore a rather "touristy" jungle, ready and waiting for visitors who wish a small taste of the exotic Amazon. A stroll through Iquitos itself and excursions in the area will open a window onto a strange world, where social values and concepts are so different. It's an instructive experience, one which breaks through the barriers of the imagination and adds a new dimension to our comprehension of everything connected with man and his nature.

South of Lima

Some of the most famous places in Peru are concentrated south of Lima. We will survey them individually along two axes. One runs down the coast to the Chilean border, more or less parallel to the ancient seashore route; the other runs along the mountain ridge to Cuzco. There is also the possibility of combining the routes, going part of the way along the coast and part of it in the mountains. The order of our survey will reflect the geographical distance from Lima. Each place is mentioned for its own merit and may serve as a basis for starting, joining, or leaving the route we present — in any direction you wish.

Transportation
All the locales to be surveyed below, both along the seashore and in the mountains, enjoy frequent bus and *colectivo* connections with Lima and with each other. There are several buses every day between the capital and each of the destinations, though we do recommend that you buy tickets a day or two in advance. For intercity transportation, local service offers you great freedom and relative speed in buses that may be less comfortable and grand than those of Lima, but are no less efficient.

The roads linking the coastal route with the Andean highway are very hard to travel, and you'll find progress rather slow. The train from Arequipa to Puno is perhaps the most comfortable way of all to complete the circle, but the Nazca-Abancay highway is also a good way of linking the mountain and coastal routes, and the trip is an experience in its own right (see "Nazca").

Warning: the mountain region of Huancayo and Ayacucho is very active with terror actions of the "Sendero Luminoso", and it is better to skip this area. In any case, do not visit this region, which is sometimes oficially closed to foreigners by military orders, without consulting about the situation there.

The Coastal Axis

Pachacámac
Thirty-one kilometers south of Lima on the Pan-American

*P*ERU

Highway we come to the remains of Peru's largest coastal city in the pre-Spanish era: Pachacámac. Francisco Pizarro's brother, reaching the site in 1533 — shortly after the Spanish landed in Peru — razed the city to its foundations, slaughtering the priests and smashing statues and magnificent buildings. Pyramids, temples, grand stone figures and similar ritual objects were damaged, and only a tiny remnant is left. Entire sections of the site, however, have been restored in recent years, and today we can once again marvel at the remains of a civilization whose primary "sin" lay in its not having been sufficiently well fortified against the Spanish. A small museum on the site displays findings from local excavations — some of gold and silver, others of stone and bronze.

A number of tour companies organize outings to Pachacamac, or you can take the bus from Plaza Santa Catalina next to Parque Universitario. The trip takes nearly an hour, and the visit to the site and museum takes about two hours. Open Tues.-Sun. 9am-5pm.

Pisco and Paracas

This small town 250 km south of Lima occupies the site where one of the best-developed coastal civilizations Peru has known blossomed about three thousand years ago. To reach Paracas, go via **Pisco**, the port city after which Peru's national brandy, *Pisco sour*, is named.

From Pisco you can travel fifty kilometers eastward to Tambo Colorado, where a pre-Incan city has survived (roofless though in excellent condition; its wall frescoes and streets are quite amazing.)

Paracas, as we said, was the center of an ancient civilization which, like many others in this area, disappeared for reasons that are still unclear.

A small archaeological museum on the site displays pottery, wood and textile artifacts, which testify to an especially high level of development. Another indication of this is the advanced mummification technique which the people of Paracas used to preserve their dead. Corpses were wrapped in fine fabrics, sealed in tightly-woven "coffins" of straw and buried on a nearby peninsula, in complex burial structures apparently meant to ensure them a pleasant wait until their resurrection.

Paracas has known strategic importance in more recent times as well. Here the Argentinian General José de San Martín came ashore to aid the Peruvians in their war of independence against the Spanish, setting up his headquarters not far away.

Today, Paracas is known primarily for the many water fowl that congregate in the area, thereby making it an important nature reserve.

Small islands scattered offshore are home to tens of thousands of water birds and thousands of seals and sea lions. Organized boat excursions set out from Paracas every morning and afternoon. The entire region has been rediscovered in recent years, with attention now devoted to the needs of the wildlife. Several companies organize boat trips to the islands; during the five hours or so of the cruise, dozens of seals swim around the boats, and it is not at all rare to see a flock of giant birds a few meters over your head. Such a cruise is highly recommended for nature lovers.

You can take the island cruise from Pisco or Paracas. The former offers more comfortable lodging possibilities and more convenient public transportation (four hours from Lima).

Ica

The city of Ica (pop. 160,000), 100 km south of Pisco, is important only as the center of the Peruvian wine industry (these wines are not highly recommended to the connoisseur) and as home to an archaeological museum. Most of Peru's wine is made in this region, but a visit to a local winery (*bodega*), is not particularly interesting. The city itself is rather humdrum; other than the palm-spangled Plaza de Armas, there is little to see here that deserves an extended visit — apart from the archaeological museum, reached by bus from the Plaza. The tastefully arranged museum displays a textile and ceramics collection, handiwork of the Paracas, Ica, Nazca and other civilizations. Mummies and skulls are also on display and will give you an impression of the manner in which the dead were treated and buried. Open Mon.-Sat. 8am-7pm and Sun. 9am-1pm. Another museum lies on the Plaza de Armas, and displays a collection of engraved stones, many of them of uncertain dates (some experts claim these are fakes). Open Mon.-Sat. 9.30am-noon and 5.30-8pm, Tel. 234-363.

Of the city's several hotels, the *Turistas* on Av. Los Maestros s/n (Tel. 233-320), which is expensive, and the Ica on calle Independencia, inexpensive are recommended. There is frequent public transportation to Lima and other cities from the central bus terminal. The Tourist Bureau (Av. Grau 148, Tel. 235-247) can provide a wealth of information and recommendations about where to go and how to get there.

A few kilometers from Ica is the enchanting oasis of **Huacachina**, a blue lake surrounded by palm trees amidst dunes. It became resort with a few hotels and restaurants, and it can be a pleasant break of your trip to and from Lima. Frequent buses connect the oasis with Ica's central square.

Nazca

Nazca, inhabited by man for more than five thousand years, has known ups-and-downs in its long history. A mysterious civilization that flourished here three millenia before Christ is apparently the one responsible for the giant figures in the desert sand for which Nazca is known. Their creators vanished without a trace, replaced by a civilization no less advanced which excelled in pottery, carving and metal working, the remains of which grace most of Peru's museums today. The Nazca civilization, which peaked around 850 AD, left a legacy of painted and decorated ceramics, wood carvings, gold jewelry and wondrously patterned fabrics.

Transportation

Nazca, 450 km from Lima, can be reached easily in about six hours by *Roggero* or *Ormeno* bus, or by *colectivos*. Try not to arrive in the wee hours of the morning, when hotels and hostels are securely locked; you'd probably have to spend the rest of the night under the stars.

From Nazca some buses continue down the coast toward Arequipa, while others head east — climbing the mountains toward Abancay, from which one may proceed either south to Cuzco or north to Ayacucho and back to Lima. It's a tough route to travel and the trip drags on for hours. Since the buses are rarely in reasonable mechanical condition, breakdowns on the road should not come as a surprise. At the same time, the scenery on the way is lovely and worth the effort. Those choosing this route can include a visit to Nazca on their way from Lima to Cuzco and the Inca area, or on their return from Cuzco to Lima via Nazca.

Food and lodging

Hotel Turistas, Jirón Bolognesi s/n. The government-owned hotel, expensive and high quality. It's staff can give you directions and information about excursions in the vicinity.
Nazca, Lima 438, near the bus terminal, inexpensive, clean and safe.

Many local residents let rooms in their homes to tourists; though rates are rather low, it's doubtful that the cleanliness will satisfy the average squeamish visitor. Several restaurants can be found downtown; most of the menu consists of seafood. There is a nice

*P*ERU

Ica — the oasis of Huacachina

restaurant near the small airport from where the flights over the desert figures depart.

What to see

Only one place downtown seems worthy of a visit: the **Municipal Museum** on the central plaza (open 10am-1pm and 2-6pm), where artifacts of the ancient civilizations are displayed; the rest of Nazca is no different from hundreds of other towns. Our main attention will be devoted to the surroundings, which are rich in archaeological ruins including temples and burial grounds. Since they are scattered all over the Nazca valley, we recommend that you avail yourself of a local guide's services and a rented car to find them.

The **Cemetery** is a unique site which shouldn't be missed; many nummies and skeletons are lying in the desert, some in weard positions, and lots of textile and pottery are all around in an excellent condition thanks to the dry air of the desert. There is no bus going to the place, and you must take a taxi (20 minutes).

The main reason for visiting Nazca is, of course, the giant paintings in Pampa Colorada. Since Erich von Danniken's book and film *Chariots of the Gods*, the remains of the fascinating Nazca paintings have achieved worldwide fame. Indeed, as you fly over the area and observe a giant spider, monkey, man-as-astronaut or bird painted on the ground hundreds of

Nasca — the cemetery

meters below, you cannot escape the strange mystery of it all: giant figures, hundreds of meters long, carved into the ground thousands of years ago. Strangest of all is the astonishing fact that the figures have meaning only from a bird's-eye view; walking along the ground you wouldn't even notice them. To compound the enigma, the entire region is desertlike and quite flat, without even a single point from which those ancient people could have admired their work and designed the figures. Numerous attempts have been made to explain the meaning of these figures, but even today the unknown outweighs the known.

The venerable German researcher Maria Reiche, who has spent decades studying the phenomenon, proposes, in her book *Mystery on the Desert*, the hypothesis that the figures were intended to have an astrological significance, perhaps a calendar; she considers them to be the work of a number of local groups, working centuries apart. A more recent theory dating from the mid-1970's, attributes the paintings to a local civilization guided by people flying in balloons. Though relics discovered in the area and analysis of the figures on the ground lend some support to this theory, it sounds too fantastic, even alongside von Danniken's claim that the paintings were made by aliens from outer space. In any event, we're obviously speaking of one of those few places in the world where our understanding has not succeeded in fathoming that which our eyes behold. Here we can only gape in astonishment and grapple with the questions for many days afterwards.

A number of observation towers have been erected in recent years, but these are far of being equal to the unforgettable experience of flying over them. The several competing companies charge pretty much the same rate, offering discounts only on rare occasions. *Aero Cóndor* is among the most reliable of the local airlines, with experienced pilots and properly maintained planes (not to be taken for granted here). *Condor* has an office in the Lima Sheraton where you can make reservations, especially recommended during tourist season. From their Nazca office they will drive you out to the little airport where the flights take off. The flights last for about 45 minutes, alternatively climbing and falling — to get a good view of the figures. Be sure to get a window seat, for otherwise it will be hard to see and even harder to take pictures. We highly recommend an early morning flight, for later the sun will glare in your eyes and the haze will interfere with your vision. You should try to fly at the very moment when the fog lifts off the desert, exposing an astounding and incomparable scene.

Onward to Arequipa

Proceeding down the coastal highway from Nazca, about three hours' driving (172 km) brings us to the fishing village of **Chala**. In this small village, with its population of under two thousand, you can intimately view the way of life of fishermen who go about their work as their fathers and forefathers did — with simplicity, speed and grace. Restaurants serve fish just hauled out of the ocean, and you can swim and tan in the sun. We do not recommend that you spend the night there, for the water isn't fit to drink and the hotels are simple and not always clean.

Continuing southward, the landscape becomes even more desertlike and arid; only after more than 200 km do we reach the town of **Camaná**, another fishing center, which blossomed in the Inca period and appears not to have changed much since (apart from having been rebuilt after suffering severe earthquake damage in the late sixteenth century).

Immediately past Camaná, the Pan-American Highway turns north-east and climbs for 132 km — to the outskirts of Arequipa, one of Peru's most beautiful cities.

Arequipa

Arequipa, 1009 km south of Lima, is a lovely city built of white granite, and the Spanish influence has not yet faded from its homes, estates and churches. Arequipa served as a major crossroads in the Inca period, for it is situated on the main highways to Cuzco from both Chile and the coast. The Spanish explorer Diego de Almagro, one of Pizarro's men, was the first Spaniard to reach Arequipa, and the new Spanish city subsequently founded beside it in 1540 eventually merged with the Incan town.

Arequipa's 650,000 residents are imbued with an unusually strong brand of local patriotism. The pride they take in their city can be seen in everything and it's largely justified — for this is undoubtedly Peru's most beautiful city and one of the loveliest in all South America. Arequipa is known far and wide as *La Ciudad Blanca* (The White City), after the sillar stone of which most of its houses are built. This white stone is quarried from the many volcanoes encircling the city, of which the most famous, El Misti, soaring to a height of 5850 m, is visible from every part of town.

The weather in Arequipa (elev. 2378 m) is ideal: perpetual sunshine and a year-round average temperature of 17°C (63°F).

Transportation

Bus: Many buses travel daily to and from Lima, Nazca and the other coastal cities. *Tepsa* runs daily buses southward to Tacna and Arica (Chile). Even though there are many buses each day to Puno, Juliaca and Cuzco, the train is preferable. For the trip to Lima, *Ormeno* and *Roggero* buses are recommended; *Morales Moralitos* buses are not recommended. Tickets should be bought at least one day in advance. The offices of the different companies are in calle San Juan de Dios and Victor Lira. Ask for the exact place of departure.

Train: Passenger trains head east from Arequipa to Juliaca and

*P*ERU

AREQUIPA

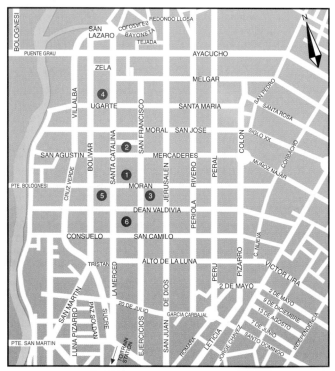

Index
1. Plaza de Armas
2. Cathedral
3. Jesuit Church of La Compañía
4. Santa Catalina Convent
5. Tourist Information Office
6. *Entel*

thence to Puno or Cuzco once or twice a day on a lovely route reaching heights up to 4000 m. Travel first-class, since the other classes are very crowded and you would be far more exposed to thieves (**Important**: see "Personal safety"!). Second-class tickets can be purchased only on the morning of your trip (get up early, or there may be no seats left) but first-class tickets

Arequipa and Volcan Misti

are available the previous day. In second-class innumerable peddlers pass through during the trip, but they are not allowed access to first-class and the buffet car. If you're not interested in eating in the buffet, stock up in advance for the lengthy trip (10 hours to Puno, 22 to Cuzco). The trip at night is very cold, so plan accordingly.

Plane: *AeroPerú* (Tel. 216-820) and *Faucett* (Tel. 212-352) both have offices on Portal San Agustín, near the Plaza de Armas. They provide daily service to Lima and Cuzco and thence to other destinations in Peru and the world over.

Tourist services

The Tourist Bureau, at Portal Municipal 112, on the Plaza de Armas (Tel. 213-101) offers courteous service and explanatory material.

The Tourist Police Station is at the bus terminal, Jerusalén 317.

Information about road conditions, service stations and the like is available from Peru's Auto Club (TACP), at San Francisco 206.

Rafting became a popular sport in Arequipa, and there are several companies that organize exciting rafting trips for a few days in the region's rivers.

Food and lodging

Arequipa's hotels and restaurants, in no short supply, are capable of meeting the needs of any tourist on any budget. Most hotels are downtown, within walking distance of the interesting sites. The many restaurants serve a wide variety of fare — Chinese, seafood and more. Typical Peruvian dishes are served at *Picanterías* — Creole restaurants famous for their cuisine.

What to see

Arequipa is known for its white granite buildings — a casual stroll through the streets will explain why. Even before we survey the sites one by one, we cannot help but marvel at the grandeur of the Spanish architecture and the professionalism of the artists and craftsmen who carried out the work. Each of the many churches, public buildings and estates testifies to the architectural magnificence of bygone days, and explains Arequipa's special quality and character better than anything else.

In the city center we find the **Plaza de Armas**, laid out around a fountain and ringed with benches on which many locals spend their *siestas*. Amid trees and flowers one can watch the passers-by and appreciate the ambience of this pleasant city. The square ends at the **Municipal Cathedral**, rebuilt in the last century in the wake of cumulative earthquake damage since the sixteenth century. Not far from it is the **Jesuit Church of La Compañía**, dating from the second half of the seventeenth century. This church, and Santo Domingo, La Merced and San Francisco churches, are Arequipa's most beautiful. The latter also houses a lovely monastery, with an impressive handicrafts market across the way.

Also downtown is the San Camilo municipal market, where various kinds of food and drink are offered alongside local artwork, household implements and the like. Not far from there is **San Agustín University**, one of two in Arequipa, with a small archaeological museum displaying a collection of local pottery and mummies.

The crowning touch of our visit to Arequipa is the **Santa Catalina Convent**. Built at the end of the sixteenth century, it served as a boarding school for the daughters of the city's elite, who were sent there accompanied by servants and lived in luxurious rooms decorated in the spirit of the place and time. Only in 1970 was the convent opened to the public. The first visitors were surprised at what they saw: entire streets, a sort of city-within-a-city existing in total isolation for centuries, wholly uninfluenced by the surrounding environment. The few nuns remaining there live in one wing set aside for them, while the rest of the convent is open to the public every day from morning until early afternoon. Highly recommended!

Excursions

El Misti Volcano has been in vogue in recent years, as more and more visitors climb to its summit. Ascending the towering peak requires hard physical effort and at least two days. It's important to bring food, suitable equipment and, most important, experience. If you lack the latter, you'd do well to practice somewhere else and choose more tranquil but no less interesting trails in the Arequipa area.

The attractions closest to Arequipa are the suburb of Cayma and the town of Tingo. Both preserve the way of life of bygone days and will give you a first-hand idea of an otherwise vanished way of life.

Colca Canyon

The most beautiful and interesting of the sites, however, is the Colca Canyon, home of the Indian tribe which gave the valley its name. They maintained independence of Inca domination almost until the Spaniards arrived. The villages of Chivay and Cabanaconde afford visitors a window on a world in which time is frozen, a chance to observe how people lived in this region five hundred years ago or more.

The road to the Colca Canyon is enchanting in its own right, with its scenery of volcanoes. At the village of **Chivay** you get to the canyon. It is 4 hours from Arequipa. 3 hours beyond Chiuay along the cnayon is the village of **Cabanaconde**.

A few kilometers before reaching Cabanaconde is the Mirador del Cóndor, from where the condors can be seen early in the mornings.

The round trip from Arequipa can be completed in one day, but you will probably miss the condors, as they are usually to be seen in the mornings only.

A recommended hike from Cabanaconde is down to the Colca Canyon. Stay the night down in the village, and climb back with another trail, that brings you to the mirador de Condores.

There is only an early morning bus from Cabanaconde back to Arequipa, and hitching is very difficult, so you will have to spend a night in Cabanaconde.

Colca Canyon

Tacna

About a six-hour trip from Arequipa, and 1293 km south of Lima, we reach the southern border city of Tacna (pop. app. 150,000), restored to Peruvian rule only in the late 1920's, after fifty years of Chilean occupation.

In the Plaza de Armas we find a monument to Admiral Grau and Colonel Bolognesi, and beside it the municipal cathedral, designed by the famous French architect Eiffel.

In Arequipa district

In the city, electronic and photographic equipment similar to that sold in Arica, Chile, is sold at low prices.

Tacna enjoys daily air service to Lima, and frequent bus connections with Arequipa, Nazca, Puno, Cuzco and other destinations.

On to Chile

Tacna, 40 km from the Chilean border, is connected by buses, *colectivos*, and trains to Arica, the Chilean port city. Buses and *colectivos* are delayed at the Peruvian and Chilean border stations, where luggage is checked and passports stamped. Generally the procedure is efficient. It is worthwhile to use the service of the *colectivos*, which are new and comfortable taxis, and which do not cost much more than buses. The border is closed at night and on Peruvian and Chilean holidays. Drivers of private cars must obtain special crossing documents, which can be purchased at kiosks. The Auto Club, on Avenida 2 de Mayo 55, will provide details and guidelines about documents, routes, service stations and so forth.

Street moneychangers can change currency for you, but their rates are low. If you're coming from Chile, you'll do well to buy *soles* in Arica or, if you must, to change only a small sum to cover basic needs until you reach Arequipa or Puno.

From Lima to Cuzco by the
Mountain Route

Peru of the past was criss-crossed by highways. The ancient Peruvian civilizations, knowing the secret of the road and cognizant of its decisive importance for dominating the area and its tribes, spared no effort in pushing them through and paving them, developing and enhancing a network of roads that occasionally reach heights at which it is difficult even to breathe. The Incans, of course, carried this to its utmost and during the fourteenth and fifteenth centuries they built or upgraded hundreds of kilometers of paved roads across mountain and valley, linking the capital of Cuzco with every outlying province of their vast empire. These grand highways (see the chapter "The Incas"), of which a significant portion has been preserved to this day, also served the Spanish conquerors and helped them reach their destinations with ease. Today's modern highways still follow the same routes.

One of the most interesting of these roads goes east from Lima to La Oroya and from there south to Cuzco. Only part of the route runs parallel to that of the Incas, though transport along it was known far earlier. Today the railroad, a traveling experience in its own right, reaches Huancayo, after which the main highway winds southward to Ayacucho, Abancay and Cuzco.

Public transportation between Lima and Cuzco foregoes this enchanting route in favor of a shorter and easier way via Nazca and Abancay. The mountain route must therefore be traveled in stages, with visits along the way to some of Peru's most beautiful cities.

Warning: The terrorist underground "Sendero luminoso" who spread fear over the local population, is currently active in the area, which leads to periodic restrictions on traffic using the road to Ayacuchuo, as well as army and police searches. Do not take this route without prior consulting about the up-to-date situation in the region.

The railroad to Huancayo
Although many bus lines link the two cities, the train (which does not run on Sundays) is the best mode of transport. The Lima-La Oroya line is the world's highest, passing through breathtaking

scenery, crossing many bridges and plunging through dozens of tunnels. The tracks wind about and climb steeply — reaching 4800 m above sea level (!!) — and in certain stretches "zigzag" in order to make the gradient negotiable.

This strange railroad line was conceived and designed by the American railroad engineer Henry Meiggs in the 1870's, though he did not live to see it built. The tremendous construction project, finished only in the 1890's by laborers brought to Peru from many countries (chiefly from China and the Orient), is one of modern Peru's most advanced engineering achievements.

The train begins its ascent almost the moment it leaves Lima, and reaches the mountain town of Chosica, a popular turn-of-the-century resort, about 40 km further. The train continues to climb past small towns, including the mining town of Casapalca (elev. 4150 m). About six hours out of Lima it reaches La Oroya, where the track splits — one line north to Cerro de Pasco (about three hours; see "The Amazon Basin — the Journey to Iquitos"), the other south to Huancayo (about six hours).

Like elsewhere in Peru, especially on trains and in stations, it is important to remember that thieves are in abundance, and to behave accordingly (see "Personal security").

Huancayo

Huancayo, the bustling commercial center of the mountain region, lies 412 km from Lima at an elevation of 3271 m. Most of its 200,000 inhabitants are of Indian descent. Their ancestors, too, lived in the city and its fertile surroundings for centuries, engaging in agriculture and handicrafts. Huancayo was important even in ancient times, long before the Spanish came. The main Incan highway passed through the city and Pizarro advanced along it on his way to conquer Cuzco. The entire mountain region is known as a politically active area, and Huancayo has been proclaimed capital of the Republic on several brief occasions.

Transportation

Buses and *colectivos* — ply the seven-hour route to Lima many times a day. Buses and trucks continue on to Ayacucho, the second-largest city in Andean Peru, and from there to Abancay and Cuzco. Direct buses to Cuzco set out several times weekly on a trip which takes about two days (longer during the rainy season). Bring a warm sleeping bag for truck rides in the mountains, since temperatures drop considerably at night. Buses head northward from Huancayo to La Oroya,

Cerro de Pasco and Pucallpa and there are also buses and trucks which set out for Nazca on the coast.

Public transportation in this area is abominable. Schedules are not schedules, tickets are not tickets ... Buy your tickets early and get to the station long before the bus is supposed to leave. Do not worry, there's no danger of its leaving early. It is just that the local passengers seem to get excited about the trip, and get to the bus hours before its scheduled departure time, and proceed to get comfortably settled along with their luggage — so that there is no room left for later arrivals. It's a local custom, and if you cannot beat them, join them — and you cannot beat them. Blend into the atmosphere, take a deep breath and fortify yourself with patience of steel.

Food and lodging
The hotels in town are of low quality and apart from the government-owned *Hotel Turistas* (Plaza de Armas) the selection is not promising. There are a great many small pensions around the train station. Be sure to check for cleanliness and hot water and remember not to leave valuables in your room.

The city is full of Chinese and Creole restaurants. Along the streets and in the markets, stalls offer local snacks. On Sundays fresh foodstuffs, brought in by Indians from nearby villages, are available at the market.

Tourist services
The Tourist Bureau is at Ancash 415; the Auto Club (T.A.C.P.) has a branch on the same street at No. 603.

Huancayo Tours, on Calle Real 543, the main street, organizes excursions in the vicinity and will be pleased to provide information on events and sites in the city and its environs.

What to see
Calle Real, Huancayo's major artery, is the scene of most social and commercial activity. It is lined with shops, offices and agencies, while sidewalks are packed with passersby and dozens of Indians hawking their finest creations — food and handicrafts.

The bulk of activity takes place on Sundays, when a gigantic market — the *Feria* — takes place, to which the villagers bring their wares. Foodstuffs of diverse kinds — cheeses, vegetables, fruit and prepared dishes — are intermingled with artwork, silver jewelry, flutes and other. musical instruments, woven fabrics, clothing of llama or alpaca wool and, above all, needle-etched gourds, produced by a technique that demands patience, precision and skill. The Huancayo market is considered Peru's finest and its prices — Peru's lowest. As in every market, here, too, you must bargain, but the final prices will probably be lower here than in Lima or Cuzco. Stroll among the thousands of vendors, men and women, size up what's available, bargain and buy. (If you are continuing southward you can buy inexpensive woolen goods in Juliaca as well, but as for the gourds — this is undoubtedly **the** place.)

Excursions

Those who reach Huancayo on a day other than Sunday or who consider the market too touristy will certainly find a visit to the nearby villages interesting. Here is where the craftsmen work and where, of course, you can buy *artesanía* (handicrafts) at slightly lower prices than in town.

Two villages, Chochas Chicas and Chochas Grandes, are the centers of the gourd-engraving art. Ask local residents to show you to the artists' homes.

You can observe weaving and embroidery in Wallwash and silversmithing in San Jerónimo. The two villages, slightly north of Huancayo, are easily reached by minibus or taxi from Calle Real.

Near San Jerónimo is the town of Concepción, from which minibuses set out for the lovely Santa Rosa de Ocopana monastery. This institution, founded more than 250 years ago to train priests for missionary activity among the jungle Indians, is built in an impressive style and is situated in an enchanting corner of nature. The monastery has a huge library, artworks and more. For a fee one can stay overnight.

The town of Chupaca, about fifteen kilometers west of Huancayo, holds a small, quiet market on Saturdays. A visit to the market, besides being an opportunity to buy souvenirs, gives you a chance to witness the local population, foods and customs and day-to-day activities, from up close.

Ayacucho

Ayacucho (pop. 100,000) was founded by the Spanish in 1539, and has served as the urban center for the area between Huancayo and Cuzco ever since. In nearby La Quinua we can visit the battlefield where Spanish loyalists were routed in December 1824, paving the way to Peruvian independence.

Ayacucho's more than thirty churches are a living testimony to the town's religious devotion in bygone years. Most of the churches — Santo Domingo, San Francisco, La Merced and the Municipal Cathedral across from Parque Sucre, for example — have magnificent altars adorned with gold and silver. These are remnants from the opulence that greeted the Spaniards, relics of an era from which so little has survived.

A university was established in Ayacucho as early as 1677 but only reopened in the late 1950's. It has since served as a center for student activity and ferment that do not always coincide with government objectives. For some reason, the *Sandero Luminoso* ("Shining Path") Maoist underground is more active in Ayacucho than elsewhere and the police react harshly and forcefully to any deviant or exceptional behavior (see "Personal security").

The market in Ayacucho is famous for the quality of its merchandise. Local Indians display a variety of jewelry, knitted garments and the like, generally similar to those available in Huancayo and with no significant difference in price. We recommend a visit to the small Historical Museum in the Simón Bolívar Cultural Center, where archaeological remains are displayed alongside items from the Independence period.

Transportation

AeroPerú and *Faucett* fly into Ayacucho every day from Lima and Cuzco. During tourist season the planes are full, so make reservations well in advance and confirm your return flight immediately after reaching town. There is passenger bus service to Lima (15 hours) via Pisco (12 hours, 374 km); from Pisco you can also continue southward along the coast. Buses and trucks cover the gorgeous 296 km route to Huancayo in about twelve hours.

Traveling overland to Cuzco, 593 km southeast of Ayacucho, requires great effort but has its reward. Several buses set out on this route every day, but they are generally crowded and uncomfortable. Make reservations as early as you can, and come early to grab a place to sit. The trip, though not supposed to last more than twenty-four hours, occasionally takes three or four times longer, especially on rainy days when whole sections of road become impassable. In addition mechanical troubles frequently cause extended delays. The local tour companies operate bus services of their own, but this is naturally more expensive.

The route to Cuzco goes by way of Abancay, a small, boring transit town, and from there continues eastward into the lovely Apurimac valley. You can make your way to Abancay separately, and continue from there on one of the many buses that travel daily to Cuzco (200 km). The most beautiful stretch is between Abancay and Anta, and it is worth your while to traverse it during daylight. If you want to reach Machu-Picchu, you can get off in Anta and proceed a short distance to Izcuchaca, where the passenger train from Cuzco to Machu-Picchu makes a stop.

The Inca Empire

For hundreds of years — from the eleventh century until the arrival of the Spanish in the early 1500's — a mighty empire progressively expanded across South America, an empire with few to match her in the history of nations. The Incas extended their rule district by district, tribe after tribe, as they pushed through roads, built cities and temples and devised new and hitherto unknown social systems. The empire's hub was the city of Cuzco, which, according to tradition was built by Manco Capac, the first of the glorious dynasty of Incas (emperors). Before setting out to explore the relics, and even before exploring today's Cuzco, one should learn something of the history of that magnificent nation, which has left a deep imprint on the Andean countries, especially Peru. This will give one a better understanding of the historical and cultural phenomenon of the Incas, which even today influences the local social order.

The Incas

Pre-Columbian communities in South America were based on unique social and tribal frameworks, and reached high levels of development. Though the remains of these ancient civilizations are spread from Mexico in the north to Chile in the south, the mightiest and grandest relics are undoubtedly those of the Inca nation. Though it lasted for only a few centuries — and its zenith lasted only a few decades — the Inca nation left its imprint on the history of the entire region, and is among the five or six best-known ancient civilizations in the world. Little remains of the Incas, due to the savage annihilation wreaked upon them by the Spanish conquest. Even so, what has survived suffices to testify to a tremendous and highly impressive empire. When we study ancient documents that have survived from the Inca period, or refer to modern research, we uncover a fascinating picture: a legendary clan which, by force of the personality of its members, founded within less than a century a mighty empire that covered about two million square kilometers — from Colombia in the north to central Chile in the south — and which numbered twenty million residents who submitted to the tough yoke of their reign. The Incas ran their giant empire with astonishing efficiency, and by disseminating their faith, they created a tremendously powerful national-religious

Machu Picchu

PERU

framework. Their swift collapse in the face of the Spanish **conquistadores** — which required no more than one dramatic half-hour — completes the story of their meteoric rise, existence and fall. If we are to fully understand the sights we will see in South America in general, and Peru in particular, we must know and understand the story of the Incas, a family which became a tribe which became an empire (until the name "Inca" became the name of the god-king who stood at the head of the Empire).

Historical sources

When we come to survey the annals of Incan civilization, we face a number of difficulties that are unusual in historical research. Unlike other advanced civilizations in the ancient world, including the Mayan and Aztec in Central America, the Incas' highly developed and efficient empire had no writing of any kind. Government decrees and business were handled orally, and proclamations were conveyed by special messengers who made use of the well-developed Imperial road system.

The only form of writing was **quipo** — "rope writing" — which, however, was meant mainly for noting dates and events rather than for daily use. The lack of a writing system, and hence the impossibility of a reliable and accurate documentation of events, apparently suited the policy of the Incan kings who habitually distorted history in accordance with their needs and understanding. They could therefore erase unpleasant events, defeats in battle, rebellions and the like from public memory, while leaving the imprint of military triumphs and spectacular accomplishments. Court poets were set to compose and disseminate ballads and folk songs praising the Incas' achievements, and these were sung at each of the many celebrations and thereby permeated the public consciousness.

The sources at our disposal, therefore, rely mainly on analysis of archaeological findings along with letters and reports of Spanish explorers who reached the area with, or slightly after, the first conquerors. Though archaeological remains are indeed abundant, we must remember that they are but a tiny remnant, for the Spaniards destroyed most of the Incas, to ensure that the Incan Empire would never again rise. Some of the surviving writings were recorded in Quechua — a local Indian language in Latin letters — and deciphered afterwards, while others were written directly in Spanish. Among the most important documents is a letter to the King of Spain consisting of 1200 written pages and four hundred drawings — a veritable treasure trove of information on the various tribes and their customs, ceremonies, agricultural methods, etc. This document was lost at some point during the intervening centuries, and only in the early years of this century did it turn up again — in the Royal Library in Copenhagen.

History of the Empire

In light of all this, it is clear why it is so difficult to determine with certainty even such basic facts as the exact origin of the Incas and when they first appeared on the stage of history. Legend has it that Manco Capac, the first Inca and founder of the dynasty, was the son of the Sun, and that he founded the city of Cuzco (Quechua for "navel of the world") in his father's name, and laid the foundations for the Kingdom of the Sun. Another version has it that Manco Capac was born not far from Cuzco, and after a grueling search along with his brothers and sisters for a suitable location for a settlement, he chose Cuzco, where in the year 1200 he and his four sisters set up their household. The family expanded rapidly and became a tribe, which began in turn to establish itself and develop in a manner similar to the scores of other tribes in the region. Small wars were frequent, breaking out because of disputes over money, division of land, etc. Usually these wars ended with the imposition of taxes on the vanquished, and their scope rarely exceeded a few kilometers at the utmost. The Incas, too, subscribed to this local approach in their earliest days, and it was only with the ascension of the eighth Inca, Viracocha, that the tribe began to evince new expansionist trends. The genuine turning point came when Viracocha's son, Pachacuti, assumed power as the ninth Inca in 1438, and in less than a hundred years — until their conquest by the Spaniards — Pachacuti and his son Topa were responsible for one of the most amazing imperialist developments human history has ever witnessed.

Pachacuti rose to power in an era when regional tensions were increasing and fierce armed struggle broke out among the three or four largest and strongest tribes in the area. The conflict reached its peak with an offensive launched by the Chanca tribe against the city of Cuzco, in which the Chancas almost succeeded in defeating and vanquishing the Incas. Pachacuti fought a heroic battle and by his personal valor emerged the victor, thereby safeguarding his regime against any internal subversion.

This victory accelerated the change in Incan attitudes. After a short period of military organization their campaigns of conquest and enslavement began, inspired by economic, religious and imperialist considerations. To this end Pachacuti quickly set up an elite force incorporating warriors from the conquered tribes. At the same time, the Incan policy of population exchange took shape, by which conquered tribes were deported and forced to accept the Sun religion, although they were still allowed to preserve their traditional dress and customs. At the same time Pachacuti began to design administrative and governmental procedures, and to erect lavish palaces, temples, and public buildings.

When Pachacuti grew old and tired from his campaigns and conquests, Topa Inca, Pachacuti's declared successor from the age of fifteen, came to power. Topa, known as a mighty fighter and a superb builder, expanded the Empire's borders northward to Ecuador and southward to Bolivia. From there it was only a short jump to central Chile (near today's city of Consititución, south of Santiago), where the conquerors were halted by logistical difficulties caused by the distance from their supply bases and by the local Indians' spirited opposition — a resistance they maintained in later centuries against the Spanish as well.

In Topa's first years of rule Pachacuti remained titular emperor, devoting most of his time and energy to domestic affairs. The father abdicated formally in 1471, however, and Topa was crowned Inca. Lust for power seemed to be the dominant impulse during his reign and Topa devoted most of his reign to training and strengthening his army, while cruelly repressing the frequent rebellions. Throughout this period, the Incan Army, noteworthy for its iron discipline and high mobility, managed to maintain relative quiet in all parts of the mighty empire, enabling the continued development and construction of the imperial capital of Cuzco.

Topa built Sacsayhuamán, a gigantic fortress looming over Cuzco and the entire region, along with many other majestic structures. His son Tital, known as Huayna Capac, was crowned Inca after Topa's death in 1493, and had nothing left to do but complete his father's and grandfather's magnificent projects. When Huayna Capac died without leaving a designated successor, the kingdom was split between his two quarelling sons. Huascar, the titular ruler, was routed by his half-brother Atahualpa in a terrible internecine battle beside the Urubamba River. This clash, one of the bloodiest the empire had ever known, ended in the deaths of thousands of soldiers and a resounding defeat for Huascar. Atahualpa entered Cuzco and became sole ruler — although not for long.

In May, 1532, shortly after his victory, he learned that Francisco Pizarro had landed on the Peruvian coast with 180 Spanish adventurers. Aware of the ancient tradition, which told of a white god who had departed from their land to cross the sea but promised to return, Atahualpa assumed that the gods had in fact come back. With great enthusiasm, he set out for Cajamarca to greet them. Following a dialogue of the deaf in a babble of languages, the glorious Incan emperor was taken captive and all his men were killed, and Pizarro received an immense ransom of gold for his release. The Incan hoard of gold was sent to Spain, where it disappeared over the years in mysterious ways. Aware of the danger involved in releasing the Inca, however, Pizarro did not keep his promise to free him, and instead put Atahualpa on trial on a charge of threatening Spanish security. The charge sheet was then greatly expanded to include various religious and ethical offenses such as adultery, idolatry, incest and so on, some of which were no more than rites of the Incan religion. The Inca was found guilty and sentenced to death at the stake. In his last moments he accepted Christianity, and the manner of his execution was therefore changed — from burning to strangling. At the end of August 1533, the Inca king was executed, the Incan capital, Cuzco, was conquerred by the Spaniards, and the glorious empire collapsed.

Another son of Huayna Capac, Manco, was crowned by the Spaniards in 1534. But Manco, who was expected to be a puppet, escaped from Cuzco in 1536 to lead a rebellion from the fortress of Ollantaytambo. Under the Spanish pressure he abandoned the fortress, and retreated to the remote wilderness of Vilcabamba. There he ruled a small rebellious Inca state. He was killed a few years later, but his sons continued to lead the state and the rebellion. In 1872 the last son of Manco and of the Inca line was captured. He was taken to Cuzco, converted to Christianity, and beheaded in the main square. This was the very end of the Incas.

Religion and customs
The key to understanding the spread of the Inca Empire is perhaps best found in their religious outlook. This took shape during the rule of the first emperors in the two centuries preceding the tribe's expansion and constituted the point from which their later conquests and domination of the neighboring lands evolved.

At the head of the pantheon stood the sun god, Inti. The ruling Inca was considered his son and earthly representative, and herein lay the source of his power: his absolute, undisputed authority in every field of life, and his comprehensive ownership of all human beings and the fruits of their labor. Inti's wife, the moon goddess Mama Kilya, was responsible for nature's cyclical manifestations, the calendar and the setting of dates for ritual events. The rain-god, Apu Illapu, and the earth goddess, Paca Mama, also had roles to play. The Incas erected lavish temples

PERU

in their honor, mainly in high, protected places. Here ritual ceremonies and prayers were conducted under the direction of specially trained priests who were "ordained" by the High Priest, the Villac Umu, who resided in Cuzco and whose authority was only slightly lower than that of the Inca himself. The priests were assisted by an order known as the Virgins of the Sun, trained from youth for their holy labors. These women made the clothes worn by the Inca and the priests, and were sworn to perpetual virginity — unless the Inca desired them as concubines.

The rites required a great many sacrifices, some of them human. At the beginning of each lunar month a hundred white llamas were sacrificed in Cuzco, while less "prestigious" animals, along with fruit, beverages, various treasures and the like, were offered at less important festivals. Human sacrifice was practiced on very special occasions such as severe drought, famine, military defeat, epidemics and — on the "brighter" side — upon the coronation of a new Inca, when two hundred children were sacrificed to the sun-god!

Divining was highly accepted as well, and the rite for consulting the oracle to ascertain the gods' wishes was an important preliminary to taking any decision. This ceremony involved various sacrifices (including children), mortification of the flesh, taking of drugs, etc. The Inca himself sometimes took part in the rite, by whose results imperial affairs would be determined.

Similar rituals accompanied the monthly holidays and festivals. The Incan nobility, cognizant of the common man's brutish soul, took pains to be generous in supplying the masses' need for entertainment and release. Festivals were set according to the religious calendar and included song, dance, eating and drinking and, of course, a religious ceremony centering around sacrifices. To this very day, a major festival which has survived from the Incan period — the sun festival, *Inti Raimi* — is celebrated every June.

The Incas believed in the cyclical nature of life, a fact which explains their great sensitivity to matters of burial. Their belief in an afterlife led to the development of a unique method of embalming and interment. The corpse was opened, the inner organs removed and the abdominal cavity was filled with special plants and treated with preservatives. Then the embalmed body was bound with knees against and chest — the fetal position — to facilitate its rebirth. For graves the Incas built clay structures shaped like hornets' nests, built directly against the mountain ridge, so that the departed one would encounter no difficulty in extricating himself from them when the time came.

PERU

Society and economy

Daily life in the Empire followed a strict and exacting code. Imperial law defined every individual's place and saw to his or her every need, including education, marriage and occupation. A complex hierarchy of greater and lesser officials guaranteed citizens' needs and rights, even as it ensured most strictly that they fulfilled their obligations to the state. Welfare institutions safeguarded the population at times of crisis, giving rise to an economic and social tranquility that increased the subjects' willingness to bear the burden and to accept the sovereignty of the conquering Inca. The emperor, for his part, understood the importance of this calm for the peace of the Empire, and always made sure to foster his subjects' rights and respond to their needs, both material and emotional. Just as the ancient Roman emperors provided "bread and circuses", the Inca made sure to provide these to his subjects — generously.

When a new area was conquered, representatives of the Inca would take a general census and calculate the unit of land essential for existence. Afterwards, the population of the region was divided into groups, and a hierarchy of officials appointed to oversee them. The land was demarcated clearly and each family received an allocation according to its size. Groups of families were organized into a commune in the manner of a Russian *kolkhoz*. The allotment of cultivated land was three times larger than that necessary for subsistence, with one third of the crop set aside for the Sun, one third for the Inca (who built up a reserve to be redistributed to the people during drought years) and one third for the family's sustenance. The land was redivided each year according to changes in family size. The Inca's deputies drew up programs for building terraces, irrigation systems, and public buildings, and the local population was required to carry these out. Raw materials and fertilizer were a government monopoly and distributed among the populace on a fair and equal basis.

The mode of living was primitive and rather modest. Houses for the "plebeians" were low, windowless, square and simple one-room affairs made of clay and thatched with straw. The occupants slept on the ground. Interior walls were smooth and unadorned, except for niches where articles and clothing were kept.

The external appearance of the Incas was ascetic: most were rather short (about 1.5 meters), strong and dark-skinned. Their clothing was of uniform style and fashioned of local materials — cotton in the coastal region and wool in the mountains. Both cotton and wool were government monopolies and were apportioned to citizens according to need. Workmen wore only breechcloths, while women wore cloth dresses that reached their ankles. Higher-class men wore shirts and pants, with leather pouches at their waists in which coca leaves and personal items were kept. Their feet were protected with sandals of wood or of llama skin. Men's hair was cut short, whereas women let theirs grow and gathered it together from behind.

Huge earrings (up to 5 cm in diameter) made of various materials, according to social status, were the usual articles of jewelry. The nobility habitually sported earrings of gold or silver, while simple folk had to settle for earrings of base metals or wood.

The Incas contented themselves with two meals per day — morning and evening. The menu was essentially vegetarian. Meat was hunted and served only on rare occasions. On a day-to-day basis the Incas enjoyed the abundant variety of local vegetables, of which some were totally unknown in Europe until the advent of the Spaniards (the most famous of these was the popular potato, first brought to Ireland from Peru in the eighteenth century and destined to become one of the most common of foodstuffs). Home utensils for cooking and eating were made of pottery or (in the case of the nobility) of gold. Cooking was done on a low flame ignited by rubbing sticks together.

The well-developed Incan road system opened the way to commerce between the Empire's various sections, enabling the people to broaden their horizons and, for the first time, to consume goods which were not of local manufacture.

The llama served to transport food and cargo. All llamas were government property. Each llama carried a fifty-kilogram load 20 kilometers per day. Thus Inca officials were able to regulate the movement of goods and supply necessary commodities to every district.

Architectural projects

Of the various remains of the Incas, their tremendous building endeavors are undoubtedly the most enduring. We can still marvel at Incan cities, temples, baths, palaces, terraces, irrigation canals, bridges and roads, all projects of stunning size, precision, and exceptional skill.

The Incas began bulding shortly after they appeared as a nation, but it was Pachacuti who gave the construction "industry" real momentum and turned it from a periodic local occurrence into an enduring historical phenomenon. The glory and focus of

Incan architecture was the city of Cuzco and its environs, which merited special attention as the center of the Empire. Cuzco was divided into twelve neighborhoods arranged around a central plaza, Huayqapata, where the most important temples stood. The Sun-Temple — Coricancha- located where the present-day Iglesia Santo Domingo stands, was one of the pinnacles of their architectural creativity and, like the Emperor's palace and the Temple of the Sun Virgins, was a source of pride for the entire nation. These structures were built of exceedingly well-fitted slabs of hewn stone which arouse amazement even in our time. Sanctuaries were built of many-faceted stones, so carefully chiseled that no mortar was required to secure them and no plants have succeeded in penetrating and taking root in the cracks between them, a phenomenon so common in other archaeological sites. All the palaces and temples were adorned with gold fashioned into various forms — wall covering, statues, fountains, religious symbols and the like. (All these, of course, were plundered by the Spanish *conquistadores*.) The small remnant that has survived is prominently displayed in museums — chiefly the Museo de Oro in Lima and the archeolological museum in Cuzco.

The Imperial rulers paid great attention to their building projects, and superb architects, engineers and skilled craftsmen — high ranking members of the Incan nobility — were engaged for them. They had access to financial resources and unlimited manpower, which they put to use in chiseling and transporting stone by the most primitive of means. Most tools were made of stone, and a few were of bronze. A level and primitive measuring tool served to determine the exact size and location of angles, and the laborers had to be precise in their work and avoid even the slightest error. Most building material was quarried in the Cuzco area and transported many kilometers to its final destination. The tremendous Sacsayhuamán fortress is made of locally quarried limestone, and the stones of its walls — of which the largest weights about one hundred tons (!) — were dragged to the site by primitive means. Tens of thousands of people took part in the task of constructing the fortress, using wooden rollers and ropes to haul the stones on ramps of sand to their final destination.

Inca engineering, however, was not confined to palaces and temples. Understanding, as they did, the importance of controlling recently conquered areas and the essential need for a transportation network reaching all corners of the Empire, the Incas created an impressive system of paved roads which extended for more 10,000 kilometers from Colombia to Argentina and Chile. Since there were no wheeled vehicles there was also no need for wide highways, so the Incas dug out narrow roadways between mountains and valleys along routes which frequently reached elevations of five thousand meters and more. These roads served for transmitting orders and transporting supplies to occupation forces at the front and for conveying government proclamations by means of the superb, specially trained courier corps. "Roadside inns" were set up to tend to the couriers' needs. The highway system was based on a coastal artery and an additional main route atop the mountain ridge, as well as hundreds of side roads between the two, by which every point of settlement, no matter how small, was linked with the capital of Cuzco. Many bridges were constructed over rivers and although these sometimes reached lengths of dozens of meters, most of them were rather weak, since they were meant to bear the weight of couriers and animals only.

To this very day, in the Cuzco area, one can see strips of mountainside carefully marked out by straight terraces. These terraces too, are the handiwork of the Incan builders, and were meant both to increase the amount of tillable land and to prevent erosion. Pisac, Ollantaytambo, Machu-Picchu and many other regions were similarly developed. The impressive irrigation systems, canals and reservoirs supported a complex and extensive economic and agricultural infrastructure, which, combined with superb military capability and the strong, all-encompassing state religion, were of utmost importance in upholding and maintaining the mighty Empire.

Cuzco — Capital of the Inca Empire

Cuzco is one of those cities where as you enter, you seem to feel the enormous impact of history on the place. A major reason for this, apart from its 280,000 strong Indian population, is Cuzco's unique architecture — a combination of ancient Incan style and grand Spanish colonial construction, a style in which entire sections of the city are built.

Whether you come by bus or by train from Puno to the station at the edge of town, or by plane to the International Airport fifteen minutes from the city, you quickly sense that Cuzco is different from other cities in Peru, that it is been graced with a special character, a unique temperament and an atmosphere significantly different from Peru's other cities.

This is an enchanting and unique city, where nothing seems to have changed in the course of the centuries. Wherever you go, everything is saturated in the grandeur of those days, each spot with its own hidden events and stories. Though remnants of bygone worlds are preserved within and around many cities, there is something special about Cuzco. This is largely due to its citizens' traditional attire, archaic customs and unusual ways, which blend in wonderful harmony with the ruined temples and palaces that confront you on every street corner. The magnificence of Cuzco and its environs cannot leave one unmoved.

Cuzco lies 3400 m above sea level, but the thin air does not seem to affect its thieves. They wait in ambush at the train station, on the streets and in the markets, waiting for the moment your attention flags, to whip away your camera, money, watch, or jewelry. Moreover, the evil touch of Cuzco's infamous thieves has won the concurrence, at least of the tacit sort, of the local police. Remember that everything said of Peru (see "Personal security") goes double and treble for Cuzco. Unofficial statistics relate that about 80% of Cuzco's tourists fall victim to theft or attempted theft. The thieves' organized activity has long since exceeded reasonable limits, but the authorities' unperturbed negligence provides them a comfortable and secure environment. Here you are on your own — so be warned! Protect your gear fanatically, for it will disappear within seconds should you fail! Leave your manners at home: when someone tries to block your path as if by accident (while his or her partner reaches for your purse with a sharp knife) shove with all your might and keep going. There is, unfortunately, no other way.

The danger of theft, however, cannot diminish Cuzco's special grandeur. Thieves aside, most Cuzcans treat visitors to their town with respect and affection. The treasures of the city far outweigh its hazards and no tourist visiting Peru should skip Cuzco.

Though your visit to Cuzco and the "classic" sites in its vicinity should take several days, a somewhat more thorough exploration, with visits to the remote and lesser-known sites, requires a week and one could spend a full month here with no effort at all. First of all we will stroll along the city's streets and after getting to know Cuzco's treasures, head out to the immediate vicinity — along the Urubamba Valley as far as Machu-Picchu. Later more fascinating routes will be mentioned for which you will have to organize yourself differently as most of these involve physical effort, suitable equipment, and lots of time.

How to get there
Whenever you take a taxi, whether from the airport or from the train station, remember to negotiate the fare in advance. When you get out, take your gear out first, for drivers have been known to take off with passengers' luggage after they have alighted.

By air
Cuzco's modern airport is an important aviation hub, with incoming flights from all parts of Peru and from La Paz, the capital of Bolivia. *AeroPerú* and *Faucett* fly several times daily between Cuzco and Lima, Arequipa, Ayacucho, Iquitos and the jungle city of Puerto Maldonado. If you are flying to Cuzco from northern Peru, choose a seat on the left side of the plane so you can enjoy the view. Planes are very full on the Lima and Puerto Maldonado routes so be sure to book well in advance. It won't guarantee anything, but it will back up your arguments at the airport when they give you the happy tidings that the plane is full and your place has been given to someone else. Confirm your reservations a day in advance and get to the airport early. Watch out for your luggage, for Peruvians have a strange tendency to "lose" it or, at best, to send it to another destination! Take everything you can aboard the plane and refrain from sending luggage separately. Flights to and from Puerto Maldonado are frequently cancelled due to bad weather and rain which prevent landing, with the result that the next day flights are even more crowded than usual.

By bus
Buses to all parts of Peru set out very frequently from Cuzco.
The three-day trip to Lima follows three major routes:

Via the mountains: first to Abancay (200 km, 8 hours), then to
Ayacucho (another 12 hours) and Huancayo (another 12) and
finally to Lima. On this route it is recommended to proceed from
Huancayo by train (see "Huancayo").

Via the coast: first to Abancay and on from there through
fantastic scenery, though on a difficult road, to Nazca on the
coast and from there to Lima. It is about thirty hours to Nazca.
Most bus companies go to Lima along this route, and the most
recommended of these is *Ormeno*. Its offices in Cuzco are on
Plaza de Armas.

Via Arequipa: travel by either bus or train from Cuzco to
Arequipa and from there continue by bus. There are several
buses per day to Juliaca, Puno, Arequipa and La Paz, traveling
a difficult and dusty dirt road alongside the railroad tracks. We
highly recommend covering **at least** the Cuzco-Puno stretch
by train (eleven hours) and continuing from Puno to La Paz
or Arequipa (see "Puno"). The train ride is lovely, following
the river through enchanting and varied scenery. We strongly
recommend that you travel first-class, where the thieves are
less menacing (see "Puno"). While first-class tickets can be
purchased the day before, second-class tickets can be bought
only on the morning of departure (from 6:30am). Moreover,
second class is crowded with peddlers and passengers so
burdened with luggage that it seems as if everyone in southern
Peru has chosen to move on the very day you picked for your
journey.

When to come
The most comfortable time to visit the Cuzco area is during
the dry season, from April to July — the weather is nice with
clear skies and an average temperature of 10°C (50°F) — but
significantly cooler in the shade. Though temperatures are a
little higher between December and March, the frequent rains
make tourists' lives difficult. You'll need warm clothing the year
round and raincoats during the rainy season.

On June 24 Cuzco celebrates **Inti Raimi** — the Incan Sun
Festival, the largest festival of its kind in Peru and second in
South America only to the famous carnival in Brazil. Tens of
thousands come to Cuzco to witness the sacrificial offering
to the Sun God, which takes place exactly as it did in Incan
times. The impressive ceremony is performed before crowds in
the Sacsayhuaman fortress overlooking the city and you must

get there early to secure a comfortable place to sit (visitors to Cuzco during this period should make hotel reservations). The festivities begin with a parade through the city streets of representatives of all strata of society, as well as bands and dance troupes, with the revelry continuing in the fortress the next day. Take into consideration that hotels and other tourist services are fully-booked at this time of the year.

Where to stay

Libertador: San Agustin 400, Tel. 23-1961. Part of the Marriott chain, a 5-star in a handsome sixteenth-century colonial building known as *Casa de los Cuatro Bustos*. Very close to the central Plaza.

Hostal El Dorado: Av. Sol 395, Tel. 23-2573. Central and very good.

San Agustín: Maruri 390, corner of San Agustín, Tel. 23-1001. Good location, good service.

Cusco: Heladeros 150, Tel. 22-4821. Central and very good.

Hostal Loreto: Loreto 115, Tel. 23-6331. One of the city's most unique. It is located on an alley branching southward from Plaza de Armas in a building whose outer walls are the remains of an Incan Temple. Moderate, recommended.

Imperial Palace: Tecsecocha 492, Tel. 22-3324. Medium priced.

Hostal Familiar: Saphi 661, clean, inexpensive and recommended.

Suecia: Suecia 332. Inexpensive, rooms can be shared, laguage can be restored.

Santo Domingo Church Hostal: can accommodate for very low prices, clean and safety. The gates are shut at 10 pm.

San Cristobal: Quiscapata 242. Friendly, recommended despite the poor area, inexpensive, basic.

Where to eat

As in many other spheres, Cuzco's culinary offerings are a cut above the South American scene, particularly that of the Andean countries. The great number of *gringos* who visit the town has given rise to dozens of eateries of various types, flavors and price levels. A number of foods are typical of the Cuzco region. Maybe the strangest of these is stuffed guinea-pig (the Spanish term is *cuy*), served whole, including head and tail. It reminds one of barbecued rat. For reasons that remain quite incomprehensible, this abomination is considered to be the piece-de-resistance at Incan feasts. Recommended only for those with strong stomachs, and we doubt about them, either.

Crisp tidbits of pork, deep-fried in oil and well-seasoned, are called *chicharrón de chancho*, and the same dish, made from chicken, is called *chicharrón de gallina*. There's a local corn stew called *locro*, often served as a first course in creole restaurants (see : "Peru — Food and drink").

Several cafés around Plaza de Armas serve breakfast, cake, ice cream and the like. The most highly recommended are *El Ayllu* on the northern corner of the square (left of the cathedral), *Café de Paris* (across the plaza), and *Piccolo*. *El Ayllu*, on Portal de Carnes 203, (left of the Cathedral), is famous for its apple cake and the classical music, where travelers from all over the world gather. All three cafés excel in superb cakes, sandwiches and ice cream. They serve as meeting places for young travelers from all over the world and the atmosphere is pleasant. Another place to enjoy drinks and light food is *Vic's American Bar*, on Calle Plateros just off Plaza de Armas, where the *gringos* gather at day's end for an evening of song and drink.

Among Cuzco's dozens of restaurants, which serve Italian, Chinese, Peruvian and other varieties of food, the favorites are those on "Gringos Street", Calle Procuradores, a narrow pedestrian mall which branches off from the middle of Plaza de Armas' northern side (across from the Tourist Bureau). Here you'll find small, intermediate-priced restaurants one next to another, each with its own special flavor — an excellent pizzeria, a steakhouse, a vegetarian restaurant and plain diners. Walk down the mall and within one hundred meters, you are bound to find at least one restaurant that attracts your interest.

More elegant restaurants are located in the better hotels and on Plaza de Armas itself. There are several restaurants behind the square, on Plaza Recogijo, among them *La Mamma Pizzería*. Furthermore, you can eat cheaply and to satiation in Cuzco, as in any city, in and around the marketplaces (be warned of sanitation!).

Transportation
Most of Cuzco's interesting sites are within walking distance of one another and can be reached without difficulty. For the more remote attractions, including those in the immediate surroundings of the city, you can hire a **taxi** on an hourly basis. Remember to fix a price with the driver before you set out! There's also **public transportation** (buses, *colectivos*, and trucks) every few minutes to the villages, towns, and archaeological sites in the vicinity, so getting there and back presents no difficulty. Organizing a small group can lower the expense of taking a taxi to the more remote destinations, facilitating the return trip as well.

Another possibility, **car rental**, is handled either through hotels or

*P**ERU*

through *Avis* (Avenida Sol 900), and *National* at Santa Catalina near Plaza de Armas.

A **train** to Machu-Picchu leaves Cuzco each morning (see below).

Tourist services

The main **Tourist Bureau** on Belén 115, Plaza de Armas, left of the La Compañía Church, will give you maps of the city and provide information about transportation and visiting hours at the various attractions. There is also a branch office at the airport. The long lines of tourists waiting to be served here make it hard to obtain detailed, patiently given advice. To visit the museums and surrounding archaeological sites you must buy a combined eleven-entry ticket for $10 ($5 for students; separate tickets for individual sites are not available). Buying it ahead of time at the Tourist Bureau will save you much time and trouble later. A Student Card will prove very useful in Cuzco, procuring significant reductions on admission fees, transportation and so on.

A special **Tourist Police** has been established to assist foreigners who have run into trouble (theft, accidents, etc.). Its office is behind Plaza de Armas on the other side of the *Hotel Cuzco* (Calle Espinar). Its members wear olive-green uniforms with white arm-bands bearing the legend *Guardia Civil Turismo*. Despite their good intentions, however, their powers are limited. If you have a truly serious problem go the investigation police, P.I.P. (offices far from downtown).

The **Auto Club** (TACP) office on Avenida Sol will equip you with maps. *Faucett* and *AeroPerú* have offices in town for buying tickets and confirming reservations. *Faucett* is on Av. Sol 567, Tel. 23-3151, and *AeroPerú* on Av. Sol 600, Tel. 23-3051.

Many travel agencies organize tours and excursions in Cuzco and the surroundings. These include transportation and guides, as well as food and lodging on longer tours. Adventure outings that include river boating or hikes through the jungles to the east are organized by a number of companies, most with offices on Procuradores. Check the quality of the equipment, the tour route, guide and prices very carefully. *Mayoc* organizes such trips and does it well. For solid and excellent tours, *Lima Tours*, Portal de Harinas 177, Tel. 22-3791, is recommended.

Tourist sites

Any get-acquainted tour of Cuzco must begin at **Plaza de Armas**: all urban affairs and events take place in and around it,

*P*ERU

CUZCO

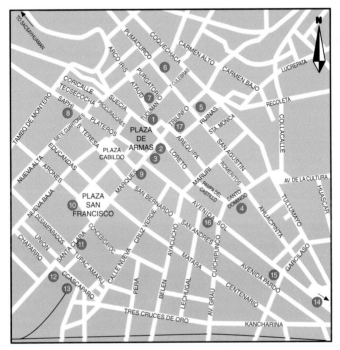

and anything you do in Cuzco will most likely either begin or end there. Most municipal institutions, important stores, offices, and the like are concentrated around the square and along the main street, Avenida Sol, which leads to the train station to Puno. The lovely plaza, packed with children and peddlers, has been Cuzco's center since time immemmorial. In the Inca period it was called Huacaypata, and some of the most important buildings and palaces were arrayed around it. Religious ceremonies took place in its center, and from it the emperors issued orders to their subjects.

In the plaza's southeastern corner, occupied by the great cathedral, the palace of Viracucha once soared, and the Snake Palace, once occupied the spot where La Compañía Church stands today (to the right of the Tourist Bureau). Nothing much remained, however, after the Spanish overwhelmed the Incas and divided up the loot. The Incas attempted to revolt against the conquerors, but were defeated. Nature and time also took their toll, and the ancient Inca city was razed nearly to the ground. The Spanish began rebuilding Cuzco in the latter half of the sixteenth century, and today it offers a rare blend of Spanish Colonial architecture and stonework of rare quality — the finest of the Incan heritage. Many buildings were built of stones salvaged from Inca ruins in Cuzco and its surroundings; the observer can clearly discern where they join up with more "modern" stones.

The **cathedral** on Plaza de Armas, one of Cuzco's largest and most impressive edifices, is a living example of this eclectic style. Built on the ruins of the Inca's palace, the viewer can easily identify the ancient foundation, while the spires are of more modern design and construction. It took almost a hundred years, until the mid-seventeenth century, to complete the maginificent building. Today Cuzco's cathedral is home to an impressive collection of statues, paintings, and historic artifacts of the city in its early days. From atop the left tower, the Maria Angola bell, South America's largest, sounds with a pleasant force heard many kilometers from the city. The bell, which weighs a full ton, was cast in 1659 from gold, silver and bronze.

To the cathedral's right is the **Triunfo Church**, the oldest in town. It was built on the site where the Spanish were trapped by Incan rebels in 1536 and were saved only by virtue of a miracle wrought on their behalf by Virgin Mary.To the left of the cathedral there is another church, that of **Jesus María**.

In the plaza's southeastern corner, to the cathedral's right, the **Tourist Bureau** occupies the spot where the "House of the Chosen Women" once stood, home of those women who faithfully supplied the needs of the ruling Inca and the nobility (see "The Incas"). To its right is the prominent Jesuit **Church of La Compañía**, considered Cuzco's most beautiful. About a hundred years under construction, it was completed only at the end of the seventeenth century after disputes and quarrels which echoed as far as the Vatican in Rome. The church's Jesuit builders erected it on the remains of the

Snake Palace, Amarucancha, home of Inca Huayna-Capac, with the aim of erecting a temple that would overshadow the neighboring cathedral in grandeur Its two soaring towers, the rich Baroque-style interior balconies, gilded altars, and collection of paintings and other works of art, indeed constitute an impressive spectacle.

From here we can set out on a walk through the most "Incan" parts of Cuzco, to get an impression of the relics of the past and to see how they are integrated into the buildings of the present. We will start with the southern and eastern parts of town.

Along the Inca ruins

Turn down Calle Loreto alongside the church and walk along the longest of the surviving Inca walls. To the left is the wall of the Chosen Women's House, and to the right — that of the Snake Palace. Shortly we will pass the lovely **Church of Santa Catalina**, built in the early seventeenth century, with a small museum inside. Continuing down Loreto and Pampa del Castillo, we reach the site of the largest and grandest of the Incan temples — the Sun and Gold Temple, **Coricancha**.

Today we find the **Santo Domingo Church** on the site. The church was built directly atop the ruins of the famous temple, and only in recent decades have archaeological excavations begun to expose a small portion of what is still considered to be the most precise, impressive and important of the Inca buildings. Coricancha had five sections, dedicated respectively to the sun, moon, lightning, thunder and rainbow (the rainbow's colors were also those of the Incas). It was here that the empire's gold reserve was kept, sacrifices were offered, astronomical observations were conducted and the important religious rites carried out. Thousands of people — all noblemen especially trained for their roles, who had consecrated their lives to the holy service — performed ritual tasks in the temple. The first Spaniards to reach Cuzco spread many legends about the temple; indeed, they found quantities of gold and silver beyond imagination: statues and fountains, altars and cult objects all cast in gold, the work of unparalleled masters of the goldsmith's art.

The few remnants not plundered by the Spanish disappeared over the years and today we can only contemplate in sorrow the remains of a world that vanished almost overnight. In various corners of the church we can discern remains of walls, bath chambers, gardens — and traces of the temple itself, at the very entrance to the courtyard of the church. The entire temple complex was designed and constructed with devotion,

At Plaza de Armas

the stones cut with an exemplary precision that arouses our amazement and admiration again and again.

Along Calle Ahuacpinta, which adjoins the church, we see more remains of walls, among them the external walls of the Sun Temple. Now, however, we turn left and head back to the center along Calle Romeritos. We pass the *Hotel Libertador*, housed in a magnificent sixteenth-century building — **Casa de los Cuatro Bustos** — and continue on **Calle San Agustín**, where the remains of Incan walls can easily be identified. A small detour to the left, to Calle Catalina, will allow us to observe the beautiful balconies of the home of Martín Concha, the last of Cuzco's Spanish governors. This house, built atop the ruins of another Inca palace, serves today as a police station.

Proceeding another block, we see on our right the **Art Museum**, which houses a collection of seventeenth-century furniture and

Cuzco — Colonial houses on Incan bricks

paintings. The building has undergone many metamorphoses, first serving as the palace of Inca-Roca (the sixth emperor) then as home of the Marquis de Buena Vista, and later as the Archbishop's residence. The museum building has an impressive facade, interior decor, carefully-crafted doors and balconies, and a handsome central patio and fountain. Visiting hours: 9:30am-12:30pm and 3-6pm.

Calle Hatunrumiyoc leads north from the museum, and in its center we find one of the most famous Inca remains — the "**Dodecagon**" (a twelve-sided stone). Here's an instructive example of the Incan stonemason's rare ability to work hard stone as if it were soft clay, and to chisel precise angles that fit exactly into the surrounding stones — with no need for mortar to hold them together, and without even the narrowest chink in between!

Continuing up the street, we come to the **San Blas church**, which contains a wooden pulpit carved from the trunk of a single tree. This exquisite piece is among the largest of its type in the entire world. Many artists and a number of *artesanía* dealers have set up shop around the church.

We return now to Plaza de Armas, but not before passing **Plaza**

de las Nazarenas. On the plaza's northeastern side are two impressive buildings. On the left is the **Nazarene Monastery**, built on the ruins of an Inca snake palace (one of its walls bears a relief of seven terrifying snakes), while on the right is **San Antonio Abad**, once a center of religious education, currently being renovated for its transformation into a grand hotel. In the middle is **Calle Siete Culebras** — "Alley of the Seven Snakes"

From here we return downhill to Plaza de Armas via Calle Tucuman, where we find **Casa del Almirante**, (the Admiral's House), today the **Archaelogical Museum**, open on weekdays 9 am-noon and 3-6pm. The building itself was damaged in an earthquake in 1950. Also worth is the **Museo Histórico Regional** in Casa Garcilaso, at the corner of Garcilaso and Heladros, open the same hours than the former, but currently closed after the damages of the earthquake in April 1986.

Calle Santa Clara and the market

Once having formed an idea of Cuzco's glorious past, especially of the Incas' impressive achievements, we need only spend a little time on the southwest side of town, an area which bustles with a different kind of activity: shops, stalls and a market. Set out from the corner adjacent to the La Compañía church on Plaza de Armas to Calle Mantas, and only one block further we come upon the **Church of La Merced**, open mornings until 10 and again in the afternoon. Here we find a collection of ritual objects, a small museum and the tomb of Diego de Almegro, discoverer of Chile.

About a block farther down the street we pass the home of the Marquis de Valleumbroso, a beautiful Colonial building recently restored after having been burned in student riots in the early 1970's. To our right is **Plaza San Francisco**, with a magnificent church of the same name, which houses a giant painting of the Franciscans. As we continue, we come to the **Church of Santa Clara** (the street changes its name after Plaza San Francisco to Calle Santa Clara) and then the **Church of San Pedro**, built in 1688. Left of the church is the station from which trains set out for Machu-Picchu, with the municipal market across the way. In fact, the entire area is one great market stretching from here southward and along the railroad track, but a stroll through this area is enough to give you the idea. The market, devoted mainly to foodstuffs and footwear, is meant for the needs of the local population. A special paragraph below is devoted to purchases that interest tourists.

A final word: remember again, especially here in the marketplace, that Cuzco takes its revenge for the depredations of the Spanish, the first foreign "tourists": no amount of defending yourself against thieves is excessive.

Entertainment

Good folk music and a rich program consisting entirely of local routines are offered every evening at *Qhatuchay*, a simple, popular folklore club on the second floor of the building with the arches along the western side of Plaza de Armas. Come early — for the Club is crowded — and have a good time until the wee hours. Recommended. Another local *peña* (folklore club), *Peña Folkloríca*, at Montero 114, is more conservative.

Several discotheques are active until after midnight. Among them we can recommend *El Muki*, on Calle Santa Catalina not far from the Church of El Triunfo. It offers disco music and drinks.

Shopping

The San Pedro market offers a rather restricted variety of local handicrafts at prices no lower than those in the stores. It is therefore best to buy your souvenirs in the shops around Plaza de Armas (the government-owned *Eppa* store at the corner of the square is one example) or elsewhere in town. In the San Blas Church area there are many workshops where local craftsmen create pottery, jewelry, wood carvings and other hand-wrought items. It is an interesting and pleasant quarter through which to meander and while strolling along you can visit a number of workshops and buy whatever strikes your fancy. A small, orderly market arranged around a large courtyard — *Galerías Turísticas* — has opened in recent years on Avenida Sol, several minutes' walk from Plaza de Armas. Its shops offer a wide selection of *artesanía* from Cuzco and surroundings. A visit is highly recommended. Bazaars are held in the Church of La Compañía from time to time, where lovely handicrafts are offered for sale. These fairs are held mainly on holiday and special occasions and there is an entrance fee — but it is worthwhile.

Wonderful markets take place on Sunday mornings in the villages of Chinchero and Pisac (see below). The two markets, particularly the latter, have earned a wide reputation which, of course, has caused prices to jump, though we must note that these very picturesque markets offer plenty of attractive buys. A visit to at least one of them is highly recommended.

It is important to note that most of the goods sold in Cuzco and the area — jewelry, woodcrafts, woven fabrics, pottery, etc. — are of local and recent manufacture. Peddlers may attempt to "prove" the antiquity of their wares, displaying moldy, torn, mud-stained or otherwise marred merchandise — just as if it has been pried right out of the hands of excited archaeologists and offered straight to you at bargain prices. Don't fall for it. It has been several decades since antiquities have been found anywhere but in museums, and those could not be bought for their weight in gold. But let it be — even day-old souvenirs have their value.

Woolen goods — especially sweaters, ponchos, wall hangings and the like — are made of llama or alpaca wool, and are brought to Cuzco from Juliaca, the regional weaving center which has its own interesting market. If that is where you are headed, delay your buying because there you will find a larger selection at lower prices.

A final word: peddlers will annoy you unceasingly as you sit in Plaza de Armas or roam the city. The ones who stay put on the ground surrounding the plaza are not so bothersome, but the others, particularly the female ones, who are always on the move with their goods, will not leave you alone for a minute. Furthermore, the moment you try to give your aching legs a respite on one of the benches in the square, the cry "*Compra me!*" ("Buy from me!") will ring out time and again.

General Information

Books and periodicals in English
A number of shops sell English-language material on Peruvian and general topics. The largest of these — on Plaza de Armas, at the corner of "Gringos Street" — offers a wide though expensive selection. Try the right-hand side of Calle Plateros, at the very exit from the plaza. Here there is a small shop with books and maps at lower prices.

Postal and telephone services
The central post office, down Avenida Sol, close to the train station to Puno, accepts letters and small parcels (open 8am-8pm). Not far at the same avenue on the left is an *Entel* office for international phone calls. The line is long and so is the wait. Calls are made from little booths in a corner of the hall. Bring a passport, which you have to deposit when you place your call.

Currency exchange
Though several moneychangers can be found in Plaza San Martín, it is best to convert money at *Banco de la Nación* or *Banco de los Andes*, both on Avenida Sol.

Camping and photographic supplies

A number of Cuzco travel and tour agencies have camping equipment to rent out to tourists preparing for hikes. Be sure to obtain a good tent, warm sleeping bag, comfortable backpack, canteen, cooking stove and comfortable walking shoes. Try the agencies on "Gringos Street" — where renting equipment is usually accepted practice.

You can buy film at the photography shops on Avenida Sol and Plaza de Armas. Special and fast films are hard to find.

Short excursions
in the Cuzco Area

The Cuzco area abounds with fascinating places to visit: naturally enough, most are related to the Incas and the remains they left behind (or, to be more precise, the remains that survived the devastation and destruction wreaked by the Spanish *conquistadores*).

We have chosen to survey four routes here, some including a number of sites that must not be missed. These are the classic sites, which clearly and distinctly reflect the Incas and their religion, culture and construction. (Before reading the sections that follow and those pertaining to the walks through Cuzco, see the chapter on the Incas.) These four routes are meant for everyone — young, energetic backpackers, families, or retired couples on their second honeymoon. They are relatively easy routes, with convenient transportation. Most Cuzco tourist agencies provide guided tours of these sites, with most of them well organized. It is important to remember that you buy a combined ticket to enter the sites (see "Tourist services"). Individual tickets are not available at most of the attractions, and without the combined ticket a visitor can expect to be sorry and frustrated — which would be a pity.

The road to Pisac

A number of the most beautiful of the Inca ruins are concentrated along the highway leading north from Cuzco to the town of Pisac, most a short walking distance from the road. To visit them, you need about a half-day walking tour, or a taxi. A third method is to take the bus to Pisac (see below), getting off at Kilometer 9 beside the Inca baths at Tambomachay, and returning downhill to Cuzco by foot. For the sake of geographic continuity, we shall survey the sites from Cuzco outwards, and if you have opted for the bus-up/walk-down method, read the following pages in reverse order.

Sacsayhuamán

About a thirty-minute walk from Cuzco, one of the largest buildings of the ancient world looms over the town — the Sacsayhuamán ("Colored Falcon") fortress, on which twenty thousand construction workers labored for more than two generations.

The enormous stones we see today, some weighing three hundred tons or more, are only a humble remnant of what was a colossal fortress that stared down on the magnificent Inca capital. Thousands of people lived between its walls. The reasons for the construction of Sacsayhuamán have never been totally clear. Conventional wisdom holds that its planning and construction began in the mid-fifteenth century and ended only several decades before the Spanish conquest. Pizarro and his men left the fortress alone during their first years in Cuzco, and only after Manco-Inca's rebellion did they storm it, take it in a desperate bloody battle, and begin the massive task of razing it. The story of the conquest is the background for many legends, and it appears that the campaign was extensive, claiming countless victims on both sides. Once Manco-Inca was defeated and the legendary fortress had fallen into Spanish hands, it took the *conquistadores* only a few months to level it, re-using its stones for their strongholds and buildings in Cuzco, situated at the base of the mountain. Today we can only walk along the massive outer wall and contemplate the stones, chiseled with astonishing precision, which the Spaniards could not budge. Then we can gaze down at the beautiful view and at Cuzco, spread out below in the valley, and remember the stormy glories of bygone days.

It is here, at this impressive site, that the Inca sun festival *Inti-Raimi* is celebrated every year on June 24 (see "When to come"). Those who come for the festivities will certainly sense the excitement of those remote Inca days very well.

Quenco — the "Zig-Zags"

Two kilometers up the road (heading out of town) on the right is an Inca temple hewn out of local stone which, according to tradition, served as a ritual center and burial site. The entire structure is cut from the limestone, with an altar, narrow tunnels and a large amphitheater, in whose walls nineteen carved benches face a six-meter high phallic monolith in the center.

Trenches whose purpose is unknown wind in zig-zag fashion (hence its name) atop the complex. Several accounts relate that they were meant for *chicha* (local rum) to flow through, while others, more macabre, tell that they were meant as conduits for the blood of the sacrifices that were offered here.

Puca Pucará
Several kilometers farther along, the ruins of Puca Pucará ("the Red Fortress") appear to our right. Puca Pucará apparently served as a sentry post both for Cuzco and for Pisac and the Urubamba Valley. From it we can contemplate a lovely landscape of hills, terraces, paths and canals.

Tambomachay
Only a few hundred meters from Puca Pucará on our left we come upon the **Baños del Inca** (Inca baths), a complex of canals and pools known as Tambomachay. In this lovely, unusually well-preserved site, we can again note the quality of Incan craftsmanship, the precision of their work and the importance they accorded to each and every detail. Pay special attention to the circular walls whose stones fit together so perfectly that even today they are hard to match. Though known as "baths", it is hard to imagine that Tambomachay indeed served for bathing, and the site, according to the best hypothesis, was meant chiefly as a "rest stop" for the emperor and his men.

Chinchero
The picturesque town of Chinchero, two hours from Cuzco, lies 3760 m above sea level. Inca ruins abound here, as they do in the entire area, but the major charm of Chinchero lies not in its past but, interestingly, in what's taking place here today. There's a lovely market every Sunday morning in Chinchero, the nicest and most agreeable in the area. Scores of Indians spread their goods out on the wide lawn of the central square and engage in barter, exchanging potatoes for onions, bread for cheese and so on. Tourists will also find enough here to empty their wallets, certainly enjoying the more pleasant atmosphere if not a large selection or lower prices. It's worthwhile to spend two or three hours here on Sunday morning, coming (very early) by bus, truck, or one of the many cars from Cuzco. A neglected church in a corner of the square was once, according to the town elders, one of the region's most beautiful.

Many tourists choose to hike from Chinchero down to the Urubamba Valley (about five hours) and hitchhike back to Cuzco.

*P*ERU

AROUND CUZCO

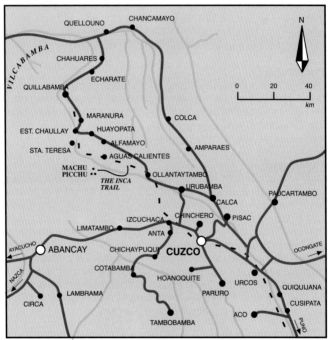

The Urubamba Valley

Along the route on which we are about to venture we find two of the most important and best-known of the Inca ruins, both highly impressive, and recommended. They are located in the Urubamba Valley, a strip of agricultural settlement that sheltered Cuzco from the north, and are very easily reached by rented car, organized tour, or ordinary public transportation.

The sites can be visited on a one-day excursion from Cuzco, or you can stop there on the way to Machu-Picchu. In the latter case, spend the night in Ollantaytambo and continue the next morning on the train from Cuzco, which stops there on the way to Machu-Picchu.

Pisac

The road that heads northward from Cuzco, passing

Sacsayhuamán and the sites mentioned in the previous section, now crosses the mountains and descends into the fertile Urubamba Valley at their base which still serves today as in the past, as the "breadbasket" of Cuzco. Its temperate climate and rich fertility account for the heavy demands of agriculture and settlement made on it, and it is certainly because of these features that the Incas invested such great efforts in constructing, fortifying and developing the valley — thereby securing the imperial capital's physical defense and food supplies.

Pisac, our first stop on the northwestern journey along the river, was and remains an important town in these respects. As we approach it, long before we cross the narrow bridge spanning the river, we discern the magnificent terraces that line the mountainside across the way and in whose shade the colorful village reposes.

The village itself is rather pleasant. Since its streets are laid out in a grid, the visitor has only to turn onto one of the narrow cobblestone alleys and walk straight to reach the square at the far end, right at the foot of the mountain. The plaza, shaded by enormous trees, is the location of the famous market held every Sunday morning, with hundreds of food items, handicrafts and souvenirs changing hands. Neither in quality nor in price is this a bargain market, but the large selection and abundance of sound and color certainly justify your coming this far.

Buses traveling the 32-kilometer route from Cuzco to Pisac in less than an hour, run frequently early Sunday morning, and on weekdays there are several buses each day. Most buses set out from Calle Saphi, but you will find cars and small trucks (*camiones*) headed in that direction from other places, such as Plaza de Armas. Get to Pisac early, for everything is over by afternoon and the characteristic tranquility is restored. Pisac offers a number of places to sleep, but *Hotel Pisac* (in the plaza) is the best. Its second-floor rooms are comfortable and clean.

The ruins
Above the village are found the remains of one of the largest fortresses built by the Incas. By foot it is an hour or two of exhausting ascent on a path beginning in the village (turn left at the fork, for the right-hand path is much steeper). An alternative route, paved only in recent years, is a road leading to the base of the temple in the center of the fortress. There's no regular transportation, so you have to persuade a villager to take you up, which, of course, requires the customary haggling over price.

Once up there, however, all is forgotten. Wander among the

ruins of towers, pass through ancient residences, observe the high terraces (most of which are still cultivated today), and visit the Sun and Moon Temples. If you have come by vehicle, you will first see the ruins of buldings generally considered to be the quarters for the priests and acolytes of the temple. Note the niches in the walls where ritual articles and icons were kept. Higher up, prominent in its grandeur, is the Sun Temple, built of black granite slabs, with an impressive sundial at its center.

The temple, known as Intihuatana, was used for religious rites and astronomical observations. An area in its center was dedicated to *Inti*, the sun. Beside it, in keeping with the dualistic Inca tradition, is the Moon Temple. At the structure's southern end we can clearly discern baths fed by waters from the canal which runs alongside. The temple was protected on all sides by ramparts and towers, some of which we passed on the way from the village below. A narrow path leads north from the temple to an area uncovered only in recent years — Kallacasa, a storage facility and housing for the plebians. Opposite the temple on the rock face of the mountain to the west (past the arroyo), we see the city's burial ground, the largest of its type. The Incas buried their dead — mummified in fetal position — in conical clay structures built along the slope. Though access to the place is rather difficult, most of the graves have been visited by relic-hunters, a fact which explains the holes that make the mountainside look like a sieve.

From here we return to Pisac continuing down the Urubamba Valley, preferably via the footpath, so we can observe the scenery, the remains of defense towers and the terraces.

The Road to Ollantaytambo
From Pisac the road continues northwest, more or less parallel to the river. Buses pass through every few hours, picking up passengers at the entrance to Pisac. You can try to hitch a ride or get aboard a truck while waiting for the bus. After about nineteen kilometers of lovely scenery we reach **Calca**, the valley's largest town. There's no special reason to spend time there, apart from walking along its streets for a short while.

Another nineteen kilometers away is the village of Yucay, and another three kilometers brings us to **Urubamba**. The road from Cuzco also reaches Urubamba, and the two combine northwest for another twenty-one kilometers — till our next stop.

Ollantaytambo
Ollantaytambo (elev. 2800 meters), one of the most exceptional towns in Peru, is situated 72 km from Cuzco. It is approximately

two thousand inhabitants dwell in a town whose houses and streets have been preserved exactly as the Incas left them when fleeing the Spanish. Here Manco-Inca battled Pizarro's men fiercely in the futile rebellion of 1536, ultimately having to escape by a ruse to Vilcabamba, where he was finally killed by the persistent Spaniards. Today we can see the remains of the strong fortress where Manco took refuge and from which he attacked the besieging Spanish. Note the rare quality of its construction, its advanced strategic planning and the organizational, military, and economic abilities it reflects, all of which are truly difficult to comprehend.

Ollantaytambo can be reached from the Urubamba Valley, or by bus and train from Cuzco (trains from San Pedro Station to Machu-Picchu and back stop here). Transportation to the village is rather frequent, with buses, trucks and tourist cars making the trip several times per day. When coming from Pisac, it is usual to spend the night here before continuing by train to Machu-Picchu; the same holds true for those getting off the train here on the way back from Machu-Picchu en route to Pisac. In any event, there are a number of food and lodging possibilities — all very basic. Next to the train station there is a sort of small hostel, *Albergue*, run by some "gringos", where guests sleep in shared rooms. The *Parador Turistico* is a small, clean hotel on the central plaza, and it has a small restaurant on its ground floor. The *Alojamiento Yavar*, with clean and very basic accommodation, is also nearby. Around the square there is always someone willing to direct you to a place to spend the night but, again, do not expect too much. A floor, too, is considered a respectable place to sleep in this village. For the more energetic, of course, there is the possibility of pitching a tent at the edge of town.

Once settled we can tour the village. A short stroll down the narrow lanes, between the simple stone walls, will suffice to give an impression of the way in which the village was built and it is crude and unsophisticated when compared with the grandeur and precision of the fortress. Most of the houses were meant for simple folk and are piled together in a sort of courtyard style along the streets, with the doors of the various houses opening onto the court. It is interesting to see the canals that carry water to the houses, and the windowless outer walls encircling the village.

At the edge of town we can clearly make out a massive terraced structure — the magnificent fortress where Manco-Inca took refuge. Its construction seems to have been begun by Pachacuti, but he did not have time to finish it before the Spaniards arrived. Entire wings, especially the upper sections

PERU

(which apparently served as a temple) still seem to be in various stages of construction. Climb the hundreds of steps leading to it and walk around. The enormous stones, each weighing several tons, were brought here from a quarry located on a cliff across the river! Imagine the means and skill needed to transport them several kilometers to this site — bringing them down the slope, crossing the river, and dragging them back up the precipitous slope.

From here we can contemplate the surrounding landscape and get a fuller picture of the fortress' strategic importance. The roads to the Urubamba Valley and to Cuzco immediately come into view. A little past the temple are the ruins of houses that apparently served the local population and the defenders. Behind them a rampart wall which demarcates the western wing of the fortress is visible. By moving slightly away from the wall on the path, we reach a place which apparently served as a prison: four cells hewn of stone, equipped with holes suitable for threading chains at the height of a man's hands and feet.

Machu-Picchu
Of all the sites in Cuzco and its surroundings the most well-known and impressive is the Lost City, the only Inca city preserved intact — Machu-Picchu. Legends were current in Latin America, Spain, and the rest of the world about the existence of such a city somewhere in the depths of the jungle but it was only in 1911, after years of searching, that it was discovered. Overnight it became one of the most famous and exciting sites of all the relics of the ancient world.

Tens of thousands stream here from all corners of the world, seeking to understand the special secret of this strange place which stood desolate for centuries, blanketed in a thick mantle of wild jungle growth that concealed it from the eye of man. To this day we do not know exactly why Machu-Picchu was abandoned, and how its existence could have eluded the Spaniards, who razed to the ground everything they came across. Some attribute this to the fact that the city was secret then as well while others explain that the Incas did not have a written history, and customarily omitted unwanted details from their oral chronicles. The latter view hypothesizes that something in the city's history displeased the Incan emperors, who ordered it erased from the national memory — thereby consigning Machu-Picchu to the depths of oblivion and saving it from destruction. The Incans did themselves a disservice, but they gave us and posterity the privilege and pleasure of beholding this special place with our own eyes and endowing the city with eternal life.

At the site of Machu Picchu

Auzangate

How to get there

The only way to get to Machu-Picchu, apart from hiking (see "The Inca Trail" for information concerning the foot path) is the train that sets out each morning from Cuzco. Since it takes on passengers at stations along the way, there's nothing easier than getting aboard if you've come directly from Abancay or the Urubamba Valley. Two trains run on this line and both are packed. Of these, the tourist train is more expensive (about three times the price) but also faster, more comfortable and — no less importantly — safer. The Cuzco — Machu-Picchu line is infamous for its plague of thieves, who are more easily spotted against a background of foreigners. The ride lasts nearly four hours, about an hour and a half less than on the cheaper local train. Those who wish to save by taking the local should at least go first class, for second class is very crowded and noisy, marring the atmosphere of the trip. Buy tickets at the San Pedro station (opposite the market) a day in advance and get to the station early. Even so, you will have to fight to get a seat!

The train zigzags its way out of Cuzco, for the steep incline and sharp curves make a direct course impossible. As mentioned this stretch is a thief's paradise, so keep an eagle eye on your gear. We recommend a flashlight for the evening return trip and for when the train passes through tunnels, for when darkness strikes so do quick-handed thieves.

Upon reaching your destination, after a lovely journey, you'll find a great many buses waiting in the adjacent lot to take you up the mountain to the entrance gate. There are not enough buses so here, too, seats go to the speedy. Otherwise you'll have to wait almost an hour! Climbing by foot is exhausting and does not save any time. Another possibility, highly recommended, is to reach **Aguas Calientes** ("Hot Waters"), a village 1.5 kilometers before Machu-Picchu, the night before.

Food and lodging

You can stay at one of its small hostels in Aguas Calientes. Here you will find several agreeable restaurants and a few simple hotels, as well as hot springs which make bathing a pleasure. Get up early the next morning and make your way to Machu-Picchu on foot. That way you will get there much earlier than the train, and also enjoy the privilege of exploring the site while it's quiet and serene, before the swarms of people invade it.

The government tourist company runs a hotel next to the entrance to Machu-Picchu, but it is not large and to spend the night there you must have reservations. The self-service restaurant is relatively high-priced, and the lines are long, so it's best to bring your own food.

Visiting the site

To explore Machu-Picchu properly, a thorough tour of its various sections is needed, with careful attention paid to construction, street layout, shape of the temples, agricultural areas, etc. We'll explore the site systematically, noting as we go along its architectural wonders, the complexity of its social system, and the strength of its defenses. The well-tended lawns, neat trails and specially-constructed footpaths everywhere do not mar the authenticity of the place to any great degree.

We enter Machu-Picchu through the gate, pass a sign commemorating the city's discoverer, the American Professor Bingham, and pay the admission fee. Now, standing at the beginning of the trail, we behold the city of wonders in its full grandeur. To the right and left, above and below, are row upon row of carefully-crafted terraces where its citizens apparently grew their crops. Incidentally, one hypothesis argues that Machu-Picchu was set aside for the Sun Virgins, since the skeletons uncovered here display a ratio of three women for every man. Glance to the left, upward, to see a special structure accessible by steps farther along the path. The large number of bones that were found at the top of the stairs, far from the city center, has led scholars to believe that this site was a cemetery. Slightly behind it is a hewn stone on which corpses were placed to dry in the sun before mummification. If you turn around, the city in its full glory comes into view. The left section, the higher one, was set aside for ritual tasks and religious rites while the right side was residential. Look also to your left and downward — apart from the stunning view, you will also notice the steep slope that protected the city from potential attackers.

Return to the staircase and head down. Turn left onto one of the alleys and notice the buildings, all similar, and the narrow walkways between them. Soon we reach the Sun Temple, where again we see exquisite stonework, and can marvel at the giant altar stone in the temple's center. A number of mummies were found underneath the stone, in a place called the Tombs of the Kings. Continuing in the same direction we reach the nobility's quarter, with a number of gigantic carved stones in its center. From here it was possible to gaze down on the valley separating the city's two sections and see what was happening there. To the left of the quarter we can clearly make out the remains of the quarry that supplied the city's building material.

In Taquile

Climbing on, we reach one of Machu-Picchu's most important sites — the Temple of the Three Windows. Though we notice the massive wall opposite us, it is impossible not to be especially attracted to the wall on our right, which runs eastward. It is made entirely of one block of stone, in which three large windows have been carved with precision.

We continue along the path. Shortly after this temple we come to Machu-Picchu's central temple, from which the path leads to the large sundial, the most beautiful and perfect of those which have been preserved. Though it is not known exactly why the sophisticated installation was built and what purpose it served, similar sundials, with faces pointing precisely to the four corners of the earth, have been found at every Incan site discovered, and they were undoubtedly of great significance in Inca life. Whether it was a clock, an astronomical facility, or a tool of some other kind, its importance cannot be overlooked and we cannot help but marvel at it.

Now we need only to continue to the other side of town and wander among its ancient houses. Notice how the construction blends into the terrain and how the builders utilised the stones in the area. At the edge of the quarter, there is a facility where prisoners were held and tortured to death. We see niches of a man's height in which detainees were held, and rocks on which they were executed.

That basically covers a tour of Machu-Picchu. The well-planned city, with its temples, fortresses and remarkable construction, testifies to an extraordinary civilization which once flourished here. A tour of the city sheds a new light on this civilization which dates back to pre-Spanish America but which still exerts an influence on the area today, five centuries later.

Those who still have the energy, should not miss the climb to the top of the cliff above Machu-Picchu — Huayna-Picchu, and enjoy the awesome view of the lost city and the incredible views around it. The steep climb takes about an hour, and the path crosses amazing gorges.

Another fine view-spot of Machu Picchu is from where the Inca Trail comes to its end. You can also make the half-hour scenic walk along the trail to the Sun Gate (Intipunku).

Extended Tours in the Cuzco Area

An adventurous visitor can spend weeks in Cuzco and its surroundings without being satiated. The area offers scores of mountain and river and jungle tour routes. It is impossible to mention them all, due to constraints of time and space, therefore only four have been selected — one for its popularity, another for its uniqueness, a third for its touch of mystery and the fourth, along a mountain track, is overwhelming in its beauty. Each lasts a number of days, and the visitor will require suitable camping gear, excellent physical condition, time, resourcefulness and orientation skills. The first route, the Inca Trail, is the most popular and easiest to follow of the four. The second, the jungle route, usually requires an organized tour, and the third, a journey to the last Incan city, requires preparation and special organization, and we mention it only to whet your appetite. The fourth, the Auzangate trek can be done on horseback. You must prepare each of these outings carefully and precisely, making use of the most up-to-date and reliable maps and local information.

The Inca Trail

One of the most interesting ways of reaching Machu-Picchu — an experience in its own right — is the hike (three to five days) along one of the most famous and popular trails in South America. This route, beginning at Kilometer 88 of the railroad and ending in Machu-Picchu itself, is one of the hundreds of roads that crisscrossed the Inca empire. Most of these roads, have been widened, and have become major highways, with no surviving trace of bygone days. Others, especially those in mountainous, isolated areas, were abandoned and have disappeared, buried for centuries under sand, rock and vegetation. Only a few have survived and it's a special experience to hike along them. The Inca Trail, the main highway from the Urubamba Valley to Machu-Picchu, is the best-known.

Remember before setting out that this is a difficult hike, more than fifty kilometers long, at elevations sometimes exceeding 4000 m above sea level. You must have suitable lightweight gear, food, maps and good spirit. Get off the train at Kilometer 88, cross the river, pay a few dollars at the entrance — and start walking.

The trail was discovered in 1915 but only several decades later was it made fit for tourists. It crosses mountains and valleys, with alternating climbs and descents. The first section is the hardest, and includes the famous climb to the first range. Afterwards the going is easier. The trail is simply paved with Incan relics. On the way there are a number of archaeological sites, among them Sayacmarca and Huiñay Huayna, considered the best of the Incan antiquites in the region.

Approaching Machu-Picchu from this direction is an extraordinary experience: as you round the bend of *Puerto del Sol* (Sun Gate), the entire city suddenly appears, stretching out below.

Many choose to spend the last night of the trek at Puerto del Sol. Thus one can enjoy the fabolous sunrise the next morning, and a visit at the site early, before most tourists arrive.

To the eastern jungles

Several hundred kilometers east of Cuzco is a vast land of jungle. Very few people live there — only a few tens of thousands — and even fewer visit. It is a forsaken, isolated stretch of territory, a place where standards and values are utterly different, an alien, strange world. Here we find a mixture of untamed nature and human settlement, wildlife and Indian tribes together with oil drillers and prospectors.

Puerto Maldonado

This town (population app. 22,000) is the largest settlement in the region, and an apealing jungle town. The harsh tropical climate, the wilting heat (up to 40°C/104°F) and the oppressive humidity fail to tarnish its extraordinary charm and should not deter one from the experience of visiting and exploring the area.

The town itself consists of several unpaved streets lined on either side with small houses. Near the river you'll find straw huts, homes of Indians who abandoned their tribal lands in the area and moved to the town. In the center of town is a broad Plaza de Armas, surrounded by a number of shops, a small hotel, a bank, a café and so on.

How to get there

You can reach Puerto Maldonado on flights from Cuzco, daily with *Transamazon* or 3 times a week with *AeroPerú* or from Lima, daily with *Faucett*, 3 times a week with *AeroPerú*, or by truck (three days in good weather and up to two weeks in rainy periods!), or by boat (only in an organized framework). The rivers leading to the town, Río Tambopata and Río Madre de Dios, are very rough and quite deserted. Only canoes or rubber dinghies are able to navigate the rivers, and then only with suitable equipment and a guide. Such trips are rather uncommon and very expensive (hundreds of dollars).

Flights tend to be cancelled on rainy days and are otherwise usually packed to the last seat. Make reservations well in advance and be sure to confirm. Even then, nothing is assured! The Peruvian companies are most unreliable and tend to overbook heavily. Get to the airport early.

Where to stay and eat
Wilson: Jirón González Prada 355, clean, reliable, inexpensive.
Tambo de Oro: Av. 2 de Mayo 277. Inexpensive, very good.
Hotel de Turistas: Av. León Velarde s/n, near the Río Tambota. Expensive, very good service.
Moderno: Av. Billinghurst 359. Inexpensive, very basic.

The *Hotel Wilson* has a good restaurant. Along the main street, too, there are a number of restaurants, cafés and stands with excellent snacks and cakes. Restaurants serve some extraordinary dishes, such as *sopa de motelo*, an excellent turtle soup, or grilled fish served with slices of grilled plantains. Castanas nuts, sold in most shops, are almost a national food here. Prices in Puerto Maldonado, as in every isolated jungle town, are very high — as much as twice those anywhere else. Rain or storms force prices even higher, for the town depends on outside supplies, for which the demand and consequently the price, rises when bad weather delays a shipment.

Excursions
In Puerto Maldonando you can get around by foot or on a scooter, an easily-driven vehicle which you can rent on the main street. You can take it out of town, into the farm areas near town and into the forests. Be sure, however, not to stray off the main road, for the thicket is misleading and it is very easy to get lost.

Puerto Maldonado is the starting point for regional outings, meant to introduce you to the area's two highly exceptional phenomena: its nature and wildlife and its people. To behold the former in full bloom you've got to get out of town — preferably by boat — several dozen kilometers up Río Tambopata or Río Madre de Dios, or downstream toward Bolivia. A jungle touring center, *Explorers' Inn*, was erected in the late 1970's about sixty kilometers (three hours) up Río Tambopata. Hikes set out from here into the bush and you can observe birds and wildlife (if luck is on your side) and visit Indian tribes that are totally cut off from civilization. It's a nice, if somewhat touristy place, and from there you can walk through the tangle of trees and form an impression of the wealth and density of the flora.

On the other side of Río Madre de Dios there is an enormous nature reserve. To explore it, however, you will need a guide and lots of time. At the harbor you can rent boats for any objective and any direction, at a range of prices. By taking advantage of this you can go up and down the rivers, visit Indian villages and even reach the town of Riberalta, Bolivia (be sure to make border-crossing arrangments in town before setting out!). While cruising along the rivers, you can see animals coming out to quench their thirst, crocodiles dozing on the riverbank, turtles laying their eggs, and so on.

An encounter with the jungle people, too, is very interesting. You can meet Indians whose dress, language and way of life have not changed in centuries and no less interesting are the young prospectors, who pan innumerable kilograms of sand every day in feverish search of the precious metal. Try to stop in protected areas during extended river outings and stay out of the water, which can be infested with crocodiles and other unpleasant surprises.

If you have time on your hands and have an adventurous spirit and the willingness for a different kind of experience, this is the place for you.

Parque Manú

Parque Manú is an area of the jungle with abundant wildlife. It is accessible from Cuzco by car, or by sailing upstream from Puerto Maldonado on the river Madre de Dios. The trip is done by canoe and takes about a week.

In Huascar street in Cuzco there are truck owners who are willing to take one, for a fee, to the village Shentuya, a day's ride from Cuzco. The road is very difficult, mostly unpaved, and starts out from the high mountains where it is cold, ending in the tropical heat of the jungles. The inhabitants of Shentuya are Indians, and those among them who have large canoes will take you on a few days' cruise up the river Madre de Dios and Río Manú, which is one of its tributaries. On the Río Manú there is a large concentration of wildlife — alligators, monkeys, parrots and more. It is worth spending some time at the lakes near the river, which have lovely hiking trails around them.

After the trip along the Río Manú one returns to Madre de Dios, and from there one can return to Shentuya and from there back to Cuzco, or continue down the river to Puerto-Maldonado, from which there are several regular flights a week to Cuzco. In the latter case, the owner of the canoe will sail as far as the town of Colorado, a gold hunter's town, and from there canoes depart daily for Puerto Maldonado, an additional 12 hours sailing away.

One needs a permit from the National Parks authority in order to tour Manú Park, and this is usually obtainable in Shentuya. It is generally only issued for a few days, but can be extended at the station authority on the Madre de Dios river.

Espíritupampa

One of the most adventurous tour routes which was opened up only in recent years and which has achieved growing popularity is the journey into the thick of the jungle, where the remains of the Incas' last refuge — Espíritupampa — were discovered in the depths of Vilcabamba about twenty years ago.

Bingham discovered the site as early as 1911 while searching for the ruins of the vanished city to which Manco-Inca fled when his 1536 rebellion against the Spanish failed, and where he was captured several years later. Upon discovering Machu-Picchu, Bingham attributed the stories of the vanished capital to that city and the ruins of Espíritupampa were again swallowed up by the jungle. Only when it became clear that Machu-Picchu could not be Espíritupampa (due to its location, architecture and — mainly — the fact that the city was intact, while Manco's city had been abandoned and burned) did Espíritupampa's star rise again. In 1964, after prolonged research and excavation, evidence was found to confirm that this, and not Machu-Picchu, was Manco Inca's last bastion. Even though the city was abandoned and desolate for centuries, the legends of Espíritupampa were passed down from father to son, ever since the Spanish conquest. Only since the mid-1960's, when an American adventurer named Savoy succeeded in returning to the site and proving that the city had existed after the Spanish conquest as well, did it become clear that Machu-Picchu was not the legendary capital of Vilcabamba, but rather, by all appearances, that it was Espíritupampa.

Reaching the site is a difficult and complicated matter requiring ten days or more. The route passes through desolate areas totally cut off from regions of human settlement. Jungle, mountains and rivers surround the hiker on all sides and a harsh climate, a multitude of mosquitoes and the terrain add physical nuisances to the spiritual experience. Come well equipped — with food, first-aid equipment, mosquito repellent and enough local currency for your needs (dollars will prove worthless). We recommend taking along a local guide and before setting out, make detailed inquiries in Cuzco concerning the safest and most convenient way to go.

Auzangate

Cuzco lies in the heart of the Andes range, and therefore a variety of possibilities for mountain hikes exist. Among these are the Salcantay and Apurimac routes, but the most enjoyable is probably that which goes around Mt. Auzangate whose summit is 6384 m high. This route is particularly enjoyable when done on horseback. The hike takes about five days and the path climbs to heights of 5000 m above sea level, which makes breathing difficult. But it is not only the great height, the beauty itself is breathtaking: majestic peaks, and glaciers which descend into many enchanting lakes, each different from the other in color.

For some reason this area is colder than other areas at similar elevation, and after sunset there is no enjoyment in walking because of the intense cold. Try to complete a day's walking early, in order to eat and snuggle up in a sleeping bag inside a good tent by nightfall. Some relief from the cold is found in the hot springs at two places along the route. Nothing is more luxurious than bathing in the hot water, when the outside temperature is hovering somewhere around freezing point.

The route begins in the Indian village of **Tinki**, or at **Ocongate** 8 km away. You can get here on one of the trucks from Cuzco which depart from Avenida Huascar and Calle Garcilaso, several times weekly. The trip, which takes about 8 hours, is difficult and tiring. In either of these villages you will be able to hire horses and grooms who also serve as guides. Be sure to check the horses — a sick or tired horse is liable to ruin such a trip. Do not expect thoroughbred Arab stallions, for the horses in these high mountains look more like mules. Take a horse for your gear, which better be packed in big sack and not in backpacks.

Lake Titicaca

One who studies a map of southern Peru, in the immediate area of the Bolivian border, will certainly notice the broad lake — Lake Titicaca. At 3810 m, this is the world's highest navigated lake with regular transportation. Its maximum length is almost 200 km and is about 70 km wide, while the center it is some 300 m deep.

A place of honor is set aside for Lake Titicaca in the history of the regional peoples, who attributed various and sundry qualities to it and its waters. According to the most important of the legends, it was here, on the Island of the Sun on the lake's Bolivian side, that Manco-Capac, the first Inca, was created and from here he went to Cuzco to found the capital of the empire-to-be. The many islands that dot the lake are populated by colorful Indians. A visit is highly recommended.

Puno

Puno (pop. 100,000), the Peruvian city on Lake Titicaca's western shore, serves as capital of the Peruvian Altiplano and is the center of most activity in, on and around the lake. This pleasant city has a number of restaurants and small hotels, all within walking distance of the central plaza. Recommended hotels here are the *Ferrocarril* across from the train station, *Lima* and *Europa*, the latter being especially popular.

Puno's center is Plaza de Armas, with its Cathedral dating back to the mid-seventeenth century. From here it is not far to the port district, where boats set out to the islands (see below) and the municipal market, where there is a tremendous variety of local *artesanía* of wood, pottery, metal and above all, wool including the best llama and alpaca goods brought to Puno from nearby Juliaca, where they are made and sold here at rather attractive prices.

Puno is known for its festivals and dances, which are best during the first half of February when a giant carnival, rich in dance, costumes, song, music, food and drink is held in town. In the surrounding area you'll find that some occasion is celebrated almost every month. Try to take part.

Transportation

Juliaca is linked by railroad with Arequipa and Cuzco and many taxis travel between Juliaca and Puno. The trip is short (45 km) and not expensive. The daily trains to those cities are a paradise for thieves: beware!! (see "Personal security" above). Always remember: Peruvian trains do not run on Sundays. The trains out of Juliaca are very crowded and you must get your tickets early. The wait at the ticket counter sometimes lasts several hours! Second-class tickets are obtainable only on the day of departure, while first-class and buffet-car tickets can be bought a day earlier. We highly recommend traveling in these cars, which are far more secure against thieves. Saving a few dollars on the fare is liable to cost you many times over in misery and loss of expensive gear. The train to Cuzco covers the 400 km in eleven hours of gorgeous scenery, passing towns and villages, mountains and rivers. It makes dozens of stops along the way and at each of them crowds of locals will disturb your rest by offering bargains on various articles, food and the like. The closer you get to Cuzco, the more interesting the landscape (both natural and human) becomes, but unfortunately you've got to focus your attention on things closer at hand, keeping an eagle eye more on your gear than on the scenery. When you reach the terminal, get off last, only after the platform has emptied. When you're jostled in a crowd, thieves will have a golden opportunity to slice your baggage and empty it out. Get off in an organized group, the larger the better, have your flashlight ready and hold your gear in front of you (see "Cuzco: Transportation").

The trip to Arequipa is no different. Here, too, you'll need eyes in the back of your head. Remember again: no security measures are overdone along these routes!! The trip to Arequipa, too, takes eleven hours, passing through scenery that is interesting though not as intensive as that on the way to Cuzco. To Arequipa there are night trains, on which you can reserve a place in a sleeping car.

The roads running parallel to the railroad to Cuzco and Arequipa are not recommended. A number of companies run buses over them, but the vehicles are antiquated, uncomfortable and much slower than the train. They are worthwhile only on Sundays, when the trains do not run.

To Bolivia there are several routes by lake and land. Ferries cross Lake Titicaca to Copacabana (Bolivia) every day and from the harbor you can find transportation to La Paz with no difficulty. Local bus companies also provide direct service to La Paz once or twice daily. A beautiful and recommended way of going between the two countries is via Yunguyo (see Bolivia: "Copacabana").

The Islands

Most people who come to Puno do so on their way from somewhere to somewhere else — some from Bolivia, others from the Peruvian coastal trip and still others from Cuzco. All of them stay in town first and foremost in order to leave it for a visit to one or more of the islands in Lake Titicaca.

Two especially interesting islands, **Taquile** and **Amantani**, are a few hours' lake voyage from Puno. Both are inhabited by Indians who have an affinity for tourists and their money. Both islands can be reached by boats that set out early in the morning from the port at the edge of town. (It's a good idea to get there before 7am). The two islands have a number of Indian villages organized into communes that buy and sell locally-produced *artesanía*, of a quality and uniqueness that are not to be encountered elsewhere. Taquile is the more popular of the two islands, while Amantani, the more remote, is quieter and far less commercial. Neither island has a hotel, but spending a night there is highly recommended. Many islanders will invite you into their homes and put you up in clean rooms for a pittance. Remember to bring a sleeping bag and a little food.

Sunrises and sunsets on Lake Titicaca are famous for their exquisite beauty. The entire sky blazes in a fiery scarlet which bursts through the clouds as far as the horizon. Enchanting!

The boats that take you to these islands will also go — by request — by way of the Uros Indian settlements. The Indians live on **floating islands**, actually mats of reeds (which grow densely in the shallower areas of the lake) which they have compressed with their feet, with great persistence, into more-or-less rigid surfaces (be careful not to tumble into the water while walking around on them). Several hundred Indians live in rickety reed structures on dozens of islands such as these, which drift about on the lake currents. They live by fishing and raising domestic fowl and a few vegetables, making some extra money on the side by selling lovely woven fabrics to tourists. The Uros travel between their islands in tiny reed boats, probably very similar to those common on the Nile in the time of the Pharoahs. The little vessels even take them on their rather infrequent voyages into town. A visit to the Uros is very interesting and you should insist that it be included in the price you pay the boat owner for your passage to the large islands.

Juliaca

Juliaca, 45 km north of Puno, serves as an important crossroads, where the railroad branches off to Cuzco, Arequipa and Puno.

Flights from Lima and Arequipa also touch down at the city's airport.

Juliaca is especially renowned as the regional center of most of the weaving done in the Peruvian highlands and products made of llama and alpaca wool are sold here at lower prices than elsewhere in Peru. In the city center, next to the train station, there is a rather large market offering a broad selection of merchandise. If you're hunting for genuine bargains, however, walk a few blocks to the dirty, crowded municipal market, where you'll find plenty of sweaters, ponchos, wall hangings and the like at lower prices.

Vocabulary

English	Spanish	English	Spanish
good morning	*buenos días*	train	*tren*
hello/good bye	*hola, adiós*	subway/ underground	*metro*
good evening	*buenas tardes*	railway station	*estación de tren*
good night	*buenas noches*	ticket	*billete*
please	*por favor*	taxi	*taxi*
thank you	*gracias*	car	*coche*
pardon, excuse	*perdón*	plane	*avión*
yes	*sí*	airport	*aeropuerto*
no	*no*	boat/ship	*barco*
what...?	*qué...?*	port/quay/ wharf	*puerto/muelle*
when...?	*cuándo?*		
where...?	*dónde?*	slow	*despacio*
there is...	*hay*	fast	*rapido*
there is not...	*no hay*	gas	*gasolina*
What is the time?	*Qué hora es?*	gas station	*surtidor de gasolina*
How are you?	*Cómo estás?*		
far	*lejos*	hotel	*hotel*
near	*cerca*	hostel	*albergue*
big/large	*grande*	room	*habitación*
small	*pequeño*	toilets	*servicios*
new	*nuevo*	bath/shower	*baño/ducha*
old	*antiguo/viejo*	restaurant	*restaurante*
left	*izquierda*	café	*café/bar*
right	*derecha*	table	*mesa*
first	*primero*	chair	*silla*
last	*último*		
open	*abierto*		
closed	*cerrado*	waiter	*camarero*
entrance	*entrada*	breakfast	*desayuno*
exit	*salida*	lunch	*almuerzo*
		dinner	*cena*
		water	*agua*
bus	*autobus/ omnibus/ colectivo*	drink	*bebida*
		wine	*vino*
		beer	*cerveza*

English	Spanish	English	Spanish
juice	*jugo*	road, highway	*carretera, autopista*
milk	*leche*		
butter	*manteca*	street	*calle*
jam	*dulce*	avenue	*avenida*
cheese	*queso*	square	*plaza*
eggs	*huevos*	alley	*callejuela*
bread	*pan*	esplanade	*paseo*
salt	*sal*	bridge	*puente*
pepper	*pimienta*	monument	*monumento*
sugar	*azucar*	fountain	*fuente*
gravy	*salsa*	church	*iglesia*
soup	*sopa*	palace	*palacio*
salad	*ensalada*	fort/castle	*castillo*
fish	*pescado*	town/city	*ciudad*
meat	*carne*	village	*pueblo*
chicken	*pollo*	museum	*museo*
steak	*bife/churrasco*	park	*jardin público*
grilled meat	*asado*		
mixed grill	*parrillada*		
chips/fries	*papas fritas*	east	*este*
dessert	*postre*	north	*norte*
cake	*torta*	west	*oeste*
fruit	*frutas*	south	*sur*
ice cream	*helado*	valley	*valle*
bread	*pan*	mountain	*montaña*
menu	*menú*	range	*cordillera*
hot	*caliente*	hill	*colina*
cold	*frio*	forest	*bosque*
bill	*cuenta*	river	*rio*
receipt	*recibo*	falls	*cascadas*
		lake	*lago*
cinema	*cine*		
theatre	*teatro*		
pharmacy	*farmacia*	Sunday	*Domingo*
shop, store	*tienda*	Monday	*Lunes*
post office	*correos*	Tuesday	*Martes*
hospital	*hospital*	Wednesday	*Miércoles*
police	*policia*	Thursday	*Jueves*
embassy	*embajada*	Friday	*Viernes*
		Saturday	*Sábado*
market	*mercado*		
how much does it cost?	*cuánto cuesta?*		
		January	*Enero*
expensive	*caro*	February	*Febrero*
cheap	*barato*	March	*Marzo*

English	Spanish	English	Spanish
April	*Abril*	17	*diecisiete*
May	*Mayo*	18	*dieciocho*
June	*Junio*	19	*diecinueve*
July	*Julio*	20	*veinte*
August	*Agosto*	21	*veintiuno*
September	*Septiembre*	30	*trenta*
October	*Octubre*	31	*treinta y uno*
November	*Noviembre*	40	*cuarenta*
December	*Diciembre*	50	*cincuenta*
		60	*sesenta*
		70	*setenta*
1	*uno/una*	80	*ochenta*
2	*dos*	90	*noventa*
3	*tres*	100	*cien*
4	*cuatro*	101	*ciento uno*
5	*cinco*	110	*ciento diez*
6	*seis*	200	*doscientos/as*
7	*siete*	300	*trescientos*
8	*ocho*	400	*quatrocientos*
9	*nueve*	500	*quinientos*
10	*diez*	600	*seiscientos*
11	*once*	700	*setecientos*
12	*doce*	800	*ochocientos*
13	*trece*	900	*nuevecientos*
14	*catorce*	1000	*mil*
15	*quince*	2000	*dos mil*
16	*dieciséis*	million	*un millón*

The Spanish language

Spaniards stress that they have very much in common with Latin Americans. Those reply that in fact, they share almost everything, but the language...

The grammatical rules are the same for all Spanish speakers, and people with a basic knowledge will find the way to manage out, but the pronunciation can differ a lot from one region to the other, and so can many words. For instance the same bus rolling the streets is called "*omnibus*" in Uruguay, "*colectivo*" in Buenos Aires, "*micro*" (masculine) in northern Argentina, "*micro*" (feminine) in Chile, "*bus*" in Peru.

As for the pronunciation, in Buenos Aires and Montevideo the "*y*" and the "*ll*" have a very hard sound (like the French j). The word *calle* (street) is pronounced "*caye*", while in these places it is pronounced "*caje*" (as the French j). In Ecuador and northern

Peru, the "*ge*" and the "*gi*" sound like the "*gue*" and the "*gui*" in Venezuela, and so on.

j is pronounced *ch* (as in Scotish *loch*)
h is always silent
ñ is pronounced as *ni* in *union*
ai is pronounced as *i* in *hike*
oi is pronounced as *oy* in *boy*
au is pronounced as *ou* in *loud*

Nevertheless, this should not deterre you from trying to contact the people in their language, as this is the best way to get to know the continent.

I NDEX

*I*NDEX

INDEX

*I*NDEX

NOTES

NOTES

NOTES

QUESTIONNAIRE

In our efforts to keep up with the pace and pulse of South America, we kindly ask your cooperation in sharing with us any information which you may have as well as your comments. We would greatly appreciate your completing and returning the following questionnaire. Feel free to add additional pages.

Our many thanks!

_____

To: Inbal Travel Information (1983) Ltd.
18 Hayetzira Street
Ramat Gan 52521
Israel

Name: _____

Address: _____

_____

Occupation: _____

Date of visit: _____

_____

Purpose of trip (vacation, business, etc.): _____

_____

_____

Comments / Information: _____

_____

_____

_____

_____

_____

_____

_____

_____

_____

_____

_____

_____

_____

_____

INBAL Travel Information Ltd.
P.O.B. 39090 Tel Aviv
ISRAEL 61390